Learner
Services

1 1 NOV 2008

2 9 JAN 2013

- 4 MAR 2015

2 4 MAR 2015

2 0 OCT 2016

A FINE WILL BE CHARGED FOR OVERDUE ITEMS

Shoot the Damn Dog

By the Same Author

Love, Aways
Concerning Lily
Lovesick
Good Grief

Shoot the Damn Dog

A Memoir of Depression

Sally Brampton

BLOOMSBURY

First published in Great Britain 2008

Quote on p. vii from *Siddhartha* by Hermann Hesse, translated by Hilda R. Rosner. Peter
Owen Ltd, London. Quotes on p. 74 and p. 223 from *The Crack-Up* by F. Scott Fitzgerald
used by permission of David Higham Associates Ltd. Quote on p. 86 from 'Summer in
Algiers' from *The Myth of Sisyphus* by Albert Camus, translated by Justin O'Brien (Penguin,
1955). Translation copyright © Justin O'Brien, 1955. Reproduced by permission of Penguin
Books Ltd. Quote on p. 138 from *The Cocktail Party* by T. S. Eliot used by permission of
Faber & Faber Ltd. Quote on p. 145 from *Peanuts* (15.07.94) by Charles M. Schulz used
by permission of Peter Knight. Quote on p. 174 from *Illness as a Metaphor* by Susan
Sontag (Allen Lane, 1979). Copyright © Susan Sontag, 1977, 1978. Reproduced by
permission of Penguin Books Ltd. Quote on p. 255 from *Wind, Sand and Stars* by Antoine
de Saint-Exupéry, translated by William Rees (Penguin Books, 1995, first published as 'Terre
des hommes', 1939). Translation copyright © William Rees, 1995. Reproduced by permission
of Penguin Books Ltd.

Bloomsbury Publishing Plc,
36 Soho Square, London W1D 3QY

www.bloomsbury.com

Bloomsbury Publishing, London, New York and Berlin

A CIP catalogue record for this book is available from the British Library

ISBN 9780747572411
10 9 8 7 6 5 4 3 2

Typeset by Hewer Text UK Ltd, Edinburgh
Printed in Great Britain by Clays Limited, St Ives plc

The paper this book is printed on is certified by the © Forest Stewardship Council 1996 A.C.
(FSC). It is ancient-forest friendly. The printer holds FSC chain of custody SGS-COC-2061

FSC
Mixed Sources
Product group from well-managed
forests and other controlled sources
Cert no. SGS-COC-2061
www.fsc.org
© 1996 Forest Stewardship Council

For Nigel Langford and Sarah Spankie

Enjoy when you can, and endure when you must.

                    Johann Wolfgang von Goethe

Happiness is a how, not a what; a talent, not an object.

                    Hermann Hesse

You desire to know the art of living, my friend? It is contained in one phrase: make use of suffering.

                    Henri-Frédéric Amiel

Contents

Introduction
Don't Look Down

*The mind is its own place, and in itself, can
make heaven of Hell, and a hell of Heaven.*

John Milton

This is a memoir of depression. It is also my story, because I
believe that we learn through stories.

We learn that we are not alone.

My story is no better or worse than the next person's, just
as my depression was no better or worse, although it felt like
it at the time. I thought I had no hope of ever making it back
to that place I called life. I thought, too, that I was the only
one who felt that way. Depression feels like the most isolated
place on earth. No wonder they call it a disease of loneliness.

If you are reading this book and you feel that way too then
you are not alone. I understand how you feel. I think that
anyone who has suffered from even mild depression understands how it feels. Yet we forget that others understand our
suffering. We withdraw, isolate or shut down completely. We
lose ourselves in our selves, and in the illness.

It doesn't have to be that way. If we connect with even one
other human being who truly understands, we take one step
out of the illness. Life is about connection. There is nothing
else. Depression is the opposite; it is an illness defined by
alienation. So I offer this book by way of connection. I offer it

too, as a source of hope. I hope that by sharing what I was like, what happened and what I am like now, that it may bring somebody else comfort.

I am not an expert, except by experience. For nearly four years, I lived with depression, day and night. I thought I would not make it through. I thought, without wishing to be dramatic, that I would die. I wanted to die. At one time it was all I wanted.

It is not something to regret, or to be ashamed by. Wanting to die (or 'suicidal ideation' as the experts would have it) goes hand in hand with the illness. It is a symptom of severe depression, not a character failing or moral flaw. Nor is it, truly, a desire to die so much as a fervent wish not to go on living. All depressives understand that distinction.

I no longer want to die. I am well. I would go so far as to say that I am happy. They say that happiness can't be measured. Perhaps not. Like depression, it is unique to the person. But just as we can encourage depression to recede, so we can encourage happiness to emerge. To begin with, I had no idea where to look. My training in the art or experience of happiness was intensely poor. The last place I thought I would find it was in myself.

My recovery was slow. I felt like I was learning to walk again. Very often, I tripped and stumbled. Some days, I could not manage more than a few steps. But every day I tried and slowly I clambered out of that pit of total despair. There are no miracles. Getting well, and staying well, takes time, dedication and full attention. It means taking responsibility for our own emotional health and happiness. It requires rigorous honesty and constant self-examination. It needs humility, patience and willingness. It sounds like hard work, and it is. But it is nowhere near as hard as living with severe depression.

You might say that this is a spiritual book. In some ways it is. It is a spiritual book, written by an atheist. As a recovering alcoholic once told me, 'Religion is for people who don't want to go to hell. Spirituality is for people who've been there.'

I make no apology for that. You can take from it what you need and leave the rest. In my own recovery from severe depression, I have drawn on various disciplines from modern therapy, through Buddhism to the Twelve Step programme – the spiritual approach practised by Alcoholics Anonymous. I have taken help from psychiatrists, therapists, friends and perfect strangers. I have discovered comfort in literature, science, and gardens – most particularly, my own.

It is also a practical book, inasmuch as it offers ideas about what might work. There are no promises, only suggestions. In my travels through depression I have tried eating in certain ways and swallowing handfuls of vitamins, amino acids and essential fats. I have done yoga, massage, meditation, homeopathy, acupuncture and bioenergetic feedback. I have had healers standing over my head, drawing bad energy from my neck, and others describing angels at my table. I have tried every form of therapy and read every book on depression I could lay my hands on. Certain phrases, from spiritual leaders, poets and writers, I have muttered like mantras, hoping to absorb serenity by sheer repetition. It does not all work, of course, but some of it does and about that I can tell you. Again, you can take from it what you like and leave the rest.

As to whether the depression will come back, it is every depressive's fear. It might. It might not. I have no way of knowing. I still get low but I have discovered that if I can meet that difficulty, I can go some way to heading it off. The most important thing is not to become trapped in fear. Depression is a paralysis of hope. One thing I know is true. Try never to abandon hope for if you do, hope will surely try to abandon you.

So here is my story. It travels here and there in time. Sometimes, it goes backwards because, as the Danish philosopher Søren Kierkegaard pointed out a few hundred years ago, 'Life must be understood backwards, but it must be lived forwards.' He also said 'Don't forget to love yourself', for which I rather love him. My story stops too, now and then, to give direction or, at least, useful ideas. It is not neat or tidy but then, neither is my mind. And nor, as it happens, is a life.

It starts on the morning of my fiftieth birthday. It seems like a good place to start. Every day without depression is a good place to start.

I wake early and sit in bed with a cup of tea and think. Not about anything in particular, it is my way of untangling the chaos in my head and establishing a sense of peace and order for the day ahead. I do this every day for half an hour, and then I meditate for twenty minutes. It's a routine I've got into since I was ill. I don't know how or why it works. I just know that it does.

My bedroom is white and filled with light, with French windows leading straight on to the garden. The light is important to me; it fights the darkness in my head.

In his seminal book on depression, *The Noonday Demon*, another depressive, Andrew Solomon wrote, 'To wage war on depression is to fight against oneself.' He's right, although on first reading I took the phrase to mean that in depression one becomes one's own enemy. In the intense self-hatred encountered during an episode of severe depression, I think that's true.

I hated myself so much that I tried to kill myself.

These days I believe that it wasn't myself I hated, so much as the self I became during depression. I wanted it dead.

It is two years since I emerged from depression and I no longer want myself dead. I want myself alive. I am no longer my own enemy. Depression is the enemy. The monster lives at my gate. My hope is that, with sufficient effort and luck, I can keep it there. And if that means behaving in ways that I once thought uncharacteristic, such as getting up at six in the morning to meditate, then I will.

Once I have meditated and set my head in some sort of order, I look at myself in the mirror. To see, I suppose, if I look any different now I am suddenly older. I see the same blonde hair, the same blue eyes and the same childishly snub nose. I am not wearing my glasses, so I am a little blurred. Then again, even without that merciful soft focus (one of Mother Nature's kinder compensations for age) I am my most unreliable witness. There is too much history attached to my face, too many memories are butting at the edges of my reality. I cannot see myself. What I can see is that the marks of depression are no longer on my face. These days, I find it easy to spot a depressive. The illness is scrawled across them like graffiti.

My daughter, Molly, takes a photograph, to mark my birthday. 'Open your eyes, Mum,' she says.

My eyes are very deep-set and inclined to disappear entirely if I don't pay attention.

'They are open,' I say.

'Well, open them some more. Look surprised.'

I do, because I am.

I am surprised I have made it to fifty when I once thought I'd never make it at all. I am surprised that I am sitting peacefully in the garden in the sunshine. I am surprised that my daughter, who is fifteen, is beautiful and abundant and taller than I am. Most of all, I am surprised that I am happy, that I have the capacity for happiness again.

When I was very ill, and Molly was nine, she used to leave notes Blu-tacked to the wall above my bed. One said, 'Dear Angels, Please bring my mummy all the joy and happiness she deserves.' I cried when I read that note because I knew that I deserved none.

I would not wish depression on anybody. And yet, it taught me a lot. I have not become suddenly mawkishly grateful for my life but I am more interested in it, more engaged you might say. When you have spent long years in the dark, there is joy in seeing the light and pleasure, above all, in the ordinary.

I look out at my garden. It is not my first garden, but it is the first that I made myself. When I was very ill, before it even existed, dreaming about this garden kept me going all through the long dark nights, and darker days. Planting it, putting my hands in the earth, have been both therapy and a connection to the future. Even at my most despairing, I kept planting. Even in the darkness, it seemed to me an act of optimism, of hope.

When I was really ill, I was living in a flat without a garden. It is symptomatic of how little pleasure I could find, even in things about which I am passionate, that I bought that flat. But, though I could scarcely get out of bed and getting dressed was a superhuman feat, my friends pointed out that every time I managed to venture out, I returned with a plant; a geranium, a pot of jasmine, a box of lavender. It is that same jasmine that now covers the wall beside my kitchen, filling the room with scent each summer, while cuttings of the original geranium bloom in pots outside my shed. When I found the garden it was a mess, a beauty sleeping under a weight of laurel, privet and brambles thick as a man's arm. A little maple, which now has peonies at its feet, still bears an S-shaped kink in its trunk, where it fought to reach the light. I love that tree.

Once I had cleared the worst (me, a man with a van and back-breaking days) I started to lay out the garden using a tape measure, a can of spray paint and bits of string. It was a very hot summer, so I was generally out in the late evening in my nightdress. I must have looked like the local loony (well, let's be frank, I was the local loony) but my neighbours are too charming ever to have mentioned this.

Now the garden is beautiful. I watch the light lift and the light fall, witness the spring come and the summer go. When I feel, as I sometimes do, that all hope has fled, it is a gentle reminder that when something dies, something else must take its place. I love nature for her serene indifference, her insistence at taking everything at her own, sweet pace. The daffodils will unfurl their yellow trumpets in their own time, no matter how often I insist that they, and the spring, hurry along. The roots, hidden beneath the earth, will slowly unfold as they are meant to do, just as life will unfold as it is meant to do. No amount of fussing or fretting on my part will change that. There is freedom in that understanding. And there is joy, too, in knowing that beauty is inevitable, in the slow blooming of a rose, in the smell of newly mown grass, in the warmth of early summer sunshine on our backs.

When I said to friends that I was writing this book, they said, 'Why are you doing this to yourself? Don't you remember how sick you were? Are you mad?'

Well, yes.

So why am I writing this book? I'm writing it because, although I dislike the confessional, I was (and continue to be) so repulsed by the stigma around depression that I determined I must stand up and be counted, not hide away in shame. If I have any talent, it is the ability to communicate, and to get published. So I wrote a personal account of my suicidal depression for a newspaper, the *Daily Telegraph*. In return, I got 2,000 letters and every one of them said, 'Thank God I'm not alone.'

I cried when I read those letters. I knew just how they felt. In reading those letters, I felt less lonely too. It was then that I knew I had to write this book and not just for other people but for myself. I never want to feel so alone again.

When that article was published many people said I was brave. Perhaps, although I don't believe that confronting an illness is necessarily an act of courage. The stigma surrounding depression just makes it seem that way. I wish I could say it was bravery that drove me to pin myself like a butterfly to the pages of a national newspaper, but it was actually anger.

I admit that my anger took me by surprise. But then, so did depression. I had never thought about its implications, or its consequences. The more I inhabited it, the more I came to see the fear and the shame surrounding it. The more depressives I met, the more I came to understand that we are not simply fighting an illness, but the attitudes that surround it.

Imagine saying to somebody that you have a life-threatening illness, such as cancer, and being told to pull yourself together or get over it.

Imagine being terribly ill and too afraid to tell anyone lest it destroys your career.

Imagine being admitted to hospital because you are too ill to function and being too ashamed to tell anyone, because it is a psychiatric hospital. Imagine telling someone that you have recently been discharged and watching them turn away, in embarrassment or disgust or fear.

Comparisons are odious. Stigmatising an illness is more odious still. Bad enough to be ill, but to feel compelled to deny the very thing that, in its worst and most active state, defines you is agony indeed.

It is an illness. That is its beginning and end. It is neither a moral flaw nor an immoral state. It is not a matter for shame, guilt or secrecy. I wish that I had known that when I first became ill. I wish that I had not spent so long trying to manage the unmanageable because I was so ashamed. Or ignorant. Or both.

There is no correct medical term for the illness of depression. It is known, variously, as clinical, major or severe depression. I shall, for the most part confine myself to the description 'severe depression', simply because I think the term describes the illness best.

When finally I ended up in front of a psychiatrist, unable to stop crying, unable to function, wanting only to be dead, he said, 'If you had pneumonia, would you try to cure yourself?'

No.

He shrugged. 'So why do you think you can cure your own depression?'

Why? Because I thought I could manage my own mind. It never occurred to me that I was suffering from an illness over which, by that time, I had little or no control. I knew nothing about depression. All I knew was that I had fought my head for a year, and I had lost.

'You are ill,' he said. 'You are very, very ill.'

At the time, it felt like the nicest thing anybody had ever said to me. I wasn't mad. I was simply sick.

When I say this, later, to a fellow depressive, he smiles in recognition and says that when his psychiatrist told him that if he refused to go into hospital voluntarily, she would have to consider sectioning him – putting him there by force – he was not frightened or angry. He was relieved. 'I was ill. I needed to go into hospital. I could stop pretending that I was coping.'

Sometimes I think depression should be called the coping illness. So many of us struggle on, not daring or knowing how to ask for help. More of us, terribly, go undiagnosed.

This, of course, is my story. Everyone's experience of depression is unique. I can only say what happened to me in the hope that it might throw some light on somebody else's suffering and help them too. It might, too, help those who love somebody suffering from depression better to understand what it is they are going through. If it has helped me in any way it is towards a better understanding of myself as well as my inherent vulnerabilities. Otherwise, I'd leave them well alone. Contemplating one's own navel has a limited appeal. I'd sooner get on with living, which is the antithesis of depression.

But I can't, and there's the truth, just as nobody who lives with a severe, recurrent illness can afford to ignore themselves or their symptoms. I keep an eye on myself, a benign objective focus that, I hope, takes my illness – rather than myself – seriously. Neither am I (nor do I ever want to be) a professional depressive, always defining myself by the melancholia that seems to dog my heels; the black dog as it is sometimes known. Frankly, I'd happily shoot the damn dog and be done with it; but I have come to accept that it is both unkillable and, in some sense, unknowable. Certainly, it often takes me by surprise.

The part of myself that I prefer (of course) is the part Molly calls my, 'usual happy self', just as real as the depressive part of my nature, which I think of as my shadow self. I am, inherently, an optimist. I love life. I enjoy people. I have many good friends. I value friendship above all else and it was my friends who sustained me through the long dark days of depression. While my inability to reach out and communicate with them drove me almost mad with grief, I knew they were there even when I was incapable of speaking to them. And they were still there when I emerged and for that I am indescribably grateful.

So I am not an expert but simply somebody who suffers from depressive illness who is writing a book. My path through depression is neither right nor wrong, it is simply mine.

Nor can my account, in all honesty, be complete. Depression, as my psychiatrist told me when first we met and I complained at my inability to think myself out of it, depresses every single cognitive process. Concentration, memory, logic, reason, even the interpretation of facts and actual events are all interrupted.

'If we did a test on you now,' he said, 'I can guarantee that your IQ would be down by at least thirty points.'

It is as if the mind draws a veil across itself. There are parts of my memory of that time that are still missing, including books that I supposedly read. When I came to look at them again I discovered that they were almost entirely unfamiliar. It is the same with films. Parts of them are eerily familiar, so much so that I get an immediate sense of déjà vu, but I have no recollection of the beginning or the end or even the middle of the story. There are conversations I have had, or that people have told me I have had, that are quite blank to me and I am apt to grow confused about the chronology of months, or even years. Mercifully, some might say, for depression is not a place to linger.

By contrast, other parts of my memory of that time are still acute enough to mean that I have only to pass certain places or smell certain scents to feel intense pain. It returns at an almost cellular level. It is as if both my body and my mind remember, and I believe that depressive illness is both physical and mental, that the body is capable of holding on to memories and experiences that the mind wishes to forget.

I doubt I am alone in being haunted by my illness. All depressives remember how sick they were, how sick some of us still are.

1

Myself So Far

I was gratified to be able to answer promptly. I said I don't know.

Mark Twain

Before I tell you about my depression, I should tell you something about my life so far. Or perhaps that should be myself so far.

I was born in Brunei, but I am English. I grew up in many different countries. After Brunei, we moved to Brazil and from there to Aden, Oman and Angola. We spent about three years in each country, with brief intervals in England. My father took a job with Shell after the war and was posted abroad. We followed wherever his work took him.

I went to a boarding school in England from the age of eleven, but saw nothing of this country other than the school. It was not home. Home was in whatever country my parents were living at the time. I came to live here fully when I was eighteen. I have two brothers, one on either side of me in age. The eldest is Michael and the youngest is Tony. They, too, were away at school for most of our childhood.

Dad comes from South London and is the eldest of four. His father, Reg, was a Cockney, born, as he was proud to say, within the sound of Bow bells. Reg worked as a handyman; then moved to the country to run a petrol station. Or, at least, it was my grandad's version of the country: a small bungalow set in front of a set of petrol pumps in the middle of a lorry park on a busy roundabout outside Norwich. This was long before self-service so Reg was out all hours in his flat cap and his brown cotton coat. It seemed to us that he was always happy, a practical joker, teaching his budgie to talk nonsense, chasing us kids around his bungalow with his false teeth out, his gummy grin reducing us to helpless giggles.

My grandmother Maisie was pint-sized, barely reaching five feet tall, with red hair and blue eyes. She kept everything, her house, Reg, their four kids in apple-pie order. And she made a mean lemon curd.

My mother is also a Londoner, but posher, born in Richmond. Her father, Phil Ray, was an actor, working in music hall and on the stage. Later, he found work in films and television, playing mostly bit parts in over forty films from *Sons and Lovers* to *Dracula: Prince of Darkness* and *Frankenstein Created Woman*. He always turned out a good priest and was a regular on *Dr Who*, *Z Cars* and even, fleetingly, in *Hancock's Half Hour*. A shy, quiet man, with a melancholic streak, he loved to act because, as he said, it allowed him to be somebody else.

His greatest passion was my grandmother Dorothy whose stage name was Jackie, and who was a dancer and a model. Hugely elegant, despite never having any money, she made all her own clothes, including her hats and coats, and taught me to sew. I spent a great deal of time with her, every weekend that I was allowed out of boarding school in England, while my parents were abroad. When she died, my grandfather made a shrine of photographs of her in one corner of their flat. And then he just quietly faded away.

My daughter, Molly, is also a Londoner. And so am I, if only by adoption.

I am blonde with blue eyes, stand five feet seven tall and weigh 140 pounds, more or less. I would prefer it to be less.

I love fashion, perhaps influenced by my grandmother, and studied it at Central Saint Martin's, where, having taught for many years, I am now a visiting professor. I still love good clothes.

After college, I wrote about fashion for *Vogue*, where I started my career, having won the *Vogue* Talent Contest. I then worked for the *Observer* newspaper, where I was fashion editor for four years.

I am a mother, to Molly, whom I love very much, and who loves me. 'This much,' as she says, her arms open wide.

I love words. And books.

I am a successful journalist. Successful in that people pay me to write for them, for which I am always grateful. As a child, it never occurred to me that people would give me money to do what I love best.

I am a successful novelist. Successful inasmuch as I have written four novels, all of which sold modestly but well. Or, at least, well enough for a publisher always to ask me to write another.

I was a successful magazine editor. In the mid-1980s, I launched *Elle*, which I edited for four years. It was a gratifying and immediate hit and established a blueprint, or so it is said, for a new attitude in women's magazines. Ten years later, I edited another magazine, *Red*, for a brief year and with far less success. Some people loved it, others loathed it. I console myself that nobody seemed indifferent.

I am less successful at relationships. I have been married twice, which is not something I am pleased about. At least, I am not pleased about the failures, rather than the marriages both of which, at the time, I liked very much. I remain close friends with both my ex-husbands.

I am in love with and loved by somebody, and hope that I am better at loving him than I was at loving my husbands. I suspect that he hopes so too.

Gardening is my passion. So is good food. I love to cook. There are few things I like more than to feed my friends.

I am, in all these ways, blessed.

I am also a depressive.
It doesn't quite fit, does it?

2

Bedlam and Leeches

Be kind, for everyone you meet is fighting a harder battle.

Plato

A little while ago, I was driving a close friend, Nigel, to have a scan. He had suspected tumours in his lungs and his liver.

'Obstacles' they called them, and marked the request URGENT. He puts on a funny voice as he reports this to me, camping up the word. We both know what it means, obstacles to life, but have a silent pact not to say it.

We arrive at the clinic. Nigel disappears through double doors marked with a big red STOP sign. I watch him go. I am in pieces but I smile, foolishly, for he cannot see me. We have been in a clinic together before, a psychiatric clinic. It is where we first met. We are both childishly fond of telling the story at parties. 'We met in a loony bin.' People never know whether to believe us. But when we laugh, they laugh too. It is only funny because it seems unbelievable. We don't look like the sort of people who suffer from depression. But I've been in three psychiatric units. Nobody in there looked like the sort of person who suffers from depression. It is no respecter of type. Or gender. Or class. Or money. Or success.

Nigel has been a huge education for my daughter, Molly.

She knows that I met him in a mental hospital. She met him there herself, when she visited. And she loves him.

'If he's mad,' she says, 'then I love mad people.'

'Not mad, darling, just depressed.'

'Whatever.'

When Nigel and I first met, we were both madly, and I use that word advisedly, suicidal. Nigel's preferred method of killing himself, or planning to kill himself, was to drive his car fast into a wall. He had all the bends and speeds around his house worked out in his head. He knew all the best corners.

I was in the hospital because I was a danger to myself. I was as capable of killing myself as I was of making a cup of tea. At the time, I could not say which I would prefer.

We got to know each other unusually well, bound together by our illness and by an abrupt, if not altogether welcome, vulnerability. If there is a faster way to intimacy than depression's catastrophic disintegration or the absolute honesty demanded by group therapy, then I have never met it. Not all friendships made in psychiatric units survive, of course. Why should they? We are people first, depressives second. There are other, more important, ties that bind than a mutual mental illness.

After we left the hospital, we remained friends as much for our devotion to books and gardens or the latest reality TV show as our intimate understanding of suicide. These days, we rarely discuss our illness. We are not, as Nigel is quick to point out, 'a pair of neurotic ambulance chasers'.

Nonetheless, it is the bleak, unwelcome shadows that depression sometimes throws at us that keep us stuck so fast. We can talk to each other at times when we can talk to nobody else. We can say things we could say to nobody else.

One day, soon after we left hospital, Nigel telephoned. I was down in the black pit and I was crying. He listened to me for a while in silence. That silence was unutterably consoling. He will never, as others do, try to persuade me out of my own reality. He won't tell me I feel something that I don't.

When I was very ill, I became so tired of people telling me that things would get better. I felt, always, that I must try to comfort them by agreeing. Either that, or stay silent. There were no words to explain the depths of my despair. I didn't understand it myself.

When I had stopped crying Nigel said, 'I think what you need is a nice drive in the country.' Remembering his chosen method of suicide, I asked him how he was feeling that particular day. He laughed.

Nigel walks back through the red stop sign doors. He smiles at me, despite the circumstances in which we find ourselves, and says that we have to return in an hour, to pick up the results and take them to his GP. We smile at each other almost all of the time. We are usually cheerful in each other's company. It is as if we have taken an unspoken pact of reassurance. We also both know that each of us is capable of smiling and talking cheerfully while at the same time planning our own deaths. Even so, we depend on each other not to die, at least not on purpose.

It is a beautiful day, sunny and warm. We go to a café, sit outside. He eats carrot cake; I have a lemon muffin. My dog begs for crumbs. Halfway through his carrot cake, I ask him if he is frightened. They'd done more tests the week before, scans on his bones. His ribs have been hurting badly. We both know what that means but we have never before said it out loud.

'No,' he says, 'I'm not frightened of cancer or dying. You know me, and dying.'

Yes, I know him and dying. Suicide is his default setting. It's never too far from his mind. He uses it, he thinks, as a release mechanism. It is an escape hatch, if not in fact, then at least in thought. 'Dying,' he says, 'feels like nothing against the fear of going through another episode of severe depression. I don't think I could do it again.'

Nor do I. I don't think I could cope with the severity of the depression that claimed and destroyed four years of my life. Four years. It seems so little in the scheme of things.

So there you have it. My life in two choices. To be happy or to die.

I choose happy.

It sounds flippant. It's not. If I choose to look up and not down, it's because I know what waits below. I am a depressive. It took me a long time to say those words out loud. Just as it took me a long time to come to terms with my illness.

All illnesses need to be managed and in that, depression is no different. It is a complex treatment, just as wellness is a complex and fluctuating state of being. Both need managing. Both need constant awareness. I mean by wellness, not just a physical robustness but also an emotional wholeness; a complete engagement and connection with life.

While there has been a shift in attitude, there is still a common belief that depression is simply a chemical imbalance of the mind that requires chemical intervention. I don't dispute that. In its acute phase, depression certainly needs medication. At that stage, nothing else can touch it. Once out of the acute phase it needs a great deal more.

I am not against antidepressants – far from it. Drugs can and do save lives. They can and do transform lives. But depression is not a singular illness and it requires more than a singular approach to alleviate it and keep it at bay. Most psychiatrists admit that antidepressants are a palliative, not a cure.

Listen to Martin Seligman, Professor of Psychology at the University of Pennsylvania; 'The dirty little secret of biological psychiatry is that every single drug in the psychopharmacopoeia is palliative. That is, all of them are symptom suppressors, and when you stop taking them you're back at square one.'

Antidepressants are not the miracle workers or the 'happy pills' our culture suggests. They did not, for example, work for me.

I thought that if I went into hospital, I would become well. I thought a pill could make me better. The failure of both to do either was almost more catastrophic for me than the illness itself. Far from making me better, it sent me into a despair from which I thought I would never emerge. If the great panacea of the twenty-first century could not help me, what could?

After months of medication and two stays in psychiatric units, my psychiatrist admitted that he was stumped. I have something known as treatment-resistant depression. In other words, it resists all chemical attempts to alleviate it. It was only when I was better that he told me that, in his experience, antidepressants are effective on only thirty per cent of the people to whom he prescribes them. Later, I discovered that opinions vary on this, as they do on almost every area of depressive illness, but that most experts agree that for a significant number of people, antidepressants are completely ineffective.

Far from being a panacea, psychopharmacology is a ludicrously inexact science. Its reputation as a modern miracle is based on the thirty per cent for whom antidepressants effect an almost magical cure of near remission. For the next thirty to forty per cent of people suffering from depression, it is touch and go. They may need to try two or three or even four antidepressants to discover the one that works for them. Then, for the last thirty per cent, for people like me, antidepressants have no effect at all.

'Why,' I asked my psychiatrist, 'don't you tell us that?'

He shrugged. 'Because I am in the business of bringing hope to my patients.'

I applaud his sentiment, but I also know that there is nothing more hopeless than the depressive who believes they are beyond all help and who does not know or understand why.

When I first became depressed, all my trust was in modern medicine. Like most people, I believed the myth of happy pills. You get depression, you take drugs, you get better.

When that remedy failed, I thought, in some obscure way, that it was my fault – that it was me who was failing modern medicine and not the other way around.

Sadly, I am not alone in this. According to research published by the Clinical Neuroscience Research Centre in Dartford:

> Around 5 million people in the UK experience depression at any one time. Whilst many people make a full recovery about thirty to forty per cent are resistant to conventional therapies. For them their depression is an enduring, debilitating disease and for some, the only treatment options left include psychosurgery and ECT.

I recall a day in my psychiatrist's office. I am slumped on the sofa, shaking and crying. My psychiatrist's expression is severe. More than that, he seems uneasy. The prognosis, he says, is bad. I have been severely depressed for an unusually long time, around eighteen months, which is long enough for my condition to be regarded as 'chronic'.

He suggests that we try ECT (Electro Convulsive Therapy) but I saw a friend I made in the first psychiatric unit I was in suffer its consequences with apparently little benefit. Her memory, she complained, was shot to pieces. I am set against it, and say so. I want my memories, good and bad. He frowns, a tiny jolt of impatience framing his eyes. He is a scientist. He wants to make me well, not whole. At least, that is my interpretation and I wonder, for a moment, what the whole of me is. If depression is a part of me, perhaps I must simply accept it as it is. Except that I know that I cannot go on like this. He knows it too. He is trying to help.

'How does ECT work?' I ask.

'We don't know. We just know that, usually, it does and that the memory loss, usually, is short term and short-lived.'

I sigh. There are far too many 'usually's in his sentence. 'But there are no guarantees?'

'No,' he says, avoiding my gaze.

Then he tells me a story, about being on a train journey with a friend with whom he attended medical school. The friend is a heart surgeon. My psychiatrist is trying to explain his work, and some of the difficulties he daily encounters. I suspect that I am one of those difficulties. After a while, his friend the heart surgeon exclaims, 'It must be like being in an operating theatre, preparing to make the first incision and somebody shouts, "No, make the cut over here." Then another calls, "No, over here." Then a third voice joins in, "Over here!"'

'In cases like this,' my psychiatrist says, 'it is trial and error.'

I am a case. I am a trial. And I am an error.

'Poor you,' I say, when what I really mean is, poor me.

There is, he says, another treatment for the chronic, a lobotomy. Not the ancient hacksaw version of Hollywood myth but a modern refinement, involving needle-fine wires. These days it goes by the more reassuring title of psychosurgery. But the success rate, among the chronic, is only twenty per cent.

I say nothing. I think he must be joking. I hope he is joking even though I can see that he is not. We return to the subject of my medication. So far we have tried five different varieties and two combinations of others. I feel like I am in a sweet shop. Let's try some of the blue ones. No good? Well, how about some blue with some pink? Or how about a few of the yellow?

My psychiatrist, in a desperate attempt to break the pattern of resistance, loads me with more and more drugs. He is nothing, if not an optimist. I think that all psychiatrists must be optimists. They could not stay in their profession if they were not.

At one time, I am taking the top dose of the SSRI anti-depressant Venlafaxine which is often given to treatment-resistant patients. On top of that I take 1,000 mgs of lithium daily. Lithium is usually prescribed for bipolar depression (manic depression) from which I do not suffer. The reason I am taking it is because a body of research from the States suggests that loading lithium on top of a mega dose of an SSRI might, in some cases, break the resistance.

It does nothing for me, other than make me so physically ill I think I might die. I shake so badly I can scarcely stand. My mouth is filled with a sour taste so repulsive I cannot eat. Even water tastes foul. The depression does not shift.

I am sicker than ever and it is two years since I took my first antidepressant, prescribed by my GP. She stuck a pin in a book. 'Let's try this one,' she said. Ten months later, I was hospitalised with severe clinical depression. In the hospital, the doctor took one look at the level of antidepressant I was taking and laughed out loud.

It was not my GP's fault. She was doing, in a limited time and with a limited knowledge of the new drugs that constantly appear on the market, the best that she could. The hard-pressed GP will be confronted with one new case of depression at every surgery session. One in every three people attending a GP's surgery has significant psychological symptoms. Even so, our understanding of major depressive disorder is so limited that only sixty per cent of those presenting with it will be detected and only ten per cent of those diagnosed are referred on to specialist services.

It is not that science is failing us. It is simply that the solution is as complex and multifaceted as the illness itself. For every theory of its causes, there is another to contradict it; for every new treatment, there is another that dismisses it as ineffective. This is not deliberate obstruction. Depressive illness, as well as being complex, is highly individual. What works for one person does not work for another. And often there is no explanation why this is so. Scientists do not know why one method or drug might work, where another does not. They know that, for some people, SSRI antidepressants work, but they have no real idea how. Or what the long-term effects might be.

But there is hope. It is just that we need to look further for it than in a handful of pills. We need to see depression holistically, as an illness of mind, body and soul (I hesitate to use that word but I can think of no other) and treat it accordingly.

John F. Greden, MD, the Rachel Upjohn Professor of Psychiatry and Clinical Neuroscience in the University of Michigan Medical School calls depression the 'under' disease – as in underdiagnosed, undertreated and underdiscussed. As for its treatment, he is on record as saying,

> If by 'cure,' you mean totally eliminating the condition for ever, I would suggest that's not the way we should think about it. Indeed, it is probably inaccurate for most. If you're asking, can you bring people with depression to a state of remission, well-being and normal functioning, and can they remain there, then the answer is a resounding yes.

I believe that, just as I believe that there is no one theory or therapy or drug that can make you, or me, better. Or keep us better. There is no simple cure or magic remedy and there are no happy pills, much as we would like to believe in them. And we do like to believe. I have lost count of the number of people who have said to me, as if it is both an admission of defeat and the end to all their problems, 'I suppose I had better go on antidepressants.'

Well, why not? If they work, then wonderful. Every weapon in the fight against depression is worth considering and there may come a day when a daily pill is all that's needed. Until then, for those like me who find that antidepressants are of little or no help there is a different path.

It is not easy, but it is possible. It embraces the various talking therapies and the daily disciplines of walking, yoga and meditation. It uses love and trust and faith – not purely spiritual faith, but faith in life itself. It requires acceptance, humility and a willingness to be open as well as constant self-examination and lacerating honesty. Those are all the tools that I have used to get better and I know that they work. Not just on me but on the others who use them too. Even those who find that antidepressants are an answer to their prayers may find some of the methods in this book useful.

The relapse rate for depressives relying on medication alone is eighty per cent. Nobody knows quite why. Some schools of thought believe that the brain becomes habituated to a particular drug, which then loses its efficacy. Still others believe that the illness mutates or that it is not a singular illness but a cluster of conditions that, at any one time, need different treatments. The illness, like the cure, remains a mystery. When I said to my psychiatrist that it seemed to me that we were no further along than bedlam and leeches, he said that at least we knew what leeches did.

It was that, more than anything, which brought me to the writing of this book. I may have, as the scientists put it, 'an enduring, debilitating disease' but I prefer to think of it as an illness that never entirely leaves us but can, with full knowledge and attention, be managed with some degree of grace.

Nigel got his test results back and they were OK. His liver is fragile after many years on a great deal of medication. He still swears by it to control the depression he has suffered since he was in his teens. I don't, but anything that keeps him away from those sharp corners is fine by me too.

3

Throat Monsters and Other Terrors

*Where am I? Who am I? How did I come to be
here? What is this thing called the world? How did I
come into the world? Why was I not consulted?
And If I am compelled to take part in it, where is
the director? I want to see him.*

Søren Kierkegaard

I am walking down the corridor in my flat. The monster is at
my throat, claw stuck fast. I cannot eat. I can scarcely
breathe. It is ten months since I was diagnosed with severe
clinical depression, months without beginning or end. Time
moves like treacle, running thick and heavy through my days.

I hate this flat. It is beautiful, a mansion flat two floors up
with high ceilings and ornate fireplaces, but I know that
behind the façade, the walls are running with tears. My tears.
Pain has seeped into the plaster.

The flat is laid out in two parts, with a long, narrow
corridor connecting the two. At one end there is a large,
light-filled sitting room and two bedrooms, Molly's and
mine. The rooms are painted cream and white, testament
to an earlier time when I tried to decorate myself out of the
dark.

My bedroom is small; kept dark by the linen curtains which
I made myself and which I keep shut fast against the day. The

white duvet cover has scorch marks in it from the cigarettes I smoke in the dead of night when I am dragged from sleep by some unknown, unseen terror, but too dazed with sleeping pills to know what I am doing.

At the other end of the corridor is the kitchen, and my study, where I rarely go. Sometimes I venture in to sit at my computer in front of the dead, blank screen and flick idly through my piles of books. They are dusty and sad, with a long neglected air. I never stay in there for long.

The kitchen is huge and half finished, as if somebody has abandoned it in despair. They have. It was me. I decorated half of the flat and then I simply gave up. There are no units, just a few rudimentary cupboards; the fridge is ancient and most of the shelves in it have collapsed. The hot water tap is stuck fast. I haven't the energy to call a plumber. I'm not sure that I even know how. Sometimes this strikes me as odd. I used to head up a staff of forty and handle a budget of millions. Now, I can't even call a plumber so I wash up by boiling a kettle for hot water. I no longer think that's strange. I think it's normal. When they come to visit, I see the way my friends look at the kettle and then at me. I don't know how to explain, so I say nothing.

As I walk down the corridor, I keep my hands pressed to the wall because I am shaking so hard I can hardly stand. The next thing I know, I am flat on the ground, my face pressed into the carpet. I think, how did this happen? Did I stumble and fall? I have no recollection of it. It was as if some great hand took me by the throat and flung me to the ground. If I hadn't been here, I wouldn't have believed me. I tear at my throat, uselessly, trying to pull the monster away. I think, I will die now. There is no other way.

Or, just one. Vodka. When the pain is this bad, I know of no better anaesthetic than vodka. No prescribed tranquilliser comes close. Believe me, in the past few months I've taken them all, with my psychiatrist's blessing.

He does not bless alcohol but then he's not in the state I'm in. Nor, oh lucky man, has he ever been. Sometimes I think only those who have suffered severe depression should be allowed to treat those with severe depression. I am sick and tired of theory. I have put on a stone in six weeks. My body feels spongy and heavy, weirdly unfamiliar. It is as if my flesh has been pumped full of a thick viscous liquid. I complain about this to my psychiatrist.

'You should not put on weight on these particular pills.'

'Well, I have. And I hardly eat.'

'There is no evidence to suggest that this medication affects the metabolism.'

I say, 'I am the evidence.'

Just as I am the evidence that antidepressant medication does not work. Or at least, it does not appear to work on me. We have tried four different types; nothing seems able to lift this dark despair. The most recent makes me shake so badly that at times I can't hold a cup of tea or a pen. I cannot even write my own name. It also, if that is possible, makes the throat monster worse.

'It may be the illness reasserting itself,' says my psychiatrist.

'Perhaps it's the medication,' I suggest. 'I think it's poisoning me.' I don't show him my tongue, which is coated a deep, dark brown from all the chemicals I daily ingest.

My psychiatrist frowns. Paranoia is a symptom of extreme depression. I hate my medication. I am never happy.

Once the irony of that thought would have made me laugh.

He says, 'The shaking and the throat may be symptoms of anxiety, which often comes with depression.'

'I don't suffer from anxiety. It's the side-effects of the medication.'

I have been in two psychiatric units. I have seen severe anxiety disorder at first hand. I have, at least, been spared that.

He says nothing.

'This is all bollocks,' I say.

I am not a patient patient.

*   *   *

I stumble to my feet and inch along the corridor, hands pressed fast to the wall to steady myself, and knock a framed photograph askew. I collect black and white photographs. There are Norman Parkinson's women, serene, glacial and unaccountably chic and Andrew Macpherson's modern girls, smiling and sexy. There is Matt Dillon, from an early photo shoot I did with him on *Vogue*, when he was just another handsome boy and not a famous movie star. And there is Bruce Weber, photographer, filming in Cannes.

I love them. They are beautiful. Now, I knock past them clumsily, as if they do not matter.

My kitchen looks peculiar, as if it is both intensely familiar yet a room I scarcely know. I scrabble in the freezer, pull out a bottle of ice-cold vodka and pour a measure into a glass. My hands are shaking badly. Some of the vodka spills on the wooden table, which I used to polish weekly, with beeswax and soft cloths. I leave the wet puddle, allow the ethanol to eat into the wood. I haven't the energy to find a cloth.

The vodka burns at my throat but gradually, the heat penetrates and the claw lessens its grip slightly. What time is it? A little after ten in the morning. I try to remember what ten in the morning means, how it feels. But I cannot. Time means nothing to me any more. I stagger back to bed, and try to sleep. Try to pass out. I don't want sleep. I want oblivion.

There's a pounding in my ears. It's muffled as if somebody has put a sack over my head. I open my eyes. My bedroom is dark, the curtains drawn to block the sun, which is shining merrily. I hate the sun. When the sun is shining, I should be happy. I should. I should.

The darkness gathers in my head. It is black, this day. Blacker than black, heavy and suffocating. And the monster is still at my throat. Its form is that of a serpent, with a thick, muscular tail covered in scales that wraps round and around my neck, pulling tight. At its head there is no mouth or eyes, just a single bird's talon, a black claw tipped with sharp silver. The claw sinks into the front of my throat and hangs fast. I try to reduce its horror by giving it a name, the throat monster. Various therapists suggest that I go one step further and try to befriend it. I think this is facile and ignore their suggestions. I don't want a cute cartoon, a puppy dog living in my throat. I don't want it to be my friend. I hate it. I want it to go away. I want drugs, to stop it. Where is modern science when I need it? Why is so little known about mental illness? What is it I am suffering from?

Grief, said a therapist. Unexpressed grief. It's got you by the throat.

Don't be absurd, I said at the time. Don't be so fanciful. But when I am alone and the monster is tearing at my throat, I think that, whatever it is, it's going to kill me.

According to my psychiatrist, the monster is not real. He tells me this apologetically, as if I know it already. Which I do. Of course it is not real. It's not even a monster, but a somatic manifestation of my illness, a mere, clinical symptom of major depressive disorder. The throat monster has a proper psychiatric name, he says, but not a name I'll like. It is called *Globus hystericus*, a psychological term for 'lump in the throat' given to it by Freud. Of course, it must be Freud. Of course, it must manifest most often in women. My psychiatrist's expression is grave. He knows that I resent that association of hysteria and women.

Even so, I am comforted by the word 'symptom' and its cool, empirical note. The reality, even if the lump in my throat is not actually real, is not comforting. It hurts, like a knotted rope thick around my neck, the knot pressed hard to my windpipe. And it never goes away. It is the sensation you get when you are struggling to hold back tears, the tight, aching ball that grows and grows even as you try to swallow it down. I read, somewhere, that crying can relieve the symptoms. It can't, or not for me anyway. I cry and I cry. I cry so much that sometimes I am astonished there is any water left in my body.

I close my eyes. Time passes. I don't know how much time. Is it day or is it night? I hear kids shouting on the streets.

'Fucking wanker.' School must be out. The shouts are too loud, banging in my head. I put a pillow over my face and push it down to cover my ears. I feel suffocated. The monster rears in my throat. I take the pillow away again.

The shouts diminish, gradually. It is so dark. Why is it so dark? Am I awake? Am I alive? I am. Fuck. I want more vodka, I want a sleeping pill, I want anything to stop me being awake, or alive, but I force myself out of bed to make a cup of tea and a cucumber sandwich. It is the only thing I can eat. That's if I eat at all.

I slice the cucumber thin, shave butter off a cold block, and lay it on squares of foamy white bread. I hate white bread. Don't I? I used to. I cut the crusts off, slice the sandwich in neat triangles, and put it on a white plate.

Once I have made the sandwich, I don't know what to do with it, or where to go. I stand in the kitchen for a while, staring at the plate, at the steaming mug of tea. I remember this mug, remember buying it and how it had to be white and of a certain thickness of china and the handle must be curved just so.

I was standing in Heal's, during the sale, and I bought six mugs, at half price. They came in a thick brown cardboard box, held shut by wide black staples. It took me hours to get those staples out.

A friend called the other day.

'How are you?' she said.

The sun was shining, the sky a merciless blue. It was only eleven in the morning but I had been awake since three twenty. I was in bed because, as usual, I could think of nowhere else to go. I said that I was feeling low. Low is the depressive's euphemism for despair.

She said: 'How can you be depressed on a day like this?'

I wanted to say: 'If I had flu, would you ask me how I could be sick on a day like this?'

I said nothing. She meant well.

People send me cards. The images on the front are inoffensive watercolours of flowers or bland, abstract art. Inside, they write that they are sorry to hear that I've been unwell. That they have always thought of me as 'such a strong person'. My sickness has a moral tone. I am reduced, made feeble. I think, well there is some truth in that. I am a shadow of the self I used to be.

I feel caged, suddenly, impossibly restless. It goes like this, inertia and then profound agitation. I must do something. But what? My daughter, Molly, is with Jonathan, her dad, for three more days. She lives with him for half of the time.

I miss her so.

I am so glad she is not here. The effort of trying to be that person she knows as Mummy is overwhelming.

I want to say to her that I am sorry, I am sorry that it is me who has taken her mother's place. I want to tell her that she deserves better, that she should have a mother like the mother I used to be, who laughs and bakes and loses gracefully when her daughter cheats at Monopoly. But I can't. I can't tell her that her mother has gone, that her mother is lost.

It would break her heart.

And so I struggle on. I drink some tea, retching against the taste, the monster tightening in my throat as if in sympathetic recoil. I pick up the sandwich to take a bite, but abandon it halfway through.

There must be something I can do. Should do. I always did something. I was never still. There was always work to be done, a deadline to meet, a child to look after, a house to run, a garden to tend, books to read, films to see, friends to enjoy. There was never enough time.

Now, there is too much. And there are too few people. And I feel that they have nothing, any longer, to do with me.

I look at the sandwich, at the perfect half circle my teeth have formed. I must eat, I know, but it seems such a laborious process, to pick up the sandwich, to bite, to chew, to swallow.

I get up and look out of the window. People are walking briskly up and down the road. I try to imagine what I would do, if I were out on the street. Where would I be going? I can think of nowhere. The newsagent's, perhaps, to buy a news-paper. Have I read a newspaper today?

I used to write for the newspapers. Almost all of the nationals, in fact. What was it I had to say? I can see myself, sitting at my computer, head bent, writing furiously, hands flying over the keys. I can't imagine what must have been in my head to make my hands go so fast.

I look at the bed. I can see no newspaper. Not that I ever read them. I can no longer read. It is the greatest tragedy of my present existence. By the time I get to the end of a sentence, I have forgotten the beginning. Words are no more than patterns on a page. Sometimes, it is better. Sometimes I can manage a few paragraphs, but later I can never remember what it is they said.

It is like being bereaved, this lack of reading, like losing an old and dearly beloved friend. A lifelong friend. I used to read four or five books a week.

I remember reading something by Goethe, about losing reading and losing oneself, and how it struck me at the time.

My creative powers have been reduced to a restless in-dolence. I cannot be idle, yet I cannot seem to do anything either. I have no imagination, no more feeling for nature, and reading has become repugnant to me. When we are robbed of ourselves, we are robbed of everything.

That's right, I think. Depression is the great thief.

When I was a child my mother was forever telling me to get my head out of a book and go outside and get some fresh air. Molly is like me. She reads all the time. I never tell her to get her head out of a book. I know the pleasure, the transport, the pure delight that reading brings. Before I was ill, I used to worry that I spent too much of my time with books, living in other people's lives. I used to think it was, perhaps, because I didn't much like my own. Perhaps that's it then. Perhaps depression is simply inhabiting your own life. Or perhaps it's simply too much reality.

No, this is mad thinking. All my thinking is mad thinking, these days. Round and round it goes, dipping in and out of perspective but always present, never still.

These days I only buy a newspaper because I want to be normal. I want to be a person who reads a newspaper. Besides, it gives me something to do, somewhere to go. Every morning, I go out to get my newspaper and cigarettes. This morning I didn't. This morning was a bad morning. Or was that yesterday? I try to remember. No, it was this morning. I had a bath. I managed that but then I was shaking so badly with the medication I had to lie down. Or, at least I think it's the medication. It's hard to tell.

Why do they call it a 'mental' illness? The pain isn't just in my head; it's everywhere, but mainly at my throat and in my heart. Perhaps my heart is broken. Is this what this is? My whole chest feels like it's being crushed. It's hard to breathe.

I am sitting on the floor, in my bedroom, curled up against the cupboards. I have given up on the bed. I hate the bed and its soft, suffocating embrace. I would like to leave this room, but I can't. I feel safe in here. Or, as safe as I feel anywhere, which is not very.

How fucking stupid is that? I can't leave my own bedroom. Me, who used to fly across the world and get on a plane without a moment's thought. I have been getting on and off aeroplanes on my own since I was ten years old. I am fiercely independent. I am fierce. Or so people tell me. Used to tell me. I never used to be so afraid. When I was one of his editors, I used to stand up against Rupert Murdoch, arguing with him. I used to be so brave. I used to be somebody.

I am still somebody.

Aren't I?

But who?

I am somebody who can't leave her bedroom, somebody who can't walk across a road to buy a newspaper. I start to cry. I hate crying. I hate these tears that come, unbidden, at any time of day.

My cat, Bert, comes and sits next to me and purrs. When I do not respond, he gently bats my wet cheeks with his paw, first one side, and then the other. He keeps the claws sheathed so his paw feels like a velvet powder puff.

Clever cat.

He used to be a hunter, a champion mouser, when we had a garden. Now he follows me around the flat, turning somersaults for my amusement or butting his head against my idle hands, demanding attention. He cries a lot too, his calls echoing through the apartment.

I never used to cry. I hardly ever shed a tear. I spent a whole life not in tears. And that, according to one therapist, is my problem. Is this all it is then? Is this simply forty years of collected tears?

'Have a good cry. You'll feel better.'

Stupid, I think, furiously. Stupid.

I remember a nurse, in the psychiatric unit. She was Jamaican, wore her hair in braids fastened with bright glass beads. They hung in a brilliant curtain over the stiff shoulders of her starched white uniform. Her nose was perfect, straight and beautiful, and she had a wide, white smile.

She held my hand at four in the morning, as I cried. They'd given me sleeping pills, enough, they said, to fell an ox. I had to take them sitting in bed because they were so strong. They said I might pass out if I took them standing up. Two hours later, I was still wide awake, walking up and down the empty corridors, up and down, trying to walk away the tears.

The nurse came and got me, led me back to my room and put me in bed, then sat with me, holding my hand.

'Have a good cry,' she said, 'you'll feel better.'

I shouted at her. Her bright smile dimmed, and went out. I

hated myself for shouting, but it seemed so important to be understood.

'It won't,' I shouted. 'Crying won't make me feel better. I cry and I cry and I never feel any better. Why does nobody understand that?'

Why does nobody understand that these are tears without a beginning or an end? I thought sadness had a beginning and an end. And a middle. A story, if you like. I was wrong.

She said, 'Has something happened?'

I ducked my head, plucked at the sheet. 'No,' I said. 'Nothing has happened.'

She patted my hand.

I must stop this, I think. I must stop these tears, stop these thoughts. Perhaps if I stand up, they will stop. Perhaps if I get dressed, perhaps if I try to be me, they will go away.

I take off my nightdress. It is old soft white linen. I have always collected vintage linen. Now it is tattered and stained and sad. I no longer launder and starch it. I am still in my nightie at four in the afternoon.

It is shocking and, shockingly, I don't care.

I pull on an old cashmere sweater and leggings. They are black. The sweater is large and comforting. The leggings are baggy and comfortable. I have been wearing these same clothes for weeks, months even. I used to work in fashion, to write about it weekly. I love good clothes. My wardrobe was once filled with designer labels. Some of them remain. I look at them and think that if only I could get those clothes on, that I might, once more, become me.

I try, sometimes, but I look awkward, uncomfortable, as if I have put on a stranger's clothes. So I take them off again.

I feel frightened, suddenly. No, terrified. This is not fear. This is black, consuming terror.

'Tell me,' says my therapist, 'what you look forward to in the day.'

'Taking my sleeping pills at night,' I say. 'Oblivion.'

Not that it lasts very long. I am awake again at three

twenty. Always three twenty, never three ten or even three thirty. My eyes snap open and my mind clicks on, as if somebody has pressed a switch. And on it goes, on and on. And it repeats the same thing, over and over.

I want to die. I want, so badly, to die.

I lie on the floor in my bedroom and scream, as if the walls could hear me.

'Will somebody help me? Will somebody please help me?'

But there is nobody there. I don't want anybody there. I don't want anybody to see me like this. I don't want anybody until the terror gets too much, until I know that I am a danger to myself.

This is one of those times. And so I make a call, to Sarah, my closest friend. We have been friends for more than thirty years. We have seen each other through successes and failures, through damaged romances and unaccountable bliss. She has seen me at my best and at my worst.

And so I call her. Poor Sarah. My poor, sweet Sarah. She gets phone calls from me weekly, sometimes daily. She gets calls when I can no longer contain the pain or the sadness alone.

She must be so bored of me. I am so bored of me.

'How's it going?' she says. She is at work; she is the deputy editor of a magazine. The office is open-plan. It is difficult for her to talk. Sometimes I call her and just cry, because I cannot speak.

I imagine her sitting at her desk, the phone pressed hard to her ear as she searches for words to say to me, words that will betray neither of us in the busy impersonal world of work. I can hear the murmur of voices all around her, the shrill summons of phones, the lovely noise of life going on.

For a moment, I can't speak. 'Not good,' I manage, finally.

Her voice is gentle, concerned. I hate that concern. I hate that it is me who is making her feel that way. 'How not good?'

I hear my voice, rusty from lack of use. It sounds slow, as if I am talking underwater. 'Bad,' I say.

She knows from the sound of my voice how close I am to the edge. 'I just have to clear something up here. I'll be with you in an hour, less if I can.'

'OK,' I say, because it is all I can manage. I can't even say thank you.

I lie on the floor in my bedroom and wait. I can't imagine why she would want to be with me, can't imagine what she could do for me. She is even more powerless than I am over this thing. Today I can't honour it by calling it an illness. Today it is just a thing that neither of us knows or understands.

I hope she won't be long, just the sight of her comforts me. I need her to be with me, even if there is nothing she can say. I am terrified she will give up on me, that this thing will drive her away. Every depressive has that fear. Why would anyone want us? We don't even want ourselves. Sometimes, we try to drive the people who love us away. Not because we don't want them with us, but because we cannot bear for them to see what we have become.

She arrives, bringing life with her. I can smell it, sharp and clear, on her coat. Then, just as suddenly, it is gone, absorbed by the dull, dead world of depression. My bedroom smells like a sickroom, stale and sad. I wonder if Sarah can smell it too. Once, there would have been scented candles burning on the mantelpiece, a fire lit, lights shining in every room. Now, one solitary lamp casts a dim pool on the table by the bed. The rest of the flat is in darkness.

Sarah is lovely, her cheeks pink and her eyes alive and sparkling. Her hair is thick and auburn, her coat black, soft leather. 'Hello, friend,' she says, crouching down to hug me. I am still on the floor.

Tossing her handbag aside, she sits on my bed. 'Has something happened?' she asks. Her voice is gentle with concern.

I duck my head, suddenly conscious that I am wearing the same, stained leggings and sweater, that my hair is matted from sleeping, my face shiny with half-dried tears and that the circles under my eyes look like bruises, purple and violent.

'Nothing.' I shake my head, 'Nothing has happened.' And it's true. Nothing at all has happened in my world that day. Just me. I have happened.

'Just a bad day then,' she says.

I nod mutely. I have summoned her from her work, brought her all this way to tell her nothing. It is unforgivable. I am unforgivable.

'I can't do this, Sarah. I can't do this any more.' I mean, stay alive. I can't stay alive if this is what living is. I start to cry. She lays her hand gently on my head, strokes my hair. She is used to me crying by now. She knows there is nothing she can do.

I wrap my arms around myself, to stop the pain, to stop the tears. My whole body is racked with it; I am shaking with tears. The monster is at my throat.

'If I was an animal,' I sob, 'they'd shoot me, to put me out of my misery.'

'No, Sal,' she says, 'they wouldn't. Really, they wouldn't.'

I look up at her face, at the terror and the love in it.

It still makes me cry, to think of it now.

She told me later that she always used to cry, when she left me. She used to drive home, tears pouring down her face, saying the same thing out loud, over and over again. 'This is not life threatening. She is not going to die. My best friend is not going to die.'

I imagine her driving through the dark streets, crying, chanting aloud to keep the bogeyman away.

4

Self-Absorption and Symptoms

Life is short and we have never too much time for gladdening the hearts of those who are travelling the dark journey with us. Oh be swift to love, make haste to be kind.

Henri-Frédéric Amiel

Before I became ill, I had no idea that severe depression has definite symptoms just like any other illness. Nor do most people. And that's where the stigma around mental illness becomes dangerous. Our unwillingness to discuss it openly creates a damaging ignorance. We know the obvious symptoms of physical illness and seek help accordingly but we rarely take our emotional temperatures or check the balance of our mental health.

Usually, we only act when things become too difficult to bear. By then, we are sometimes sicker than we need have become, and often too lost to help ourselves. Many depressives say they find a second episode of the illness easier to deal with simply because they know the symptoms and get help earlier.

As with most other illnesses, if the early warning signs are caught early enough and treated accordingly, it may be possible to avert the full-blown disorder. Or, at least, to head off some of its most devastating consequences. A reactive (as in a reaction to life events) or moderate depression is much easier to treat than major depression which, once it is present, can assume an independent, violent life of its own. Nobody quite knows why.

The origins of depression are both vague and complex. The symptoms, however, are not and it is as well for us all to know them, so we can seek help sooner rather than later.

So here they are, as defined by *The Diagnostic and Statistical Manual of Mental Disorders, Fourth Edition (DSM – IV)* which is used by most psychiatrists and mental health experts to diagnose depressive disorder.

Mild to moderate depression includes the first two symptoms and at least one other. Severe depression is the first two symptoms and at least five others. For depression to be diagnosed, the symptoms would occur together and for at least two weeks without significant improvement.

1. Depressed mood most of the day, nearly every day, as indicated by either subjective report (e.g., I feel sad or empty) or observation made by others (e.g., appears tearful). In children and adolescents, this can manifest as irritable mood.

2. Markedly diminished interest or pleasure in all, or almost all, activities most of the day, nearly every day (as indicated by either a subjective account or an observation made by others).

3. Significant weight loss when not dieting, or weight gain (e.g., a change of more than five per cent of body weight in a month), or a decrease or increase in appetite nearly every day. In children, this could show as a failure to make expected weight gains.

4. Insomnia or hypersomnia (sleeping excessively) nearly every day.

5. Psychomotor agitation or retardation nearly every day (observable by others, not merely subjective feelings of restlessness or being slowed down).

6. Fatigue or loss of energy nearly every day.
7. Feelings of worthlessness or excessive or inappropriate guilt (which may be delusional) nearly every day (not merely self-reproach or guilt about being sick).
8. A diminished ability to think or concentrate, or indecisiveness, nearly every day (either by subjective account or as observed by others).
9. Recurrent thoughts of death (not just fear of dying), recurrent suicidal ideation (thinking about it constantly) without a specific plan, or a suicide attempt or a specific plan for committing suicide.

I wish I had sought help more urgently, wish I had known or even understood the symptoms. I waited – for a year – for my mood to lift, telling myself that I was just a bit low or tired, waking day after day convinced that soon I would be right again. In that state of passive ignorance, I had no idea of the demons that were waiting for me and that, once they captured me, would not let me go without a catastrophic struggle.

They finally got me in the January of 2001. By then, I was lost. Each day hurt, each breath, each step I took. I wanted only to be dead. It was the only thing I could think about.

Sometimes, the final realisation that you can no longer function or continue with life is called a breakdown. It's a phrase rarely used by mental health professionals; it's considered too patronising or demeaning. It's sufferers themselves who use the expression most often, perhaps because it perfectly describes that state of total collapse. You no longer have control over anything: thoughts, emotions, sleep, appetite. You are, quite literally, broken down. To me it felt like the total disintegration of everything I had ever known about myself.

Someone once asked me how it felt. I lost my balance, I said. It felt as if I lost my balance. I fell flat on my face and I couldn't get up again. And if that implies a certain grace, a slow and easy free-fall, then you have me wrong. It was violent and painful and, above all, humiliating.

People rarely discuss the absolute humiliation of severe depression, the punishing helplessness, the distressing, child-like impotence. When well-intentioned friends and family say to the depressive, 'pull yourself together', they may as well be saying it to the baby crying in its cot.

We cannot. It is not that we don't want to. We simply can't. But, unlike the baby in the cot, our adult brain is sufficiently engaged to know that we should, to believe that if we tried hard enough, we could. Then every attempt and every failure brings with it its own, additional depression, its own pro-found and hopeless despair. And every contemptuous glance, every irritated sigh from family and friends drives us still further out into the cold, black night.

Depression has its own pathology and self-absorption is part of that pathology. Telling somebody who is in the grip of severe depression that they are being selfish and self-pitying is like telling somebody with asthma that they have breathing difficulties. It is meaningless except as a statement of fact or an expression of the symptoms affecting them. They are lost in a place without boundaries or borders, where the concept of self has no meaning. They have lost their very self.

The first time I truly realised how lost I had been was when I was better, and out walking with a friend. It was a beautiful, sunny day and we had not seen each other for some time. I was talking fast, falling over my own words, trying to cram all my news into the short time we had stolen away from work and children. When we were parting, she grabbed me in a fierce hug. 'You're back,' she said, 'you're really back. Welcome home.'

Until then, I had not realised how far I had gone, or how long I had been away. I understand it when people say they just want us to be 'back to our old selves' and the terrible confusion of coming up against the stranger standing in our place. I've been around enough depressives, myself included. There have been times when I've wanted to shake them (myself) or shout at them (or myself) to snap out of it. I understand those gauche, clumsy attempts to bring us to our senses, know they are born simply out of fear and frustration. Most of all, I know how those emotions make unintentional bullies of us all.

Even, of depressives themselves.

Here's an example. I am sitting in group therapy, in a psychiatric unit. There are twelve of us. We are each expected to speak; a therapist is present to guide the process, to stop any one person from dominating the group, and to encourage others who retreat into silence.

We sit on moulded, grey plastic chairs in a circle, facing the therapist. The walls are painted in cream gloss with a green border, the shabby carpet is a utilitarian grey. The room is cold, empty save for a flipboard. There are no potted plants to fill the emptiness, no paintings to add colour to the walls. The atmosphere is clinical. There is no suggestion that we are here to do anything but work.

We are, literally, a motley crew; a disparate bunch of people with nothing in common but our illness. We look peculiar, some shabby, some smart, according to our status in the hospital. Some of us wear coats. A few are dressed in suits, the women in formal skirts and high heels. They are the outpatients, attending what is known as 'after-care', which is a daily, two-hour session of group therapy, designed to make the transition of leaving the psychiatric unit and moving back into normal life as seamless as possible. They look glossy and polished, as if they do not belong in here with us, the inpatients. You would not, if you passed them in the street, point them out as mental patients.

By their chairs are handbags or briefcases, plastic carrier bags filled with paperwork and sandwiches, bottles of water, cans of Coke. This is lunch, to be snatched on the run after the therapy session, before an afternoon at work. We are not allowed to eat or drink during group; nothing is allowed to distract us from the task in hand – which is us.

They are the elders of the group; they know
served their time and done well enough to be g.
privileges. They have been allowed to take a step
world.

The inpatients watch the outpatients with a m.   .ɔt
envy, respect and fear – of leaving this safe, cloistereu community and going back out there, into that place where the
terrors and pressures of life conspired to bring us down. How
would we manage out there? How does anyone? Some of us
may have run our own business, some of us are husbands or
wives or parents. We have all, at one time, managed our own
lives.

Now we are too frightened to walk down a street alone.

I am an inpatient, dressed in a pair of old jeans and a
hooded top, bare feet shoved carelessly into old, battered
trainers. There is a strict dress code for inpatients in this
hospital: dressing gowns and slippers are not allowed. We
make jokes about it, someone suggests a sign for the door:
'No Jim-Jams here.' You can be as mad as you like, but
you've got to get dressed in the morning.

Some of us have brushed our hair. Often, the first sign of
life, or a coming back to life is a comb dragged through hair
or a shaky lipstick line. Some days, I could not manage to
brush my teeth, on others I would achieve a passing semblance of mascara and eyeliner. It does not go unnoticed.

'You're wearing make-up! Well done! You must be feeling
better.'

It is halfway down my face before we have even finished
group therapy. Nobody cares. Tears are normal in a place
where normal has many different interpretations.

Susie is talking. She is frail and intensely thin, suffering
from an anxiety disorder so violent that she used to vomit
into wastepaper bins at work, which was in a bank. Young
and pretty, with brilliant dyed red hair, she has a manic laugh
and an addiction to fluorescent trainers, fluffy pink jumpers
and false nails painted a glittery mauve. Susie worries about

everything: her mum, her brother (with good reason, he is a soldier, posted to Iraq), her sister, her niece, her mum's dog, her future, her past. Most of all, she worries about her cleverness.

She stops me in the corridor one day. 'I'm not like you, Sal. I don't know words. I don't know how to say what's in my head.'

I say that, even though I do know words, all the words in the world still cannot explain what's in my head. Susie laughs so hard I think she's heading for another panic attack.

'We're right ones, we are,' she says, at last. 'Right fucking loonies.'

'It's what's in your heart, Susie. That's what matters,' I say.

Her blue eyes fill with tears. 'That's not right either,' she says. 'My heart's not right at the moment.'

'It is, Susie,' I say. 'It is.'

And I know that it is because, after we leave the hospital, I take her into my house, sometimes for days, sometimes for weeks. I like to have her there. She likes to be there. 'It's like a holiday,' she says, 'from my life.'

She scarcely takes up any room, and there is no spare bed to give her so she just curls up in the corner of the sofa like a small, elegant cat. On the table in front of her is a mug of tea, a packet of the rich tea biscuits she loves and on which she seems to exist, and a constant cigarette, smoking in the ashtray.

She never seems to sleep at night, although she has pills to knock her out. I am usually awake too, despite the pills I take to stun me into sleep, and often I will stumble groggily out of my room and see the dead blue light of a television flickering under the door and know that Susie is staring at the screen, the sound turned down so low (she does not like to disturb me or Molly) it's a wonder she can hear anything at all.

What she likes most is to clean. I always know when Susie is feeling low. Her head appears around my door and she says, 'Sal, is it all right if I hoover?'

The flat sparkles, but we can never find anything. Susie likes all surfaces to be clean of everything, not simply dust.

'Has Susie been cleaning again?' Moll asks when she gets home from school and searches, fruitlessly, for a book or a clean T-shirt.

'Yes.'

Moll nods sympathetically. 'Must have been a bad day.'

Susie's hiding places are creative. But they make sense to her. Her mum often telephones to say, 'Can you ask Susie where she's put the shampoo? I've searched all day and I still can't find it.'

Susie and Molly love each other. I often find them curled up together on the sofa, heads bent towards each other as they chatter endlessly or clutch each other in helpless laughter.

'I don't think Susie's a grown-up at all,' Moll says.

In group therapy, Susie's words are jumbled, often interrupted by tears. Sometimes the tears win and she sobs helplessly, unable to speak. After a while she starts to shout, at herself.

'Shut up, shut up, you're pathetic,' she cries. 'Stop crying, you're being ridiculous.' Every fresh outburst brings a fresh spate of tears until, frustrated and humiliated, she begins to slap herself in the face, at first gently, and then harder and harder.

'Stop it! Stop it!' she shouts.

Slap, slap.

'Shut up!'

Slap, slap.

Finally, the therapist says to Susie, 'Why are you doing that?'

Susie keeps crying but she stops slapping herself. Nobody moves to comfort her or offer her a tissue. Or, some do, but the therapist stops them with a warning glance. In group therapy, to comfort somebody is to get them to shut up. The goal is to get them to express their feelings, however painful. The way to do that is to leave them alone. It sounds tough. It is tough. Our instinct is to comfort somebody who is distressed. It is hard not to obey it.

After a long while, the therapist looks at the rest of us. 'Would anybody like to say anything to Susie?'

I look at Susie, her hands clenched across her face, knuckles white, as she fights the urge not to hit herself. I used to do the same thing, slap myself to stop my own tears.

'If I was crying,' I say, 'would you tell me to shut up?'

She lifts her face from her fists in astonishment. 'No, of course not.'

'Then why are you doing it to yourself?'

'Because I hate myself when I'm like this. I want me to stop.'

I understand that. I wanted me to stop too.

So, we've heard it all. We've heard it from friends, from family, from meaningless strangers. But, most of all, we've heard it from ourselves.

Pull yourself together.

There are lots of people worse off.

It's not that bad.

Get over yourself.

Get a life.

I did not, could not, blame anybody who offered me such advice. It was no more than I told myself daily, even hourly. I developed terrible pains in my face. It took me a long time (and a dentist) to realise it was because I kept my jaw clamped tight. I was gritting my teeth to get through the days.

Only once did I answer back. It was a bloke on a building site, just trying to be cheery, just being normal.

He called out: 'Cheer up love, it might never happen.'

I turned on him and I said: 'Well, it fucking well has happened. And what are you going to do about it?'

I might just as well have hit him. He was shaven-headed and built like a brick shit house but he spread his hands beseechingly and blushed. He said nothing. Nor did I. I was trying too hard not to cry.

There were men like him in the hospital. One was a cab driver, huge and burly. He looked like a hard man but his expression told another story. He was terrified his mates would discover he was in a loony bin. He did not want to share his feelings or tell us how he felt, which was bad. Very, very bad. He thought about dying, about hanging himself by the neck. 'I don't understand,' was all he said.

The group murmured in assent. Nor did we.

None of us understood why we had been singled out for depression. None of us knew how we came to be shut away in a psychiatric hospital, compelled to spill out our emotional guts to strangers. It was not the way we saw ourselves. It was not the way that we wanted others to see us.

5

Losing My Balance

*The greatest danger, that of losing one's own self,
may pass off quietly as if it were nothing; every
other loss, that of an arm, a leg, five dollars etc., is
sure to be noticed.*

Søren Kierkegaard

If there is one fact about depression on which all the experts
agree, it is that there is no single cause but rather a number of
contributory factors that come together and may trigger a
depressive episode in people who are vulnerable.

I say, may, because nobody knows which combination of
triggers is liable to be explosive nor why one person should be
affected when another, given the exact same set of factors,
should remain untouched.

But it is generally agreed that major depression is the result
of a number of difficult events (known as stressors) that,
coming in quick succession, affect the chemical balance of the
brain. Depression, literally, changes your mind.

Those stressors may include a relationship breakdown, the
loss of a job, the death of a loved one or financial problems.
Loss of any kind seems to be a significant trigger. Depression
often runs in families so there may also be a genetic suscept-
ibility – but it is a predisposition rather than a predetermination. It does not mean that everyone with depression in the

family is destined to develop the illness. Nor is everyone who experiences difficult events destined to become seriously depressed.

My descent into depression was steady, textbook, even. I began to wake, every morning, at twenty minutes past three. My head was an alarm clock, set to the minute; to the not-so-sweet spot.

Early morning waking is one of the classic symptoms of depression, but I had no idea so I paid it little attention. I had a lot on my mind and anyway, I have suffered from insomnia since I was a child, although it used to be of the not being able to get off to sleep variety.

This was a new form. I fell asleep as if I had been hit over the head, too fast, too violently. And then, a few hours later, I was awake again and always at the same time. I began to dread the clock, my startled, suddenly awake eyes staring at those luminous hands that always pointed at the three and the four; pointing the way, I began to imagine, towards hell.

I felt odd in other ways. Food tasted strange, or dry, like dust. I lost weight quickly, about a stone in a few weeks. I was pleased in a vague, detached, way although I sometimes thought I should be happier about losing weight without even trying. In those odd moments of clarity, I was surprised by my lack of pleasure. I was thin and in my world, thin was good. I worked in magazines. I went to fashion shows. People told me how fabulous I looked while all the time I wondered who this stranger was who inhabited my skinny Earl jeans.

I lost interest, too, in everything that I had once loved. My garden deserted me. It grew, unwatched and unappreciated. I felt indifferent to it and it, in turn, seemed indifferent to me. It did not seem to matter whether I was present or not. After a time I became resentful, feeling that the flowers mocked me, blooming in defiance of my listless misery.

I did not pay much attention. My mind was on other, more important, things. If I could not sleep or eat or garden, it was for a reason. My ten-year marriage was dying and crawling painfully towards its conclusion. My husband, Jonathan, and I had begun to bicker destructively.

'Does everything I do annoy you?' he asked.

'Yes.'

He turned away.

I put my hands on my hips, addressed his reproachful back. 'Well, that's what you wanted to hear, isn't it?'

He said nothing but I could hear, in his silence, the acid bite of my words.

We had developed our own sad pattern. I attacked, he withdrew. There was no war, more an empty sense of defeat. Our misery was played out in a sniper's no-man's land, and there seemed nothing we could do to change the view. Or perhaps it was that neither of us wanted to.

My life had changed in other ways. I had gone back to working in magazines, as the editor of *Red*, after a decade working as a writer in absolute peace and quiet. I was not used to so much noise, or the incessant, urgent demands of a staff of thirty, and found it, frankly, difficult.

I had worked in magazines before; I loved the drama and the chaos of them. It did not occur to me that this time it would be different. Perhaps it was simply that I was older or perhaps it was merely my state of mind but I found the consuming obsession with celebrities and shopping trivial and infuriating. It was fine, in its place; but its place, to my mind, was small.

I thought, too, that I understood the Machiavellian politics of office life. I thought, even, that I enjoyed them. I ignored the way they stuck, like the food I ate, in my throat.

My marriage finally ended. There was no real resistance, just the occasional flurry of emotion; as much out of politeness or habit as regret. I found a flat and moved out. Jonathan could not, he said, face moving himself. He finds it hard. I do not, having spent my childhood doing it; or at least, I thought I didn't, but that understanding came later, by which time I was drowning in an emotional backwash I could neither handle nor understand.

I found a flat near the house so Molly could move easily between us. It was difficult, but curiously easy. We talked about it a lot. We stayed close friends.

Jonathan went to see a therapist, about the marriage breakdown and other things. It did not occur to me that I needed to. I thought therapy was for other people but I was up to my neck in the denial that, as so many therapists have told me, I am so consummately good at.

Jonathan reported back from his therapy sessions. 'He says we're so polite and considerate with each other, we're like something out of the *Guardian*.'

Yes, I thought, passionless. Dead. Beyond hope.

'He wants to know why we don't shout or throw china.'

I laughed. So did Jonathan.

'Has he understood nothing at all?' I asked.

Jonathan shrugged.

At about the same time, I fell in love. Absurdly, insanely and catastrophically in love and with somebody I should not have been in love with. I had felt the pull of it for months, but had done nothing about it. I thought, even, that I might be going insane, thought that I was making the whole thing up. It was only, finally, when we came together that I knew that I had been right all along, that the hugeness of the emotion I was feeling did not exist in isolation.

It didn't help. I felt madder still, an insanity compounded by guilt and impossibility. Love, as the scientists tell us, is enough to change anybody's brain chemistry. And I was in love, not just with my head and my heart but with my body and soul too. The connection was inexplicable, even to myself. And so I did not try to explain it.

I was more lost than I have ever been. His name was Tom. It still is. When we met, he was with somebody else, in situation, but not emotion. We did nothing. It was like watching a car crash. There were children involved. We talked, we kissed, we made no plans. There were none to be made. There was just us, this thing that we could do nothing with, or about.

We could not even ignore it.

He sent me an email.

Suddenly that mad email I sent you doesn't seem so mad and incoherent, does it? I'll find the quote . . .

'But his flawed heart (Alack, too weak the conflict
   to support)
Twixt two extremes of passion, joy and grief, burst
   smilingly.'

Whatever we do, whatever, will be completely WRONG.

One thing. I'm glad, no, not glad, delirious, that this has happened, is happening, will happen.

Love, come what may.

I went to see my doctor for some sleeping pills. She told me that early warning waking was a sign of depression and prescribed antidepressants. I didn't believe her, told her that I was not depressed but simply tired from getting so little sleep, that I had a few too many things on my mind.

I was vaguely outraged by her suggestion that I was depressed. I am not a person who does depression. I am a person who always copes. I am strong. Or so my thinking went at the time.

She listened to me patiently then suggested a counsellor. The NHS waiting list was, at minimum, six months. I let her put my name down although I knew that, in six months' time, I would be better.

I insisted, again, on sleeping pills. She refused, prescribed me antidepressants, explaining that as the depression lifted, so my sleeping patterns would return to normal.

I took the pills. I continued to wake at three twenty every morning. I thought that she was wrong in her diagnosis. The antidepressants did nothing for me so I could not be depressed. I just had too much on my mind.

Two months later, I started to cry. I woke, crying, and I went to sleep crying. In between, I washed my face, got dressed and went to work. It still did not occur to me that I was depressed. I was just sad, about the ending of my marriage, about loving somebody who I should not love.

Four months after we separated, Jonathan became involved in another relationship. I was pleased for him. I wanted him to be happy. I knew, from my lack of jealousy or pain, that our marriage was truly over. Even so, I carried the guilt of its ending like a thundercloud. I was the one who had moved out. Was it all my fault? Had I not tried hard enough?

'You did try,' Jonathan said. 'You kept trying to talk about it but I wouldn't. I just hoped it would go away. I knew it was over, that we had been unhappy for a long time. I couldn't face doing anything about it; I couldn't even face facing it. So, thank you for being strong enough to do it.'

'That's OK.'

He grinned at me. 'I couldn't have done it without you.'

We are still good friends, even now. We see each other often and not just because we share a child. I call Jonathan in times of trouble, or celebration. And he calls me. This confuses some people. They think we are weird to be so happily separated. They wonder why we bothered. We don't. We both know we have the sort of relationship that survives separation, but not intimacy.

Nor did our friendship stop the pain of a marriage ending. It did not diminish the agony of ripping apart a ten-year marriage, a house, and a life. Perhaps, even, our friendship made it worse.

'Why are we doing this?' I said, one day, as we were packing up the family home.

Jonathan looked sad. 'Because there is no other way. We both know that.'

'Yes,' I said, and went back to packing up boxes of china and glass.

We dismantled our marriage slowly; it took us over a year to sell the house. During that time, I moved twice, into different flats, and moved in and out of the family house twice too. It was unsettling, but I was already unsettled.

I kept on taking the antidepressants. They did nothing, but my life was a mess. No drug has the power to tidy away that degree of mess.

I was physically unwell too, with an underactive thyroid, or hypothyroidism as it is known, diagnosed a year previously. 'It's only mildly underactive,' my GP said. 'Borderline. Nothing to worry about.'

And so I didn't.

Mental health professionals, however, take malfunctioning thyroid glands very seriously, for good reason. The thyroid, which governs everything from metabolism to mood function, used to be known as the gland of emotion. It is hugely implicated in depression. According to one report, twenty-five per cent of women in psychiatric units have an underactive thyroid. Often, it is only borderline, which is why its implications regarding severe depression are often missed by general practitioners who tend to regard a mildly under-functioning thyroid as bothersome but not serious. There is, too, an enormous variation in function.

As my own psychiatrist told me later, 'Normal is a piece of string. What's normal for one person is off the chart for another. And NHS blood tests for thyroxin are notoriously insensitive.'

I knew none of this at the time and, taking my lead from my GP, did not take its implications seriously even though I had felt extremely unwell before I was diagnosed. I was tired all the time and not normal fatigue but bone-weary exhaustion. I slept as if I had been knocked unconscious and struggled to wake in the morning, dragging my leaden limbs through the day. I was always cold; my fingers white and numb even during the summer, when I kept a heater going at full blast in my study. If I got too cold, I found it almost impossible to get warm again and resorted to lying in a bath with the hot water running. My arms and legs ached constantly, so painfully that, at times, I took painkillers every four hours. And my weight, which had been the same all my life, kept going up despite eating very little. Stranger still, my eyebrows started to fall out and my skin was so dry I was almost bathing in moisturiser. I felt constantly low and depressed but I was working too hard and had a small child who needed me. I was ripped in half by guilt. Of course I was depressed and tired.

'It's your age,' a locum GP said. 'You're probably meno-pausal.'

He was a young man, with ears that stuck out and were so red and shiny it looked as if he scrubbed them daily.

'I am in my forties,' I said with as much outraged dignity as I could muster in the face of his blank, young indifference.

He did not look up from his notes. 'Exactly.' His eyes flickered across the pages. 'And you have a small child and you work.' He looked over at me as if to say, what did you expect?

Eventually, my own GP put me on a small dose of thyroxin, 50 mgs a day. 'To see if it has any effect,' she suggested. My body temperature shot up. The weight fell off. My energy returned. But still, I couldn't throw off the mood, the low feeling that seemed always to envelop me like a cold, grey blanket.

When, eventually, I was taken into hospital with severe depression, they trebled the dose of thyroxin, to 150 mgs a day. The maximum dose is 200 mgs a day. The amount I had been taking was far too low, even though the blood tests my GP had done indicated that the levels of available thyroxin were back to normal.

My ruinous love affair continued. We fell more and more in love, ran towards each other and away again. We were as intimate with each other, and as estranged from each other, as it is possible to be. We did not see each other for weeks on end and then came together in cataclysmic passion.

Tom grew more and more miserable, until he was almost speechless with pain; handling his difficulties by shutting down emotionally or disappearing for days. I knew he could not bear to leave his children or break up the family even though, as he said, the relationship that should have pinned it all together was already broken. Only the surface remained intact. I did not want him to leave his children but I knew, too, that I could not bear him to leave me. He had to and so we agreed to part, again, only to come back together when the pain and longing grew too much for either of us to bear. And so it went on.

The crying grew worse. I was scarcely sleeping. I started to cry in unexpected places, at inconvenient times. One day, I cried at work. I was mortified. I never cry at work. I decided that I was exhausted, and took a week off. It was the end of June. I spent the days walking around London, wearing dark glasses, with tears streaming down my face. I walked for hours, every day. Looking back, I see that I was trying to walk my way out of depression.

I could not see colour, I could see only in black and white. I thought it was strange, but not unduly so.

Later, I found a quote from the American humorist Art Buchwald describing his depression: 'Everything was black. The trees were black, the road was black. You can't believe how the colours change until you have it. It's scary.'

And I thought, so I'm not the only one.

At the time, I paid no attention to my monochrome world. Everything was strange. My life was strange. There were no fixed points left.

After that week of near total collapse, I went back to work. I sat through meetings, flew to Milan and Paris, tried to keep my staff inspired and lively. An editor is nothing if they cannot give inspiration, leadership, a sense of belonging. A magazine is nothing without people; without the people who make it, it does not exist. My job was to keep those people happy and anyway I had grown inordinately fond of them. I said nothing about my own misery. I hoped, passionately, that it did not show.

I felt so desperate that I asked a friend who knew about such things to recommend a therapist. Back then, I was not a person who did therapy, wanted therapy, talked therapy. I used to rather despise the notion, believing it to be the preserve of the severely emotionally damaged or the simply narcissistic.

I went, but unwillingly. I told nobody. The therapist practised out of a mean little room, decorated in shades of beige and sage, the unrelentingly dreary colours of analysis. There was a vase of dusty dried flowers, a box of tissues and a woman with unkempt hair who wore, to my cynical and weary eyes, a series of unnecessary scarves. I later discovered that this mannered Bohemia seemed to be the uniform of therapists of this sort.

Even as I shrank from my surroundings and the middle-aged woman in front of me, I cried. I had no idea why.

Even as I cried, I answered questions. What did I do? Did I have children? What was my relationship like with my mother? I felt, in a surreal way, that I was trapped at a dinner party with some impertinent stranger. Worse, with a stranger who, judging from her chilly impersonal manner, I was unlikely to discover anything about. She was steeped in Freud, in the analytical methods that demand from the therapist a blank, anonymous presence intended to throw the patient (their problems, as well as any solutions) into sharp relief. It was the wrong sort of therapy for me but knowing nothing about therapy or the various sorts on offer, I did not question it or her methods. I simply found it hateful; just as I grew to hate many of the other therapists I sat facing in the months and years to come. But I kept going back, just as I kept taking the anti-depressants I thought did nothing for me. I did it because I did not know what else to do. I did it with reluctance, with no desire at all to engage. I did it because I thought that if I expressed my misery, it would go away.

A little while later, on a grey Sunday afternoon, I was sitting alone in my rented flat and feeling low. I turned on the television, for company. A photograph of Paula Yates flashed up on the screen and a voice said, 'Paula Yates is dead.' I turned the television off, and then turned it back on again, as if, by chance, I had tuned in to some unknown, extraterrestrial channel. 'Paula Yates is dead,' said the voice. 'She was found in the early hours of this morning.'

I could not believe it. I loved Paula. We had been friends for twenty years. We met when I was a young journalist sent to interview her about her book, *Rock Stars in Their Underpants*. She was well known but not particularly famous. This was a few years before LiveAid and before Bob became, as she put it, 'a saint'. And before she became, as she also put it, 'the Antichrist'.

We started talking and we just carried on, for years. I used to spend weekends with Paula and Bob in the country, just so we could talk. She made me laugh more than anyone else I have ever known, except perhaps Nigel. Depressives, when they are not being depressed, are often the funniest, most blackly comic people around.

She had been away for the summer, was full of life and plans for the future. How could she be dead? We had talked on the phone only the day before and had arranged to see each other the following week. More than that, over the past year we had spent a long time discussing our mutual difficulties, and how we were trying to handle them. And, even though Paula was in a far darker place than I was, she still kept trying to pull me through. 'We must be strong,' she kept saying, 'we'll get through this. I know we will.'

And now she was gone. I shouted at her face, laughing on the television screen. 'You promised. You promised that we'd both get through.'

Miss Marigold, I called her, because, like Susie, Paula loved cleaning, just as she loved her pink rubber gloves. She wore them with diamonds, a cocktail frock and high stiletto shoes. She wore them as you would imagine Paula would. None of it was fake; it was simply the way she was. She even wore cocktail frocks on Sunday mornings, in the garden.

She loved her pink rubber gloves because she loved to clean, to try to restore order to her somewhat chaotic life. When she was admitted to the Priory with severe depression, they sat her in the hospital garden and filled her room with torn-up pieces of newspaper. Then she was taken back to her room and made to sit there, amid the torn-up newspapers, without cleaning up.

She thought this was hysterical. 'The press kept saying I was put away for drug and alcohol addiction. Actually, they locked me up for being a housewife.'

She turned her stay in the Priory into a fine, comic turn, punctuated with stories. I remember her sitting at lunch, regaling me. Her face was free of make-up and she was wearing the tortoiseshell glasses she so rarely used in public. She looked pretty, and so alive.

'I used to walk up and down the corridor in the Priory,' she said, 'with Tiger in my arms, whispering into her ear, "You are my heroine." And suddenly, all the doors in the corridor would shoot open and all the druggies would stick their heads out of the doors and say, "Heroin? Did somebody mention heroin?" '

And then she threw her blonde head back and laughed in that hiccupping, infectious way she had.

I changed therapists, hoping for relief. I disliked the second one more, even, than I had disliked the first. She worked out of a larger room, but one decorated in the same dreary beige and sage. Her hair was set and blow dried, like a helmet. I wanted to mess it up, rumple it out of shape. She wore camel skirt suits and sat stiffly, hands clasped in her lap. She talked hardly at all.

At the time, I did not know that there are many kinds of therapy or that the particular sort she practised was wrong for me. Nor did I know that she was wrong for me, simply because I did not like her and could not warm to her.

I thought therapy was a sort of magic, that you just kept talking and the very act of talking unlocked some forgotten key. I did not know that there are good therapists and bad therapists or even that a therapist might be good for one person and bad for another. I knew nothing except that I was in pain and that I must do something, anything, to get rid of it.

Very soon after Paula died I was sacked as editor of *Red*. Almost the last thing I did before I left was to write her obituary. The management wanted more celebrities, more shopping, more make-up secrets. They wanted fewer words. I didn't argue. I knew, before they said it, that I was the wrong person for their job. I had always known it. The magazine I wanted to make, and the magazine they wanted to sell, were two different creatures.

I should have left months before; should have admitted defeat and made a graceful exit. I should have admitted I was wrong, had always been wrong in even considering the job about which they pestered me for six long months before I agreed to take it. I should have listened to my instincts and understood that I could never have done what they wanted.

Except that I could not admit it. I could, and would, admit nothing. Even as they sacked me, it was all, I said, fine. I said that it was the way of the world. It was corporate culture. It was the way magazines are. I said it was all manner of things – except the truth.

The truth was that I believed that if I was really good at anything, I was good at editing a magazine. I had believed it for years, since the success of *Elle*. I had been told it for years. So the failure of my editorship of *Red* was not simply the failure of a job. It was the destruction of an absolute truth about myself.

With it went a large part of my identity. With it came an overwhelming sense of loss, on top of all the others. I was crap at my job, I was crap at marriage, I was crap at love. I had lost at them all. A good friend had died. I had lost her too. And depression, as many experts have pronounced, is almost always about loss.

I did not know that at the time.

I left the job quickly, by the end of the week. The following Monday, I woke, as usual, at three twenty. There was a storm, rain lashed at the windows of the bleak, rented flat in which I was living. It was cold, and damp. I had run out of cigarettes and the shops were closed. I wanted to go home, to the house I had known and loved for ten years. But I was already at home. I could not go to work. There was no work. I wanted my child but I knew that in that state, I wasn't much of a mother. I wanted my friends but I did not know how to tell them what I felt.

If losing my job had been my only loss that year, I doubt I would have fallen so hard or gone so low. Loss, or abrupt and unwelcome change, causes stress, and extreme stress, according to the scientists, changes the chemistry of the brain. Those chemical changes are always found in those suffering with severe depression. Depression doesn't cause the changes. Depression reflects them. And my brain was changing, fast.

It was October. That's when it got really bad. I told nobody. I did not know what to say. I was too ashamed, and confused. I still had a place to live, money from a redundancy payout, a child I adored, friends I loved, work if I wanted it. What right did I have to be depressed?

I thought that if I opened my mouth to talk, the tears would start and they would never stop. And so I avoided talking, to anyone. I sacked the therapist, by letter. In the letter, I lied. I said that I was better, that I had no more need of her services. She wrote back. She said that I was more in need of therapy than anyone she had ever met.

I thought she was mad, or greedy, but I think now that she recognised the stress I had been through within the space of ten months. She saw the danger in that accumulation of loss and perhaps, even, that I was on the edge of a breakdown. It was just that she did not tell me. Or perhaps she knew I did not want to hear.

Three months later, I was admitted to hospital with severe clinical depression. In all those losses, I had lost myself.

6

Breakdown

I am the most miserable man living. If what I feel were equally distributed to the whole human family, there would not be a cheerful face on earth. Whether I shall ever be better I cannot tell; I awfully forbode I shall not. To remain as I am is impossible. I must die or be better.

Abraham Lincoln

People generally think of a nervous breakdown as a sudden, cataclysmic event rather than the gradual erosion of a person, a slow and sad disintegration of a human being. Inevitably there is some story in a newspaper of a man who has suddenly gone mad with a shotgun, of a woman who has driven herself and her young children over a cliff.

This is madness writ large; this is a breakdown of dramatic force but for most they happen, not with a bang, but with a whimper.

On the day I finally lost touch with reality, with my life, I had gone to see Jonathan and Molly in our family home. I had been awake, as usual, since three twenty and crying since I woke. I could see no future and neither did I want one.

But I had a child, who I had promised I would go and see. So I got dressed, which seemed to me such a superhuman feat that I was trembling with exhaustion by the time I was ready. I stumbled down the road, holding tight to the low garden walls because I found it hard to see where the pavement ended and the road began. The noise of cars was deafening and brutal. Every time one flashed past, my whole body jumped in sympathetic response, leaving me shaken and fragile.

I said nothing to Jonathan of my state when I arrived at the house. I was hoping to get through the day, just as I had hoped to get through all the others. It was January but the sun was brilliant, our kitchen filled with the cold, hard light of winter sunshine. The light seemed too harsh; I longed for the cloistered gloom of my bedroom, the curtains drawn fast against the sun.

I had, too, a pronounced sense of unreality but I put that down to the strangeness of our situation; married but un-married, friends bound together by past intimacy and that most precious of all things, our child.

In the kitchen, everything looked the same, yet utterly different. The coffee pot had been moved from its usual place and I could see, just from a glance, that nobody had wiped down the door of the fridge. It had gathered a faint yellow sheen.

I looked away. This was not my house any more.

It was Sunday morning, which, throughout our marriage, had followed a particular routine. This morning was no different. Jonathan was sitting at his usual place at the kitchen table, his back to the window. I sat opposite him, also in my usual place. Molly, as was usual, was watching television in her playroom. The newspapers were spread across the table and we, as usual, were talking.

It was all so normal, yet everything was different. Perhaps that was why I could make no connection. It looked, to me, like a scene from a play that I was witnessing. I could not say that I was even engaged enough to be watching it. Any focus was absent. I felt a sudden, claustrophobic grip of terror and of grief. Terrible grief.

Jonathan finished telling a story. 'Anyway,' he said, 'how are you?'

I was staring out of the French windows at my beloved garden, which I had spent ten years creating. I loved that garden, used to spend every moment I had in it. I knew in which corners the snowdrops would be blooming, the white hellebores bursting from bud and the viburnum flinging out its cloying pink and white scent. Once I would have been out there on my knees, watching the snowdrops push their pointed, green noses out of the hard, cold ground. I would have been welcoming the spring, celebrating every moment of extra light, counting down the lengthening of the days. Now, it seemed meaningless.

'What?' I said.

He laughed. 'I said, how are you?'

'I can't do this any more.'

Jonathan frowned. 'What can't you do?'

'All of it. Any of it. I can't get back to myself. I can't seem to make sense of anything at all.'

'Sal, what are you talking about?'

I dropped my head.

'Sal?'

And so I said the only thing I knew to be true. I said, 'I don't know how to look after Molly. I don't know how to keep her safe. I don't know how to be here for her.'

'But you're a really good mother. She adores you.'

'It's not that. It's not safe. I'm not safe. I want to die.'

It was the first time I had said it to anybody. The first time I had said it out loud. I had been struggling hard for nine months and I knew, then, that it was over.

Jonathan went very still. 'What did you say?'

I looked out at my garden. 'I want to die. That's all I want. Every single day, all I want to do is die.'

'How long has this been going on?'

I said nothing.

'Sal? How long?'

I turned my head so he would not see my tears. Why? I had cried in front of him before. We had been married for ten years. 'Weeks, months. I don't know. A long time.'

'Why didn't you say something?'

I shook my head. 'I don't feel safe.'

'Where don't you feel safe? In your flat? Out on the streets? Here?'

I raised my hands, clutched them around my head.

'Here.'

Neither of us knew what to do. It was obvious, even to me, that I needed help but I had no idea how to go about getting it. Neither of us knew a psychiatrist. Neither of us knew anything about psychiatrists and while I had seen those two therapists for a short while, I realised that I knew nothing about mental illness. I did not even know what mental illness was. I just knew that I was not right.

Fortunately, Jonathan is not a man to allow ignorance to be any impediment. 'You're going to bed,' he said, 'and I'm getting on the phone.'

When I woke, it was dark. Jonathan had, through a friend of a friend, made contact with a psychiatric hospital. They would see me the following morning for an assessment.

'What does that mean?' I asked.

'Apparently they have to assess you, to see if you need to see a psychiatrist.'

'OK,' I said, although the word made me flinch.

Jonathan made me stay in bed and cooked me scrambled eggs for supper, although I protested that I was not, actually, physically ill.

'I think it's best,' he said.

And it was. I was so tired I could hardly sit up. The eggs were perfect but the plate was scorching. I watched the eggs fry before my eyes.

'The plate's too hot,' Jonathan said.

I smiled. He never burns food, only plates. I ate the eggs, to please him. They tasted like scorched rubber.

The next morning, Monday, was grey with rain. The hospital was a place I was to come to know well in the years that followed but at the time, I was so confused and frightened I remember little of my surroundings or what was said, except it was a male nurse who conducted my assessment. He had a clipboard and the room was green. I remember that. Green is supposedly the most psychologically soothing of all colours, presumably because it is found in nature. All mental hospitals are painted green, in one way or another. I have come to hate green rooms.

The nurse asked me questions. About food. About sleep. About pleasure and about pain. And then he put down his clipboard. 'You need to see a psychiatrist as soon as possible,' he said. 'I'll see who's available.'

I met the nurse again, a year later, but did not recognise him. 'Don't worry,' he said. 'It happens all the time. You weren't quite all there when we first met. How are you doing?'

I looked around me. I was back in the hospital.

'Not good,' I said.

The psychiatrist was expecting the imminent arrival of his fourth child. He kept his mobile switched on. 'Just in case,' he said. It lent the proceedings a somewhat surreal quality; this child who was waiting to be born, and this woman who was wanting to die.

The psychiatrist was short and slightly stout with dark hair and eyes that were a little too close together. He wore a dark suit, a white shirt and an anonymous tie. His expression was neither indifferent nor sympathetic; it was simply clinical. It was as if he was conspiring to be almost entirely anonymous. Which, I suppose, he was. I was the focus of our interest, not him.

'You don't appear to be very well,' he said.

I was leaking tears; slow, grey cold water. They slipped down my face in silence. I hardly noticed them. We talked for a while. Or, rather, he asked questions, and I answered them. About my disrupted sleep, my indifferent eating, my disintegrated marriage, my ruinous love affair, my stalled career; about my family, friends, my child. About pleasure (none), pain (too much) and hope (entirely absent). It was not a conversation so much as a list of situations and symptoms.

'Do you think about death?' he asked.

'No, not death as such. I think about not wanting to be alive.'

'Have you thought about particular methods of dying?'

'I don't care. Just so long as I do.'

He nodded as if it were the most natural thing in the world for a person to say. Which, I suppose, to him it was. 'How long have you had those thoughts?'

How long? Two months? Six? A year? Time seemed to have lost all meaning.

'I don't know. I can't remember. I keep trying to sort my head out, to think my way out of this, and I can't. Nothing is actually wrong. My life is fine. I have somewhere nice to live, lots of friends, work if I want it. I don't understand why I can't pull myself out of this.'

He said that a marriage breaking up, moving house three times and being sacked from a job, all in the space of a year, didn't seem fine to him.

'Even so,' I said. 'None of it is bad enough to make you want to die. People go through it all the time.'

'It is enough,' he said, 'to send you into depression. You can't think at the moment, let alone think your way out of depression.'

I shrugged. 'Most people get depressed when a marriage breaks up.'

He looked at me in silence for a moment. 'No,' he said. 'Not like this. You have severe clinical depression.'

'Oh.'

'Now I'm going to tell you something you won't like.'

I thought he already had. 'What?'

'I think you should go into hospital,' he said, 'and as soon as possible.'

People react badly to mental hospitals. A friend told me recently that when her husband heard that I was being admitted to a psychiatric unit, he was appalled. 'Surely,' he said, 'that can't be necessary. She can't be that bad.'

No, not bad, or even mad. Just sad.

As for me, I was neither upset nor appalled. For the first time in months, I felt hope. I was going into hospital. I was going to be made better. I thought they would fix my pain, put a plaster cast on my broken head. A few days in bed, some medicine and I would be good as new.

It wasn't quite like that. It wasn't like that at all, just as a mental hospital was not as I imagined it at all. Not that I had ever spent much time imagining it. It was, to be perfectly truthful, the last place I thought I would ever find myself.

The first unit I was in took up a floor in a big London hospital. My psychiatrist chose it because the food was good. If that sounds arbitrary, that's because it was. There's little to choose between mental hospitals, even posh private ones. Food is a good enough reason although, as it turned out, it was enough to drive anyone mad. All food orders had to be placed two days ahead. As few of us there could even remember who we were, let alone what day it was, the food we had ordered on a Tuesday night for a Thursday lunch was a constant and not always delightful surprise.

Really, when it came to a mental hospital, I cared about only one thing.

'I must be able to smoke,' I said. 'If I can't, I shall go mad.' I paused. 'Madder,' I added.

He did not smile. Psychiatrists don't like jokes about madness. They've heard them all before.

'I'm sure you can smoke,' he said.

Of course I could smoke. Most depressives, as I was later to discover, smoke. There's even research that claims that of the several thousand chemicals in cigarettes, one, or several, may affect mood in much the same way as a group of antidepressant medications called monoamine oxidase inhibitors (MAOIs). These MAOIs effectively increase levels of specific neurotransmitters involved in the regulation of mood. So smoking may be a way that depressives try to self-medicate their symptoms. If private psychiatric hospitals instituted a no-smoking policy, half the rooms would stay empty.

The psychiatric unit was modern and light but the rooms had hospital beds and sharp, dark hospital smells. The windows were locked fast and the doors to the ward were reinforced plate glass with automatic locks. There was no way out. But I had a room to myself, and a door that closed, for which I was grateful. Not that it stayed closed for long. An endless stream of doctors, nurses and in-house psychiatrists eddied in and out of the room, taking my pulse, tapping my chest, taking blood, filling in forms, asking endless questions. I had no idea that depression was so medical.

On the first night, three nurses lined up at the end of my bed. They were all from the Caribbean, their black hair bound in tight, bouncing braids, their smiles white and strong and they looked so much like a hip-hop version of the Three Degrees, I could not help but smile in return.

They talked in syncopated rhythm, too, each entering on cue as the other finished speaking.

'We are the night shift.'

'If you need us, all you have to do is press the bell or come to the nurses' station.'

'But we'll be checking you every fifteen minutes all through the night,' finished the third. 'Just to be sure.'

'To be sure of what?' I asked, even as I realised that I was on suicide watch. They would be checking me to see that I had not killed myself.

'To be sure that you're happy, honey,' said the first.

Molly, then nine, came to visit me and was enchanted to discover that my bed went up and down if she pressed a small red button. We sat in the bed for some time going up and down, up and down.

'Are you sick?' she said.

'Well, I am now,' I said. 'I'm sea sick.'

She laughed for a bit. 'But proper sick,' she said. 'Are you proper sick?'

I told her what my psychiatrist had told me, that depression is an illness, like pneumonia. When it gets really bad, it needs doctors and nurses and a hospital bed to make it better.

She thought about that for a bit. 'OK,' she said.

One day, soon after I had been admitted to hospital, she turned up and announced that the kids in her school were stupid.

'Why?' I asked.

'Because when I said that my mummy was in hospital, they said not to be so stupid, that you didn't go into hospital with depression. They said all their mummies get depressed.'

'And what did you say?'

'I said that it wasn't stupid, that proper depression isn't just being a bit sad, it's an illness and sometimes you have to go into hospital to get better.'

'And what did they say?'

She shrugged. 'They were cool about that.'

I always managed to be cheerful when Molly came to visit. It was only after she left that I fell apart. Going into hospital was the easy part. Staying there, and slowly beginning to understand just how ill I had become and how serious severe depression truly is, was terrifying.

7

It's No Picnic

One should, for example, be able to see that things are hopeless and yet be determined to make them otherwise.

F. Scott Fitzgerald

The first time I had to attend group therapy, I cried. I howled. I hung on to my bed, sobbing, as three nurses tried to drag me from my room and take me to the therapy room where all the other patients were gathered.

'No, no,' I begged. 'I don't want to go in there. Don't make me.' I had not seen the therapy room, had not left the safety of my own room for the twelve hours since I had been admitted to hospital. The nurses eventually gave up, left me in a damp huddle on my bed, shaking with fear. I could try again, they said, that afternoon.

My psychiatrist was summoned.

'You seem rather distressed,' he said.

Distressed? Distressed is when you've lost your purse, not when you're locked up in the mad house. My instinct was to punch him, to deck him with a swift left hook. It was often my instinct with my psychiatrist. His language was always so temperate, so measured.

Necessary, I suppose, in the face of madness. But maddening, nonetheless.

'I don't want to go in there.'

'It would be helpful if you did,' he said.

I sighed. In what was left of my rational mind, I knew I had a choice. Except that it no longer seemed like much of a choice. Either I could not attend group therapy and go on being depressed. Or I could attend and be terrified.

I felt like I was back at boarding school. I have a horror of institutions, of being locked away. Yet I was the one who had agreed, voluntarily, to be locked away. So I lay weeping on my bed as the man in the dark suit talked. And as he talked, I knew I had a choice. I also knew it was no choice.

I was, as they say, fucked.

It's no picnic, a psychiatric ward. They fill up your time with group therapy, every morning and every afternoon, for two- or, sometimes, three-hour slots. Everybody gets a turn to speak, although not everybody does. Some days you don't want to, you just want to be quiet and listen. Some days you don't want to listen either. Or perhaps it's more that you don't want to hear.

There was a young woman in our group – let's call her Sophie although it was not her name. Sophie was in her late twenties; pretty and rosy-cheeked with auburn curls. You might smile to see her pass you on the street. Her mum and dad sexually and physically abused her from the age of eight. She ran away from home when she was fourteen. She's just found out her mum's in hospital, dying. She wants to go and see her but she's too frightened. Not just of her mother, but of her own anger.

She says her mother was certifiable, a real nutter. When Sophie was twelve, she stood in front of her and pulled out her own front teeth with her bare hands. Sophie tells the story, deadpan.

'Seems stupid,' she says, 'to be frightened of a toothless old hag.'

Her dad fucked her everywhere, up her bum, in her mouth.

He died two years ago. Sophie's having a hard time dealing with that. She says that now she'll never know why he did what he did.

Afterwards, the therapist asks us if we have any comments. What she actually says is, would we like to share Sophie's pain? Nobody could do that, not even Sophie. She's wrapped it up tight and hidden it away because it's too horrible to contemplate. The therapist wants to get it out in the open, lay it out on a slab like a piece of bleeding meat. She says it's what's crippling Sophie with depression.

When she says that, you can see the fear in Sophie's eyes.

When she says that, I feel like a fraud. What right do I have to be here? I have not suffered as Sophie has. How dare I claim her pain? Or any pain?

I listen to the others. A man has lost his job. He cannot get over it. Without his job he does not know who he is.

A woman is terrified of her children, who are very small. She says she does not know how to be a mother and they will find her out.

It took me a while to understand that there is no direct line to depression, although a history of abuse is a more direct line than almost any other. Otherwise it has no lineage, no red markers other than vague talk of genetics and predisposition, stressors and reactors. What may devastate one person will leave another entirely unscathed. It is all terrifyingly vague. Much like my head.

And then there is Jane. She's very funny, very smart and very, very sad. She cries most of the time. It's no big deal. We all cry most of the time.

We didn't become friends straight away, although I noticed her at once. It was her face, mainly. It's one of those faces that in any other life you'd say was open and friendly. The lines around her eyes say she laughs all the time. Or used to. Depression does funny things to faces; it's as if they're wrapped tight in cling-film so they take on a pale and plastic quality. Sometimes, they glitter. Then there are the shadows under our eyes, stark as violet bruises. Everybody has them.

Jane's skin is green. Not pea soup green, but that delicate shade that tells you somebody is sick. It doesn't just happen when you're sick to your stomach. It happens when you're sick to your soul.

And Jane's sick. Really sick. She's been this way for four years, although she says she has no reason to be depressed. Nothing bad has happened in her life. 'If it had,' she says, 'it might be easier. To understand,' she adds, as an afterthought.

Jane is dangerous. Not to anybody else, just to herself. Really, in a physical sense, we are only dangerous to ourselves. In every other sense, we are dangerous to all the people who love us. We destroy their happiness, their peace of mind, their certitude. Depression does not only destroy those it directly touches.

She keeps trying to kill herself. Her mum's so anxious about her she can't eat, but Jane, who loves her mum, says she can't help herself. She just wants to die. She's on twenty-four-hour suicide watch. All day and all night somebody sits outside her door, which must, at all times, remain open.

It's not just the suicides they check. They look in on everyone, at random times during the night. They never knock, which I don't like. I may be depressed but I'm still human.

'They think if they knock, it gives you time to hide the razor blade,' somebody said. I have no razor blades; they went through all my stuff when I arrived. They even took away my disposable razor. They were impressed I had enough energy to care about having hairy legs. I didn't, really. But I do now.

When they come into my room, they always say the same thing. 'You're awake!' As if that's a surprise at four in the morning in a mental hospital. I reply that I am always awake at that time. They say something about getting my psychiatrist to increase my sleep medication and then they check their charts and see that I am on the maximum dose.

'Just try to relax,' they say, 'let your mind drift.'

Relax? Drift? Have they any idea what my mind is doing? But I say nothing. They are only trying to be kind.

Jane thinks the expression, suicide watch, is funny. 'Can't they phrase it in another way? It sounds like, "hey, guys, watch me die."'

I say, 'Why do you want to die?' I am fascinated. Before I got here, I had no idea that anybody else wanted to die.

'I don't want to die. I just don't want to be here any longer. I don't mean this place,' she says, making a gesture that involves the ward. She points to her head. 'I mean, this place.'

On the second day, a doctor comes by with an official looking form, the Beck Depression Inventory. It is a series of questions that attempt to measure the severity of your depression.

I score thirty-two.

'Is that bad?' I ask.

'Anything over nineteen is severe depression. Under that, it's moderate, dropping to mild.'

'Oh.'

'But there are people here at fifty,' the doctor says.

I think he means to cheer me up. My throat closes at the idea of so much pain.

'I see you ticked that you want to die.'

'Yes.'

'How would you like to die? Cancer, Aids, car crash?'

I look at him. 'I might be depressed but I'm not mad. Pills, of course.'

He smiles. 'Some people prefer cancer. It leaves them no option. It takes the responsibility out of their hands.'

Jesus.

Eighteen months later, I understand, after I have tried, twice, to kill myself and failed. Well, obviously, I've failed. It's harder than you think to die, even when every fibre of your being is focused on death. Rehabilitation units are filled with people with shattered legs who've tried to kill themselves by throwing themselves off high buildings.

By then, I don't just want terminal cancer. I long for it. Not for the sympathy. I want no attention. I have too much of that already. I just want not to exist.

Jane's been in and out of this hospital five times. She is constantly, chronically, unrelentingly suicidal. But she is good, like most depressives, at hiding it. So good that the last time she was here, she was allowed out for a walk.

She went for a walk and then she went to a pub, where she drank five large gins. Not because she wanted a drink but because she wanted an anaesthetic. Psychiatrists call depressive drinking, 'self-medication'. Then she bought four hundred paracetamol, all from different chemists. She ripped open the packages and hid the pills down her socks, in her coat pockets and in her jeans. It took her two hours to pop the pills out of their white plastic holders. When she walked back into the ward, she was rattling.

'True dedication,' she says.

'You're nuts,' I say.

She laughs. 'No!' she says. 'Really?'

'It's the worst death. It takes weeks and then your liver finally packs up.'

'I know. They told me that when they found the pills.'

She wants to go for a walk now, but her psychiatrist won't let her. 'I'll wear slippers,' she pleads, 'so I can't run fast. I'll shuffle slowly, like a mad person. A nurse can follow on behind. I'll wear a nightie and a coat with no pockets.'

The answer is still no.

'Please. I just need some fresh air.'

She tries another tack. 'I could go out on the terrace. Sally could come with me. She's responsible.'

I know what the psychiatrist is thinking. The terrace is three floors up. Sally is clinically depressed too.

'It's not as if I was going to jump,' Jane grumbles to me later. 'I want to be dead, not a paraplegic.'

Her psychiatrist reckons this is their last chance to crack

Jane's immoveable depression. Crack: that's the word he uses. When I hear it, I think of depression as the shell around a nut. We are trapped fast inside it.

Jane's down for ten courses of ECT. Her first is tomorrow, at ten in the morning. 'When the national grid goes down,' she says, 'you'll know I'm under.'

They're going to do it in her room, wheeling in a machine and attaching electrodes to her head. She shows me where. They have to strap you down, to stop your body jerking too violently and breaking bones. Or your neck. The procedure only lasts for two minutes.

'What if it doesn't work?'

She draws a finger across her neck and shrugs.

I have a stalker. Her name is Grace. She's a tiny Spanish woman in her sixties. She wears big round dark glasses and follows me wherever I go, crying in a low whimper.

She tugs at me constantly. 'Why am I here? Why I am here?'

'Because you're sad,' I say, 'Just like everyone else.'

'But I never get any better.'

'You will.'

'How do you know?'

'Because everybody does.' I am lying. Not everyone does. But it is what I want to believe and so I say it out loud.

'No,' she cries, punching me on the arm with a tiny fist. 'I won't, I won't. I won't get better.'

It's what everyone thinks, of course. Nobody thinks they'll ever get better. They think they'll cry until eternity.

I want to buy Jane flowers, to cheer her up before her ECT. There's a certain, grim sanity in that thought. So I go to the nurses' station and ask permission to leave the hospital, to go to Sainsbury's, which is down the road.

They look doubtful.

'I'm not mad,' I want to say. 'Just sad.' Instead, I say, 'It's just down the road, I won't be long.' It's weird having to explain yourself, to ask permission to go to a supermarket. I haven't done that since I was a child. I haven't been locked up since I was a child at boarding school.

They say that they have to call my psychiatrist. I need his permission to leave the ward.

I go and sit in my room and wait.

Grace sits with me. She pulls out a crumpled piece of paper from the big plastic handbag she carries everywhere.

'What does this mean?' she says.

I look at the paper.

'It's the drugs you're on,' I say.

'But what do they mean? What are they for? Why do I have to take so many?'

Why? Why? Why? I know just what she means, but I have no answers. Since I have been here they have doubled the amount of antidepressant medication I was on, then doubled it again. My original dose wasn't enough, they said, to touch the sides. I think I'm on a lot now, but I have no way of knowing. I take my pills with blind submission. Just as I take the tranquillisers and sleeping pills they give me.

I shrug and hand back the piece of paper to Grace. 'I don't know about your drugs. I'm not a doctor.'

She subsides into a small, quivering heap in the chair by my bed. I lie on the bed and stare up at the ceiling, feeling Grace vibrate beside me. Even in her stillness, she is agitated. She suffers from severe anxiety, as well as depression.

A nurse puts her head around the door. 'You can go out,' she says to me.

I swing my legs off the bed, search for my shoes. I haven't worn proper shoes for a week. I put them on. My feet feel stiff, uncertain.

Grace is bolt upright. 'Where are you going?'

'To get some flowers for Jane. She has her first bout of ECT tomorrow.'

Grace clutches her bag in excitement. 'Can I come?'

I look at her. I have listened to her in group every day, twice a day, for a week. I know all about her dead daughter and her cold, unfeeling husband. I know that she cries all night, that she is half-blind with tears. I even know what size shoes she takes (two). But I don't know how mad or sane she is. I try to picture her in the fresh veg section in Sainsbury's. She's so small, I could fit her in a shopping trolley, like a toddler. And then I imagine losing a mad Spanish midget in a supermarket.

I'm not sure I could cope with that. I'm not sure, even, that I can cope with myself. I have not been out in the real world for a week. I think it might be a shock. All those people, those lights, the harsh cold air of reality.

'I don't think so,' I say.

She is indignant. 'Why not?' She beats at the chair with her fists. 'Why not?'

I put on my coat, resort to rules and regulations. 'You have to have permission from your psychiatrist.'

Grace starts to whimper. I feel exhausted. My unfamiliar shoes pinch. 'We'll ask the nurses,' I say.

We walk to the nurses' station. 'Grace wants to come with me,' I say, pulling wild please say no faces over the top of her head.

They look at Grace. 'Now, Grace,' they say, 'you know you're not allowed. You know what happened last time.'

I leave, without a backward glance. I don't want to know what happened last time. I don't want to hang out with mad people.

The air is cold and sharp after the cloistered warmth of the ward. Everything feels big and noisy, too bright. Cars hurtle past me, heaps of jagged metal. I shrink into my coat. Even as I shrink I think, how odd. I am not, by nature, a shrinker.

The people in the supermarket look strange, as if they have been recast to bigger proportions, painted in stronger colours. I choose a bunch of flowers, walk to a till, take my purse out of my bag, count out money, hand it over. As I do so, I marvel that I am capable of acting so normal. Except that I am not. My hands are shaking. Sweat is pouring down my back. The effort of being among people, among lights and noise is overwhelming. I want to sit down, right there at the checkout. I used to do this every week, with a trolley full of stuff and a world of recipes in my head. I used to do it and think about twenty other things at the same time. Now, it takes all my concentration to retrieve some money from my bag. I marvel at myself, at how competent I used to be.

I want to cry. I want to explain myself to the people standing around me. I want to say, 'This is not really me. I am not like this. I am like you. I am not a patient from a mental hospital. I am just an ordinary woman whose mind has gone temporarily wrong.'

And that's when I realise that all I want to be is an ordinary woman, in an ordinary supermarket, doing her ordinary, everyday shopping.

And I understand how unspeakably wonderful ordinary, everyday life is and how I long to be back there.

I grow to like group therapy. It is consoling, being with people who feel as I do. Sometimes, when the blackness eases in my head, I even feel bored. One of the therapists, let's call her Meg, bores me. She wears crêpe-soled Mary Janes, toddler shoes with little buttoned straps, and bunched cheese-cloth skirts. Her voice is very low, almost a whisper, so the group has to lean forward to catch her words.

'Attention seeker,' I think. I am picking up the jargon of therapy fast.

Meg's hair is clay red, abundant with henna. She is thin; a skinny, whispery woman with a squeaky little temper and a banal way with words. If I met her in another world, I'd get no further than hello. Now, I have to pay rapt attention to her every word. She treats us as if we were children, scolding and encouraging us in turn. I want to punch her. Cheesecloth does that to me. So does depression. I find myself stranded in sudden, almost murderous rages. I can't keep still, am filled with a fierce, restless agitation. Then, just as suddenly, I am hopeless and helpless with despair and apathy. I can find no middle way. I understand what they mean by an unbalanced mind.

Later, when I am well enough to research my illness, I discover that I may suffer from a form of depression known as agitated depression. The spectrum, major depressive disorder, covers a multitude of conditions. The manifestations of depression are not always passive and inert.

After I have tried to kill myself yet again, I discover the following passage by Kay Redfield Jamison, from her book *Night Falls Fast: Understanding Suicide*.

> The severity of depression – especially when coupled with physical agitation, alcohol or drug use, and profound emotional upheavals, losses, or disappointments in life – is far more predictive of suicide than a diagnosis of depression alone.

I can tick all the boxes: 'agitation, alcohol, profound emotional upheavals, loss.' Suddenly, I understood and just as suddenly, found it possible to forgive myself. I spent the months following my suicide attempts in an agony of guilt over trying to take my own life and abandoning my daughter. But when I read about myself in stark black and white, I understood that I was not a terrible, selfish and unfit mother. I was a walking symptom of an illness.

Jane, who took her ECT badly and threw up for two days, is feeling better. She can't, she says, remember much – or at least not much in the short-term. Who was it brought her flowers? They're very pretty.

This short-term memory loss goes after a few weeks. Long-term memory is not affected. At least, not usually. I am growing to hate the vague declarations of psychiatric treatment, the airy cross-your-fingers pronouncements. The treatment of mental health is an inexact science. But, as I am slowly coming to understand, depression is an inexact illness.

Meg bores Jane too. We decide to liven things up a little by seeing who can say loony most often. We're not allowed to say loony in the loony bin. Apparently, it's too much reality for our poor heads to cope with.

My personal loony best is five, although Jane says I cheat. 'Talking about Looney Tunes does not count.'

'Nor does saying you wore loons in the seventies.'

They don't like jokes in group therapy. Humour is a defence. I am in denial, they say, which is just another word for smartass. I use humour to hide behind, because I cannot bear to feel my feelings, cannot face the truth. I use too many words, they say. I hide behind language. I intellectualise my feelings and then explain them away.

'Stop using your head, Sally. How do you *feel*?'

'How can I tell you how I feel if I don't use words?'

'Just feel the feelings.'

'Feelings are thoughts,' I say. 'Thoughts are words.'

They sigh. I can see the word 'difficult' captured in bubbles above their heads.

'Feel the feelings,' they say, again.

And then what? My feelings are stuck in my throat. The feelings that I can't, actually, put into words.

8

Leaving Hospital

If there is a sin against life, it consists perhaps not so much in despairing of life as in hoping for another life and in eluding the implacable grandeur of this life.

Albert Camus

My psychiatrist tells me that it is time for me to leave the hospital. Not because I am better, but because my health insurance has nearly run out for that financial year. I have been in the hospital for two weeks. It has never occurred to me that I might be forced to leave and nor have I ever thought to ask how long I would be staying. When I was admitted, I was in no state to think about anything, let alone the intricacies of private medical insurance. I just thought that I would stay in hospital until I was better. Isn't that what happens when you are very sick?

I stare at him numbly.

'We need to keep the remainder in lieu,' he says. 'In case you need a back-up.'

'A back-up?'

'We may need to readmit you. And I'd like you to do individual therapy, at least twice a week, perhaps more. You will need money for that. There's a therapist I'd like to suggest.'

I ignore the suggestion. I don't want a therapist. I want to be better. I want to be a person who doesn't need therapy. I want to be the person I used to be. Hospital was supposed to fix that, to fix me. That's why I agreed to it.

I say nothing. I can think of nothing to say.

'It's early days yet,' he says.

That's the odd thing about depression. Two weeks in hospital for any other illness seems like a long time. In depression, it is nothing, a brief interlude. In depression, time loses all meaning. The average stay in hospital is six weeks. Some of the people in the unit are staying for three months or even six.

Suddenly, I feel terror at the thought of leaving these safe, airless confines.

'How am I going to cope?'

'Why do you think you can't?'

My psychiatrist looks at me with dispassionate, professional interest. His prognosis is that my depression is not so bad now, at least in practical terms. I can wash and feed myself. It is less likely that I will kill myself, although about that nobody can be sure. Least of all, me.

I look away. Of course I can cope. I am an adult. I have run businesses, houses, marriages. It is absurd to think I can't, it is my imagination, my poor deluded mind. I hear him say something about attending after-care a couple of mornings a week and getting used to life again. I imagine myself making my way from my flat to the Tube, walking free in the clear, cold air, looking like every other person on the street. Except that I am not like them. I feel too much. I think too much. I can get nothing in proportion. My emotional thermostat has malfunctioned. It is set on full alert. I imagine a red light flashing from my forehead. WARNING. WARNING. SYSTEM CORRUPTED. DO NOT ATTEMPT TO OPERATE.

I look at him and something of my panic must show in my face because he smiles at me and says, 'It will be easier than you think.'

I see that he is trying to be kind.

'Perhaps,' I say.

I have seen people leave this hospital and seen the fear and elation in their faces as they say goodbye. I have seen their terror but never felt it. Until now.

I go and find Jane.

'I'm leaving,' I say.

Her face registers nothing. 'Why?'

'The insurance has run out. I have no choice.'

'Are you OK?'

I stare down at my feet, at our feet. Neither of us is wearing shoes. We are barefoot in this asylum. Her toes are square and practical, like her hands. My nail polish has chipped, giving my feet a ragged crimson and white edge, like the frill on the petal of a carnation.

'I'm scared,' I say.

She gives me a hug. 'Of course.'

I am glad that she doesn't tell me I'll be fine.

Sarah comes to the hospital to get me. I am moving back, temporarily, into the marital home. Everyone thinks it's better if I'm not on my own. Everyone except me. I think it would be much better if I were on my own. My ex-husband Jonathan is being kind. Everyone is being kind. It makes me feel like an invalid. I'm not sick, I want to say. I'm just not myself.

Half my stuff is still at the house. The rest is at my flat, which I was in the middle of doing up when I had the breakdown. And that, I suppose, is the way I feel too – neither here nor there.

Sarah stands next to me, her hand on my shoulder. I can feel her need to take me away from all this, from mental illness and hospitals and back to the person I used to be; the person she has known and loved for thirty years. She wants it to be OK, wants this to be just a brief and difficult interlude, a sudden hiccup in an ordinary, unblemished life.

Except it is not like that. I know that this is a beginning, not an end. I linger at the door, staring at my empty room. It is just another hospital room now. I have taken away the cashmere shawl from the chair with the wooden arms. I used it to hide the cushions, which are sick green polyester. I have packed up my old American quilt, which I used to cover up the ugly woven beige and brown bed cover. The flowers in the vases are all dead.

I think back to a time when I was staying in New York, in a brown and orange Howard Johnson hotel, decorated with hideous, unerring precision. The first thing I did after I checked in was to rehang the brown and orange flowered curtains so that the cream lining faced in to the room. I could not bear to sleep amid that cacophony of colour. Every morning, the maid rehung the curtains to face the right way. Every night, I changed them back again. We never met, but we knew each other's character. Neither of us was the losing type.

'Are you OK?' Sarah says.

I step into the corridor. 'I don't know. I think so.'

We drive through the black February afternoon. London seems jammed with headlights and noise. It is very cold.

'Promise you'll call me every day,' Sarah says.

'I'll be fine,' I say.

'Really,' Sarah says.

'Really,' I say.

'I mean, really call, every day,' Sarah says, her expression faintly exasperated. She knows me too well. I don't call her every day, of course. Like all depressives, I like to disappear.

When I came out of hospital, everyone thought that I would be immediately better. I knew otherwise, but said nothing. I could feel the fragility in myself but hoped that I was wrong. If I had known, then, that it would be two years before I felt anything other than black despair, I might not have made it through. I'm glad I didn't know. If I had, I might have tried to kill myself earlier. Everyone thinks that a suicide attempt is a reaction to something. For me, it was a reaction to nothing. It was a year after I left hospital that I tried to kill myself. A year of blank and terrible loneliness. A year of no improvement.

'You have resistant depression.' That's what my psychiatrist said. I did not know, at the time, what it meant or what its full implications really were. I thought he meant that my resistance was temporary, that it was a passing phase. I did not understand that, in medical terms, it meant that no drug on earth could cure or even touch me.

I thought of a nurse in the psychiatric unit, bringing me my daily drugs. 'Time for your smarties,' she said.

I wanted to hit her. I wanted to say to her that they were powerful and dangerous drugs, not harmless sweets. I am not a recalcitrant child who needs my medicine sugared with words. I have not lost my mind, simply mislaid it.

She carried them on a white plastic tray, tipping them into my palm from a tiny cardboard cup then stood over me, gimlet-eyed, to make sure I swallowed them. Some people save them up to kill themselves. Which is pointless. The new breed of SSRI medications will not kill you. The older varieties, the tricyclics, are better for suicide, although you have to take a lot.

In those early days of my illness, I had not touched real despair, although I thought that I had. Real despair came later. Back then, I struggled hard to get better, hanging on to moments of optimism or clarity as if they were passing boats in a stormy sea. My fragility constantly took me by surprise.

Soon after I left the hospital I was standing in the kitchen at home making a cup of tea. Molly, who had just turned nine, jumped out from the shadows and said, 'Boo!'

I screamed, dropped the cup of scalding tea and burst into tears. Once upon a time, I would have laughed.

Moll shrunk against the wall in terror. 'Sorry Mum. Sorry, sorry, sorry,' she cried, holding up her arms as if to ward me off.

I longed to comfort her, to say that everything was all right but I could not speak. I could only cry in great racking sobs and shake, as if I was having convulsions. Molly fled up the stairs, crying for her father.

I collapsed, hysterical, on the floor amid the spilt tea and broken china and as I sat there sobbing, I remembered, ludicrously, a phrase from some long forgotten black and white movie. 'It's her nerves, poor thing. Her nerves are shot to pieces.'

'I am shot to pieces,' I thought, feeling that my skin had been turned inside out and now the nerves, the blood vessels and the organs were all exposed to the cold and the light. Everything hurt, physically hurt. The shaking would not stop.

Once I had quietened down, I went to find Molly. Jonathan had put her to bed. He was quietly furious. 'What was all that about?'

'I don't know.'

He said nothing. I could see the look on his face. He thought I should know.

I shrugged helplessly. 'She gave me a fright.'

'You frightened her.' His tone was accusing. I realised, then, that he thought that I was better. I had been in hospital. I was cured. I wanted to believe it too, but I knew it wasn't true.

'I'm sorry.' I did not know what else to say. How do you say to someone that you are not in control of your own senses, that you have frightened yourself as much as you have frightened your own child? I looked like me. I sounded like me. But I wasn't me.

'I'll go and see her,' I said.

'She's very upset.'

'I know.'

Moll's light was out so I knew she was on best behaviour. I longed for her to be busying herself around the room, desperately trying to be quiet as she arranged her Beanie Babies in random piles – or random, at least, to the naked adult eye.

She was humped under her duvet.

I found her blonde hair and stroked it. 'Sorry darling.'

A whisper emerged. 'You frightened me.'

'Yes, baby, I know. I didn't expect to find you behind the door.'

A small hand emerged from the duvet, a blue eye peeked out. 'Sorry, Mummy. I didn't mean to upset you.'

'You didn't baby. It wasn't your fault. I upset myself.'

She scrambled up, put her arms around my neck. 'Is it the depression thingy?'

'Yes. I'm not quite as well as I thought I was.'

'Didn't the hospital make you better?'

'They tried very hard but it takes longer to get properly well.'

'Poor Mummy. Never mind, you'll feel better soon,' she said, patting me on the back. She did that often when I was ill, her arms wrapped around me, her little hand busy on my back. 'There, there,' she murmured into my neck. 'There, there.'

It is what I used to say to her when she was tiny.

I remember little of the months between the time that I left hospital and went back in again, except that there were eight of them.

I moved back into my flat and struggled through the days and nights. Everything I did, or tried to do, was blanketed with depression. Time lost all meaning, the days and nights went topsy turvy.

There is an entry in a journal I kept erratically. It reads: 'People call. I answer the phone. In that way it is a good day.'

The telephone, which I have never liked, became a torment. I answered it less and less until, eventually, I stopped answering it altogether. My friends knew to leave a message and, when I was feeling stronger, I would call back. Feeling stronger sometimes took days or even weeks. The only person I could bear to call was Sarah and then, not as often as I should. I did not, at this time, know Nigel. I met him in second mental hospital.

'Leave me a message every day,' Sarah said. 'You don't have to use many words. Just "I'm good" or "I'm bad" or "I'm shit." Just so I can hear your voice.'

Just so she knew I wasn't dead.

Often, I lied, said that I was feeling fine even as I wondered how I could get through the next minute, let alone the next hour. If I could convince Sarah that I was feeling fine, perhaps I could convince myself. Perhaps, saying the words out loud would make them so.

Sometimes it took me hours, a whole day, to pick up the phone. Often, I practised speaking before I telephoned, trying to inject the words with just the right amount of lightness, attempting to get to the end of a sentence before my voice collapsed. If Sarah's answer machine picked up, I knew I could usually manage a brief message. If she answered the phone herself, I knew I would be found out.

She always knew if I was low, no matter how hard I tried to pretend, no matter how hard I practised the right, careless tone. I could lie to her. My voice could not.

'I thought we had an agreement,' she always said, 'I thought I could rely on you to tell me the truth.'

The truth? The truth was that I wanted, passionately, to be dead. How do you tell your best friend that? How do you tell anyone that?

I had, by then, abandoned all pretence of work. My editors, on various newspapers and magazines, called less and less. As I did not return their calls, they understandably gave up. I could not bear to explain to them that I could not write or even, by that time, read. Words made no sense to me. I made no sense to me so how could I make sense to anyone else? If journalism is about anything, it is about making sense of the world in which we live.

Words, sense, the very identity that kept me moored and

...d had abandoned me. I was lost and that ...nic. Who are you when you are no longer ...What do you do with a self that is no ...? If you don't know who you are, how do ...ng? If you cannot live as yourself, who and what is it ... are living for?

My daughter.

I went on living for Molly. She was my bright star, the fixed and living point in my dead universe.

I set myself tasks.

I would keep the flat clean. I would keep myself clean. I would look after my child. I would buy food and I would cook it, during the days that Molly was with me. The arrangement with Jonathan was that she spent five days with me, and five with him. When I was alone, I rarely bothered to eat, let alone cook. It was too much effort. Sometimes, as I ate my solitary supper of stale, toasted bread, I thought of a friend, who did not like to cook, and how she had told me that she had made herself cauliflower cheese.

'What,' I said, 'you actually cooked?'

'No, idiot,' she said. 'I ate a piece of cheese and a piece of raw cauliflower.'

That memory made my stale toast seem almost sensible.

On the days that Molly was with me, I would get myself up and dressed in the morning then wake her and get her ready for school. Once she had left, I usually crawled back into bed and stayed there. I was always up and dressed when she got home, and the flat was always clean. Mrs Twitchit, she called me, because I shook so much from the effort. And from the medication I was taking.

'There you go again, Mrs Twitchit,' she'd say, holding my hands in hers until they stopped shaking. 'Better now?'

'Better, darling,' I would always say.

We ate supper together and watched television. It was a very small television, a portable perched on a chair. I didn't have the energy to buy another, despite Molly's protestations.

She did not, bless her, protest too much. I think she understood the effort it took, just to sit in a chair. The thought of going to a shop or making a decision about what to buy terrified me. Crowds frightened me, going on the Tube frightened me. Being outside frightened me. Halfway down a street, I would start to cry, for no reason. People would stop and stare as I stood, motionless, tears running down my face.

I tried not to cry, ever, in front of Molly. I did not want to frighten her again, although sometimes, I would cry without realising I was doing it. Anything could start my tears. Moll says now that it was usually the news on television, particularly anything about children being abused.

Sometimes she would switch the TV off.

'You're crying, mummy.'

'Sorry, darling.'

'You're not to watch it any more. You're especially not allowed to watch it when I'm not here.'

She does not like me to watch the news, even now. Sometimes I catch a swift sidelong glance. I sense her tense as the reporter says a couple has been jailed for the torture and death of a child.

'Hateful,' I say, out loud. '*Hateful.*'

She likes it if I speak. When I was ill, I stayed mute. Every expression went inward, not outward. She would look up and find me white-faced and stricken, tears leaking slowly from my eyes.

I talk a lot now.

Moll played music constantly, perhaps to cheer me up. Her favourite, 'our song' as it came to be known, was Robbie Williams's 'Angel'.

'Dance with me, Mummy, please.'

And I would try. We'd turn the music up loud, and lip-synch along to Robbie, using hair brushes as microphones. To this day, I am word perfect.

Angels played a big part in chasing away the demons, both mine and Molly's. She found God a terrible trial, and still does.

'God's a poo,' she said, aged seven.

'Oh,' I said, 'and why is that?'

'It's all thou shalt not. What about, thou shalt? He's so cross all the time. I don't like him. I shan't believe in him, whatever anyone says.'

And she didn't. But she did believe in angels, and so it became the angels who looked over us. Angels, she said, were very good for chasing away depression because angels, as she announced with the irrefutable logic of a child, are light and depression is dark. The light will always cast out the dark. 'If we turn on the light in my bedroom, Mummy, the darkness goes away.'

At night, if Molly couldn't sleep, I lay with her on her bed and we summoned our guardian angels and dressed them like celestial Barbie dolls. Moll's wore silver and white (she hated pink, 'too girly') and were dressed in Vegas showgirl lamé and marabou trim with plumy white feathers. Mine were kitted out in top of the range Prada, in spun gold.

She remembers little of all this now that she is a teenager and not given to believing in angels, but I do. I remember it well and sometimes, when sleep eludes me or the black dog bites, I summon that old gold Prada angel.

9

Fine Is a Four-Letter Word

Hope is only the love of life.

Henri-Frédéric Amiel

I remember, years ago, reading that at some point in their lives one in ten people would suffer from some form of mental illness. I looked around the office in which I worked. There were forty of us. Four of us would become ill. I wondered idly who it might be.

I was never on that list.

Nor, or so they think, are most people even though the figure these days is closer to one in four. At any one time, twenty-five per cent of us will suffer from 'mental distress', as it is sometimes called.

Let us, just for a moment, look at the implications of that 'distress'. Severe depression affects more than 120 million people worldwide and more than 5 million in the UK. By 2020, according to the World Health Organisation, it will be one of the world's most debilitating conditions, second only to heart disease.

Is that distress? Or is it a major illness? The danger in polite euphemisms is that they drive the condition underground. I constantly see people struggling with severe depression, clamping down on the pain so as not to bother anyone. I know how they minimise both themselves and the severity of their struggle. Mute, pale shadows, they are gagged by polite euphemisms and by misunderstanding.

Unless we tell it as it is – it is an illness just like any other – we will never defuse the fear and secrecy surrounding it. Phrases such as 'mental distress' (which are used, and I can hardly believe I'm writing this, even by some large mental health charities) stop people getting help when they most need it. They minimise the condition, reinforce stigma and impose a burden of secrecy that causes useless and unnecessary suffering. At their worst, they are a death sentence. The fatality rate among those suffering from severe depression is fifteen per cent. Many of those who kill themselves (particularly men) do so because they are too ashamed to admit they have the illness or to seek help.

One of the many letters I received after I wrote about my own experience of suicide and depression was from a man whose son had hanged himself.

'The worst aspect,' he wrote, 'was that I hadn't known that *depression was an illness*, [his italics] so hadn't sought him out, even insisted upon trying to help.'

We are not easy to help. Nor are we easy to be around. Nobody with a serious illness is easy to be around. Although not obviously physically disabled, we struggle to get things done. Our energy levels are dangerously low. Sometimes, we find it hard to talk. We get angry and frustrated. We fall into despair. We cry, for no apparent reason. Sometimes we find it difficult to eat, or to sleep. Often, we have to go to bed in the afternoon or all day.

So do most people with a serious illness. We are no different.

It is just that we are seen that way.

'Sometimes,' says a fellow depressive, 'I wish I was in a full body cast, with every bone in my body broken. That's how I feel anyway. Then, maybe, people would stop minimising my illness because they can actually see what's wrong with me. They seem to need physical evidence.'

Like most people, I have friends who have suffered from a severe illness – one from a stroke at an alarmingly young age, another from cancer. Both were angry, frustrated and despairing. Both were disabled by a lack of energy and found it difficult to eat or sleep. Often, neither of them wanted to talk, but they still wanted the company of those who love them. Neither wanted their friends to dwell on their illness, but neither did they want it ignored.

'The people I found most difficult to be around,' says one, 'were those who tiptoed politely around my illness. There's this huge great elephant in the room and they do everything they can to ignore it, but actually they can't. Every time they bump into it, they act horribly awkward and embarrassed and it ends up being me who has to try to put them at their ease. That's exhausting.'

That awkward embarrassment is even worse around severe depression, because of its inherent stigma – not to mention its intimations of weakness and indulgence.

The question I am most often asked as a person who is so 'out' about their illness (an absurd and sad word to have to use, but true) is 'how do I help somebody who is depressed?'

The most important thing is to accept they have a serious illness. Once you do that, everything becomes easier. Treat them as you would anyone else who is ill. Understand that they will have good days and bad days. Ask them how they feel. Don't expect them to get better overnight. Talk about the illness. Don't shut them up by telling them that they'll feel better soon. They might, but on their time and not yours. Don't dismiss or minimise their condition with clumsy clichés such as 'it's not as bad as all that' or, 'you'll feel better in the morning'. Depression is not a passing mood.

Neuroscientists believe, and are beginning to prove, that depression is more than an affliction from the neck up. It is a whole body disorder. Research shows that it can lead to heart disease in otherwise healthy adults and magnify existing cardiac problems. It can also accelerate changes in bone mass that lead to osteoporosis. Bruce Charlton, a research psychiatrist at the University of Newcastle, has even put forward the theory that depression, far from being a mental illness, is entirely a physical disorder, one that is misinterpreted by the brain. Sickness is read as sadness. The low mood characteristic of depression is merely a secondary response to a physical malaise that includes lack of energy, slowed movement, lack of pleasurable appetites (including sex) and an inability to concentrate.

Charlton suggests that depression is the body's way of withdrawing to conserve energy – in an 'evolved pattern of behaviour' mediated by the immune system. 'The trouble with malaise is that you don't necessarily know you've got it, and you blame yourself for your condition of low performance. Major depressive disorder is sickness behaviour inappropriately activated and sustained.'

In that spirit, Charlton insists that antidepressants do not make people happy. They simply treat the state of unpleasantness. 'Their effect on mood is no more remarkable than the fact that it is easier to be happy without a headache.'

While scientists debate whether depression is an illness of body or mind, or both, one thing is urgently true for the depressive. The sadness that comes from sickness needs addressing. One of the most corrosive aspects of depression is despair. I know it well, and it is catastrophic. It leads to hopelessness, helplessness and a terrible, frightening sense of loneliness. It feels impenetrable and unendurable. You know that you shouldn't feel that way, but you do. It is real.

It is also, although magnified by a factor of thousands in depression, what most of us feel at one time or another. Severe depression, put simply, is an overwhelming and unmanageable onslaught of every normal, human fear and difficult emotion. It is a loss of and lack of perspective and proportion.

It is like living through a waking nightmare. What we most want is somebody to take our hand, to try to connect us back to the world. We don't expect anybody to take our night-mares away but we do need help in seeing them for what they are – as inappropriate responses.

Everyone, not just the depressive, is familiar with those fears and difficult emotions. The way to help a depressive is to share that knowledge. If you want to help them, talk about loneliness and confusion and misunderstanding. Talk about your own too, not just theirs. Don't abandon them to their illness. Share with them. Perhaps talk about a time when you felt that you couldn't connect with other people. Everybody feels that way sometimes. It is just that in depression, that feeling is magnified to become a supreme, unsplendid isola-tion.

Talk about the human condition. Talk about how fright-ening and difficult life can sometimes be. Talk about the things that affect us all, not just depressives. In depression, those feelings sometimes overwhelm us. We feel we can't climb out from under the weight of them. They are not, though, unique to depressives. They are the feelings that all of us feel.

Do it, though, with humour and wit. Life is richly comic, the mistakes we make are often absurd. Our fallibility makes idiots of us all. Our fears, brought out into the daylight of humour, are often laughable. Connecting our fears, our less governable emotions, makes them seem more manageable.

These days, when I collapse into one of my periodic bouts of depression, what I now call 'negative head', I call a friend – usually Nigel or Sarah. In that state, I used to hide myself away, too ashamed or embarrassed by my black nihilism to allow it to be seen. Now I know that the only way to bring it into proportion is to express it. If I don't, it will feed on itself until it becomes, in every sense, unmanageable. The last time it happened, I called Nigel. When he arrived at my door half an hour later, I was still in bed, unwashed, unfed and in tears. Ignoring my protestations, he cheerily made me dress and eat something, then put me in his car and drove me to a park.

As we walked, he countered every one of my negative remarks. 'That's simply not true,' he said, laughing. Or he would build one of my fears into some silly, fanciful story until the sheer absurdity of it made me laugh. Then he would confess one of his own, equally ludicrous, fears until I protested and pointed out the flaws in his thinking. At that point, I realised the flaws in my own.

I believe, completely, that life is about connection; that nothing else truly matters. People so often say, 'I don't know how to help.' This is one way – through empathy but more importantly, through connection. Don't think, as so many people do, that depressives are best left alone. They are not. Ignoring or dismissing depression only makes it worse. It never makes it better.

A friend once said to me that he didn't know how to do small talk. The very effort of it shut him up.

Do big talk, I said. Talk about what really matters, say what you really mean.

I can't, he said. People won't like it.

I used to think that way too. If I had not been trapped in the prison that is depression and forced to bust my way out in any way that I could, I might feel that way still. We are never taught that it's OK to be human and to be vulnerable, so now we've almost forgotten that it's simply the way we are. And that goes for all of us. The way that I deal with my depression these days is to talk about the way I truly feel, and not the way I think other people would like me to feel. I am rarely right about that anyway. And I have discovered that when I break the treaty of silence, I am amazed to find how many people will join me.

I know that some people find such notions of honesty and vulnerability impossible, if not abhorrent. Most of us have never learned the vocabulary of intimacy. We simply don't know how to express our feelings. Perhaps some of us don't need to but it's more, I think, that most of us are frightened to, myself included – although I have now lost that fear. There's nothing like being locked away in three psychiatric units and crying in front of most of London to help you lose your inhibitions, or that carefully constructed social self we regard as so precious.

Much of that self is unhelpful; it is a brick wall behind which we find ourselves trapped, frightened and alone. It is fear, I think, that keeps us so locked down, fear of not being, as the therapeutic phrase goes, 'good enough'.

It takes courage to be honest and open about our own vulnerability. But it is, at heart, what we all crave and need – not only to be listened to, but also to be heard. We want to be understood and accepted for the people we truly are. That's all therapy is, understanding and acceptance. It is allowing somebody to speak until they feel heard. It is an acceptance of each other and of ourselves.

There is a word that's forbidden in therapy.

Fine.

'How are you today?'

'I'm fine.'

In truth, I may be happy or sad, or anxious or irritable. I may be bewildered or lonely, perplexed or depressed. I may be elated or despondent, tired or confused.

But to you, I am just fine.

Fine, in therapy, stands for:

Fucked up
Insecure
Neurotic
Emotional

Fine is my word. It has always been my word.

I have been fine all my life. I have been fine even as my world fell apart. I have been fine as two marriages collapsed.

'It's such a meaningless word,' says a fellow depressive. 'It's a word to hide behind when you're not being honest. It's a word that reveals nothing but is designed to keep people at a distance. There's no comeback from "fine." "OK" is open to interpretation. "I'm well", means that, literally, all is well. But fine is such a non-word that it becomes a barrier to communication.'

I was fine until I had a nervous breakdown.

I was reminded of that, recently, when I had dinner with a friend, Betty. We have been friends for years and, just as she has never faltered in her friendship, she never faltered in her belief that I would get better. Sometimes I think that she held on to it long after I had let it go.

It is winter, and dark outside, but the restaurant I am sitting in is warm and garlanded with fairy lights, because it is nearly Christmas. I am early, because I always am. I suffer from an almost pathological punctuality.

Betty bursts through the door and gathers me in a hug. She has a way of bursting into rooms, as if she cannot contain her own energy. As she releases me from the hug, I register the relief in her face when she sees that I am smiling and happy. I sometimes forget the pain my friends went through, how helpless they felt in the face of my bleak despair.

We don't often discuss my illness. But, tonight, perhaps because I am telling her about this book, and how well (or badly) the writing of it is going, we do. I want, anyway, to see my depression from a different perspective, to understand what it's like to see it from the viewpoint of a friend.

'There was one night when Sarah and I were sitting with you in your flat,' Betty says. 'You were quite mad. Is it OK to say that?'

I smile. 'Yes.'

'You couldn't keep still and you couldn't stop talking. A lot of what you said didn't make sense. You were up and down like a yo-yo, running down the corridor to the kitchen then coming back, empty-handed, looking bewildered. I couldn't keep up but, as we know, running is not my best thing.'

'No,' I say, feeling faintly ashamed for the self-absorption of my former, mad self. When she was twenty, Betty was in a car accident, smashed up so badly they thought she would not live. She was in hospital for a year, had a leg amputated and now has a prosthetic leg, which makes it awkward for her to walk very far or fast. She never complains. I have never heard her utter a single word of self-pity and she radiates such good humour; you want to warm your hands against her. She is also ceaselessly and transparently grateful to the people who helped her to recover and for, in every sense, her life. It is Betty who taught me about gratitude, a quality I now try to emulate as often as I can. If there is one single mental action that can help a depressive, it is the daily practising of gratitude – but more of that later.

Betty says, 'Sarah and I hardly recognised you at all. There were glimpses of the person we knew but you, Sally, had gone. It was as if you had put up this huge big wall and disappeared behind it. You were completely unreachable.'

I say nothing. I don't remember. It is an odd sensation, to be sitting in a warm restaurant lit by fairy lights and listening to stories of a time and a person that I can scarcely recall.

'Sarah and I didn't know what to do, so we just sat there. We sat and we sat even though it was obvious you wanted us to go. In the end you almost threw us out. I called Sarah the next day. We both thought we'd lost you completely. We made a pact that one of us would call you every day and try to visit you, if we could get you to let us in. Most of the time you didn't answer the phone. We always had to leave a message, not knowing if you had got it or, even, if you were still alive.'

I do remember the phone ringing, and the terrible agonising sound of it.

'And when you did finally call, you always said that you were fine,' Betty says, 'even though we knew that you weren't.'

'But I'm OK now.' I choose the word carefully.

Betty will not have it. This is her story, as much as it is

mine. She wanted to save me, to make me better, and she couldn't. All my friends say that, how desperate and helpless they felt, and how terrified. Everyone who loves a depressive feels that terror and impotence. It is a cruel, a desperate illness and not simply for those trapped inside it.

'Yes, but you weren't OK, not for a long time. Do you remember that I came to see you in the first hospital you were in?'

I frown. I want to remember. 'No. Yes. A little.'

'You had this fixed smile. You kept saying, "This is fine, isn't it? It'll be fine now. I'll be fine."'

When she says that, I suddenly want to cry.

'And I looked around at the barred windows and I thought, "No, this is not fine. She's in a mental hospital. This is so completely not fine." Before that, you were always so bright and funny and competent. You could do anything you put your mind to with one hand tied behind your back. With both hands tied behind your back. I was so used to seeing you that way but in the hospital you were sitting on your bed with great black shadows under your eyes, pale as death. You'd obviously been crying for days and all you said was, "I'll be fine."' She looks sad, momentarily. 'And I knew you weren't but because you kept saying it, I couldn't get past that word to help you.'

'I'm sorry.'

Betty laughs. 'It's fine. Just don't do it again.'

It was Betty who handed me the words that became my mantra for months, or even years. It is a mantra that I still use, if life ever becomes difficult. And life does sometimes become difficult, whether we are depressed or not.

I was slumped on my sofa, unable to move, unable to do anything or recognise anything of my old life. She was wearing black, as she always does, and smelled of scent and good things. Her hair was bright blonde, her nails lacquered a deep red and there were diamonds on her fingers. I, as usual, was wearing an old cashmere sweater and stained leggings. I felt like we came from two different worlds. She took my hand and held it so tight; I felt the bite of her diamond ring.

'This too shall pass,' she said. 'You've got to remember that, Sal. Nothing stays the same, good or bad. It's the law of the universe. Believe me, I know.'

I looked at her silver-topped walking stick and knew that she knew. And I knew that she was right.

She took off the black sheepskin scarf she was wearing. It smelled of Chanel scent. 'Please take this,' she said, 'it will keep you safe.'

I slept with that scarf around my neck for months. It made me feel safe, even when the demons were right by my side. I still have it, folded away carefully in my cupboard. Sometimes, when I am in need of comfort, I get it out again although, these days, I never wear it to bed.

I don't use the word 'fine' any more, except when I talk about the weather. And I try to let my friends help me. I try to tell the truth.

I remember, vividly, standing in my kitchen during the days I was first battling with depression, and telling nobody how terrible I felt. Sarah was sitting at the table. We had just finished eating. I don't know what she said but suddenly, something broke in me. I put my hands to my face and I started to cry. Sarah got up and put her arms around me.

'What is it?' she asked.

I said, 'I can't do this any more.'

'What can't you do?'

'I feel so sad, all of the time.'

'About what?'

'Everything.'

'Try to explain.'

'I can't.'

Sarah hugged me. 'I think we should get you some help.'

I shook my head. 'No, I'm fine. Really I am. I'm just being stupid.'

She pulled back a little and looked me in the face. 'Sometimes,' she said, 'you are very hard to help.'

I was astonished and hurt. My friends often used to complain about my habit of suddenly disappearing for days on end or my inclination, in those moods, never to answer the phone. It did not occur to me back then that vulnerability is a pleasing or even a necessary part of friendship; that in order to be loved we must also allow the people we love to feel that we need them too.

I am better at it, these days, I hope. And if severe depression broke down that resistance in me, then perhaps it is a breakage for which I should be grateful. My psychiatrist, who I came to like and respect very much once we had got past our initial battles, said to me that he knew what it was that frightened me the most.

'What's that?' I asked. Even I did not know what frightened me the most.

'Losing your mind.'

'Well, I did. You were there.'

'Then perhaps it wasn't such a bad thing, after all,' he said.

Madness as advantage. Now there's a novel idea. 'In what way?'

He smiled at me. 'The Buddhists tell us that in order to find yourself, you first have to lose your mind.'

It is one of the most consoling things anybody has ever said to me.

10

Genetics, Family and Other Disorders

*Face the facts of being what you are, for that is
what changes what you are.*

Søren Kierkegaard

A memoir of depression is, in some sense, the memoir of a life. What made me the way I am? How are the emotional responses I learned unhelpful?

I want to stay free from depression and live my life well. To me, and this may not be the same for everyone (although I have never met a person for whom it is not true), that means looking at my own behaviour and dismantling the parts of it that keep me stuck in negativity. Or even, simply mired in the low-level discontent that stops me from fully engaging with my own life. It is a self-evident truth, so evident that it took me years to learn it, that life is what it is. It is the way we see it that causes us difficulty.

Looking at our own selves is horribly difficult to do, requiring a level of honesty and humility that can at times feel unbearable. Few people are prepared to engage with it fully but without it, I truly believe that we cannot be happy. And happiness, rather than a good-enough life, is what I aim for. It might be a stretch too far, who knows? But in the reaching I shall at least feel that I am taking some sort of action, that what I do matters, if only to myself.

My responses are, of course, all tangled up with family because they so obviously lay the foundations of our characters. Pretty well every expert in behavioural psychology agrees on that. We learn everything by mimicry, from how to tie our shoelaces to what to eat to how we respond to other people. Most of those patterns are unconscious and many are useful but others are downright obstructive.

Those tripwires to happiness need our full attention. It is not how we learned them, or who we learned them from that matters. What matters is that we have enough knowledge and understanding to put them right when they are damaging to our happiness or good relationships.

Some of those characteristics are genetic but quite how many or to what extent, nobody knows. And as we do not know but only understand that some inherent trait in our characters is due to immutable genes, perhaps the best way to deal with that is in the way that we deal with any other trait – through an examination of our own behaviour, seeing them as obstacles that are fixed but in some way passable.

I once read a theory about 'positive thinking' that seems to me to be true or, at least, made a sufficient impression on me to remember it. I have always been distrustful of positive thinking, believing it to be as fixed and unyielding as negative thinking. Yet it is the advice most often offered to depressives. That it does not work seems not to occur to those who offer it up like some benevolent panacea. Perhaps it works for them or perhaps they are a product of some positive thinking gene pool. Who knows? Anyway, here is the theory that helped me. I hope that it will help you too.

Imagine that you are driving a car, and that you are heading straight for a brick wall. If you stay in habitual or rigid thinking (the sort of thinking that says, 'this is the way I always do things') and do not change the direction in which you are headed, you will drive your car into the brick wall.

Now imagine that you are driving that same car towards

that same brick wall. Now use positive thinking to imagine that the wall is, in fact, a tunnel. It is not, of course, you simply hope or wish that it is a tunnel but it is the same old, intractable brick. You still drive your car into the wall.

You are in the same car, facing the same wall except that you use creative or constructive thinking. You see the wall as an obstacle set dead ahead and see that it is solid and immoveable. You use your thinking to change direction and drive your car around it.

Understanding that our thinking is not always helpful sounds so obvious and simple. So does changing our thinking, yet both are formidably difficult to do, perhaps because, most of the time, we never question it. We just go right ahead and do what we have always done, in the same way we have always done it. We crash into relationships, mess up jobs, ruin friendships and all because we believe that our way is the right way.

There is a saying: 'I'd rather be right than happy.'

And here is another. 'My way or no way.'

I see that wall as a symbol for an obstacle (or obstacles, there may be many) in our emotional make-up. If we go on behaving in the same way, we will crash. If we pretend that those obstacles in our character don't exist, or are something else entirely, we will still crash. But if we acknowledge them and behave in a different way, we will come to a better and safer place. Or at least we will, until we meet the next one.

I know that I have dodgy depressive genes as well as certain behavioural brick walls. Those genes are inherited from my family, as are certain of those behavioural traits, although not all. Others are down to environmental events, in other words, childhood, while still more are just the way that I am.

In order to get well, and stay well, I had to examine all of those possibilities: genes, family, childhood, and my own particular nature. I can't say that I enjoyed it. I doubt that anyone enjoys admitting their own faults and failings or the hurt that they have caused or been caused. I doubt, either, that I would have done so had I not been forced to by the absolute severity of my depression but I like the results of that ruthless self-examination. I feel calmer, easier and happier than I have ever felt, as if I have put down some tiresome burden.

Therapy helped, but it is not magic. It does not change our thoughts or behaviours. It only teaches us what they might be. It does not work unless we take from it what we have learned and put it into action. So it is not, as so many people seem to think, a piece of indulgent navel gazing. Nor is it about blaming the parents. It is, I'd say, quite the opposite. It is about understanding and accepting our parents.

There is a saying, 'it's never too late to have a happy childhood'. I'd rephrase that. I'd say, it's never too late to stop a difficult childhood from turning us into unhappy adults. A difficult childhood may have set up a series of behaviours and responses that leads us to repeat those same patterns in our adult lives. That does not mean that we have to continue those patterns.

Blame is easy and parents are sitting ducks. We can blame them, secure in the knowledge that we have reasons for our behaviour. Or we can understand how those behaviours came to be, and change them. Our parents may have (and most did) done the best they could. They, like us, are stuck in behaviours and patterns that they themselves learned as children. They may go on behaving in those same ways and drive us mad.

So, we can blame and resent them or we can understand that they behave in the way that they do because they are the way that they are. It is not up to us to change them. It is up to us to change ourselves.

The following, in a nutshell is how we might go about doing that, in a therapeutic sense. I understand that I am not responsible for your behaviour, and you are not responsible for mine. I am, however, responsible for the way in which I choose to respond to you. You may, or may not, be responsible for the way you choose to respond to me. I can do nothing about that. The only person I can directly influence or affect is myself.

Good therapy does not leave us stuck in the past. Nor does it allow us to change it. It simply helps us to understand why we do certain things, why they are unhelpful and how we might overcome them. It will not work, though, if we do not use its lessons. The hard work, the lion's share, is down to us. I have heard people complain about therapy that, 'It's all very well learning why I behave in the way that I do. That doesn't stop me behaving in those ways. I am just more conscious of them.' Consciousness is where therapy stops and we begin. Therapy can only give us knowledge. It is up to us to use it. It is not easy. Changing a habit of behaviour takes time and endless repetition. We have to, literally, learn to think in a new way. But in order to do that, we have to analyse the old way.

So, in order to understand my depression and to find a possible way out of it, I had to understand the illness, starting with genetics. While we cannot change our biological destiny, an insight into it might help us to be careful, rather than careless, of it. I have two brothers. All three of us have, to varying degrees, suffered from depression. Major depressive disorder is thought to be heritable, although to what extent, nobody appears to know. The verdicts among scientists range from 'mildly' to 'fairly'. New research suggests that women are at greater risk than men. According to a study carried out on 42,000 twins, the heritable rate of depression is forty-two per cent in women and about twenty-nine per cent in men. The study concluded that: 'Depression is a moderately heritable disorder, suggesting that genetic factors are important, but by no means overwhelming.'

In other words, it is a predisposition as opposed to a predetermination. But if there is depression present in a family, there is also the chance that a parent may be depressed and therefore may not be able to provide the best environment in which to raise a child. So, how much of it is inherited through genes, and how much through environment as a possible result of those genes, is open to debate. As the author of yet another study on genetics and depression cautioned:

> Because parents may provide both high-risk genes and a high-risk rearing environment, disentangling psychosocial and biological factors mediating the transmission of risk across generations is a challenge.

I think that's shorthand for, 'we don't really know', which is hardly surprising as there is no single gene for depression. Like diabetes or cardiovascular disease, depression is a complex genetic disorder, meaning it involves multiple genes. So you can't go around pointing fingers saying, 'There's the culprit.'

It makes sense, too, to think that a certain cocktail of genes may set up an underlying fragility that may make us more susceptible to depression when faced with certain difficulties. Whether we will be faced by those difficulties depends, to an extent, what hardballs life throws at us and also how well we have been taught to deal with them in the first place.

This is what the World Health Organisation says, in rather more scientific language:

> Depression is a complex disorder which can manifest itself under a variety of circumstances and due to a multiplicity of factors. The biopsychosocial model is useful to understand the causation of depression where biological (genetic and biochemical), sociological (stressors) and psychological (development and life experiences) factors interact to produce a picture of depression. Research during the last fifty years indicates that there is no single factor which can explain the cause for depression.

Crucially, an episode of depressive illness seems to require a number of stressors (difficult or painful events) to become active. The gene thought to be responsible for the regulation of serotonin, the feelgood neurotransmitter, is known as 5-HTT. It commonly appears as either a short or a long form. It is the presence of the short form that seems to indicate a possibility (rather than an inevitability) of depression. Researchers at King's College London conducted a study using a control group of 847 people, who they followed over twenty years. It revealed that people who carried one copy of the short form had more depressive symptoms in response to life stresses. Those with two copies of the short form were more than twice as likely to become depressed following stressful situations as those who carry the long form.

But surely, difficult or painful events are a part of everyday life? In which case, anyone with a genetic predisposition to depression is guaranteed to fall ill at some time or other. Well, no. According to biologists, there is only an inherited liability to develop major depression in response to environmental stressors rather than it being an entirely genetically determined condition.

Then there is the nature/nurture debate. Is depression the likely result of a difficult childhood and a dysfunctional family set-up, or is it simply a vulnerability that one is born with? Perhaps both. There is growing evidence that depression has a great deal to do with family patterns, as in learned behaviour. If children are not taught good coping skills or emotional strategies, they may find it difficult, later in life, to deal with problems. And, if depression is actively precipitated by stressful events or problems, those children are perhaps more vulnerable than those who have been taught how to face problems effectively.

I was not taught well. I know how to ignore problems, but not how to face them. My default setting is stoicism, coupled with an extreme self-sufficiency and independence. Now, these are all admirable virtues. They served me brilliantly well in my career and I am grateful for them.

Had it not been for the fact that I also have depression-prone genes, which renders those stoical qualities more destructive than constructive, I might never have become depressed. But I did and, more to the point, so did my two brothers. Three out of three, or one hundred per cent, is a pretty high score for an illness with a genetic liability of, at most, forty-two per cent, and seems to suggest that my particular depression is not simply the result of a mutual biological inheritance but of other, shared influences.

And so I had to look at my family, in more forensic detail that I would normally use. Not simply because I want to know what caused (or may have caused) my depression, but because I would like to see and understand the behavioural patterns that made me vulnerable in the first place. And which, if I am to avoid (or at least, diminish) further episodes, I need to change.

On the surface, we are a happy family. We hug and we kiss. We are pleasant. We can afford to be. We never engage with one another enough to be unpleasant. We do not shout. We do not fight. We do not have rows. We are, in short, like icebergs with only the top on show. The rest is private and it is in that privacy that darkness lies. Or, my darkness, at least. To live on the surface is in its own way fine and perfectly peaceable. Peaceable, at least, until something as catastrophic as mental illness intervenes.

Our childhood was spent moving. We were brought up in six different countries, in Brunei, Brazil, Aden, Oman and Angola – and England too – following my father wherever his work took him. All three of us were sent to boarding schools, which were not the benign, liberal institutions that most are today. If we were ever made unhappy by our disrupted, peripatetic childhood, we did not say so. Not to each other and rarely to our parents although I was the most vocal of us three. But I am the most volatile too although that volatility, when I look at what goes on in other families, seems a very tepid thing. We do not, as a family, ever say how we really feel. We just get on with things and if ever we did express distress, there was always our mother to say, 'Don't upset yourself.'

I am, these days, amused by that phrase; it is so beautifully English. It tells us two things. It says that the initial upset is not important enough to be taken seriously and that it is anyway, you who is upsetting yourself. It's a lose-lose situation so better to put up and shut up. It was not intended unkindly. It just shows, I think, how the details of family lore can, quite innocently, weave their way into an impenetrable emotional deadlock.

I saw this clearly, perhaps for the first time, when I was driving my younger brother, Tony, to the airport. At the time, I was still struggling with my depression and deep in therapy, so I was perhaps more conscious than usual of odd behaviour. I was also very conscious of the depression that seems to haunt our family or, at least, us children. When he was young, between the ages of about fifteen to twenty-five, my older brother, Michael, suffered badly from depression. He got no help. We do not, like most families, have any dealings with psychiatrists or therapists and this was thirty years ago, long before such things were commonplace or acceptable.

At the time I drove Tony to the airport, he was also depressed. He had lost a startling amount of weight, was deathly pale and had great black rings circling his eyes. The medication he was taking did not appear to be working. Tony's self-prescribed remedy for depression was to go off around the world, alone. He left his wife and three children behind and arranged a three-month sabbatical from his City job. The company for which he works is very formal so is not in the habit of handing out leave to senior employees but when he explained he had severe depression, they were sympathetic.

As we drove I said, 'Have Mum and Dad asked you why you are going away?'

Tony shrugged. 'No.'

'Have they asked you why you look so dreadful?'

He smiled faintly. 'Thanks and no, they haven't.'

'They've said nothing to you at all?'

'No.'

'So you've told your boss that you're depressed, but not Mum and Dad?'

'That's right.'

'Have they asked you how you are emotionally?'

He grinned, a familiar cheeky smile that held echoes of our childhood. 'Of course not.'

My parents are not uncaring. They love their children very much. It is just they do not express emotion well because it was never expressed to them. We do not knit our behaviour into patterns on our own. We learn them from our parents. And they learn them from their parents before them. We are all following a pattern that was laid down years before we were even born.

Those childhood patterns are hard to break. I still, after years of therapy, dislike saying how I really feel. The effort of it chokes me, literally, with a constriction at my throat. And there, obviously, are the origins of the throat monster. I don't need to be an amateur psychologist to know that. I've had plenty of experts to tell me. I swallow down my feelings and choke on my true instincts. I have no idea, in the classic therapeutic phrase, 'how to get my needs met'.

Why? Because, as one therapist told me, I have been beautifully trained to have no needs or, when I had them, to deny them. I needed, as a child, to feel safe, to be secure, to form lasting attachments and not only to people but also to places and things. Living between six countries over a period of eighteen years, leaving schools, houses, friends and cultures was not the best way to feel secure.

As human beings we all have to learn to adapt, it is part of our condition. As children we have to learn to adapt in order to survive because we are so wholly dependent on adults. So I adapted. Impermanence was so much a part of my childhood that to my childish mind, I became the only fixed point in my landscape. I was powerless to change the way things were and it seemed to me that my parents were powerless too. No point making a fuss, no point wishing life was otherwise.

I remember, when I was nine and we left Aden for the last time, the sight of Bimbo, our dog, snuffling happily in the garbage heaps piled on the sandy pavements outside our house.

He was the only dog we had ever owned, or would ever own. We moved too much to have pets. It was not fair to leave them behind, on us or on them. Bimbo was being sent to live with another family. I knew that I would never see him again. I knew, too, that Aden was becoming a dangerous place. There had been a bomb at the airport some weeks before. A friend of mine, a child, had been hospitalised after a piece of shrapnel was blown into her stomach. As far as my nine-year-old self was concerned, we were abandoning our dog to danger. I lay in my bunk on the boat back to England and cried. But I knew that there was nothing to be done and nothing would come of crying about it, just as I had discovered that nothing could be done about leaving my friends in Aden, my school, my house and all the other familiar things that bring comfort.

And so, as I understand it, I adjusted to constant loss as well as the inability to articulate any distress on, as one therapist described it, an 'adapted' level. The term, 'adapted child' was originally used by Eric Berne, the father of Transactional Analysis in the 1950s. Essentially it means the compliant, orderly side of us that hides anger, pleases others and generally acts the good girl or boy. The more that behaviour is rewarded (and the more that any other behaviour is punished or, more usually, ignored) the more we adapt ourselves to keeping quiet and not making a fuss. Put in another way, we adopt the position known in therapeutic terms as 'abandonment or withdrawal'.

It is not, either, only the still, pale, silent child who has withdrawn. Withdrawal takes place at a far deeper level and may be disguised by a bright, lively and social exterior – the sort of exterior that indicates compliance because compliance brings its own rewards.

Alice Miller, psychoanalyst and author of *The Drama of Being a Child*, describes the ways in which children recognise their parents' needs at a very young age and then repress their own, often very intense, feelings and needs, because he or she believes they are unacceptable to the parents. Miller writes,

> Depression is the price the adult pays for this early self-abandonment. These are people who have always asked themselves what others need from them, thus not only neglecting their own feelings and needs, but never even making contact with them.

I remember, clearly, the first obvious sign of my brother Michael's depression. We were living in Oman, a slice of land just above Saudi Arabia, and had planned to go on a fishing trip with another family. When we were about to leave, everybody gathered together except Michael, who had disappeared. We searched the house, which was quickly done, and the area immediately outside the house. We lived in the desert, but a desert made of steep ravines and gorges. The temperatures there were unbearable, sometimes reaching 130 degrees Fahrenheit in the shade. After a brief search, we asked our houseboy, Mohammed, to go out and look. Mohammed knew the terrain intimately and could run up and down the ravines barefoot, dodging the scorpions and snakes that lived there. It was not a place for a fourteen-year-old schoolboy, fresh off the plane from England, to be wandering. Mohammed came back empty-handed.

We sat and waited. The silence seemed endless.

Two hours later, Michael appeared. He looked startled to find us in the house. He obviously thought that we would all have gone on the boat trip, as planned. He said simply, 'I didn't want to go on the boat, so I went for a walk.'

My mother, who was understandably frightened and angry, asked him furiously why he had not said anything or told anyone.

Michael simply shrugged. 'I thought that nobody would notice.'

Nobody would notice. That remark has haunted me for years.

'Stop abandoning yourself,' a therapist, Elizabeth, once said to me.

'What?' I didn't understand.

She explained it like this.

Every time you feel sad and swallow down your tears, you abandon yourself.

If somebody hurts you and you pretend that you are fine, you abandon yourself.

Every time you don't eat, or fail to feed yourself, you abandon yourself.

If you are tired, but refuse to rest, you abandon yourself.

If you drink too much and poison yourself with alcohol, you abandon yourself.

If you don't ask for what you need from somebody with whom you are intimate, you abandon yourself.

The times when you resent putting somebody else's needs before your own are the times when you are abandoning yourself.

If you don't ask for help when you need it, you abandon yourself.

'You suffer,' Elizabeth said, 'from a failure of care.'

From who?

'From yourself,' she says. 'And before that, from your parents. They are the ones who should have taught you how to take care of yourself.'

A failure of care. It sounds so harsh. And at the same time so childlike. Both things are true. An inability to take care of oneself or soothe oneself is a sign of immaturity. It is a failure of understanding, or of teaching. If you are not taught as a child how to take care of yourself, you do not know as an adult. The pattern becomes ingrained. You are now an adult inhabited by a child. The child pleads, the adult overrules. You deny yourself proper care.

There are, of course, many theories about the effects of childhood on later, adult depression but this particular idea rings true about my own. If nothing was constant, it was better not to become attached and better not to need. If you are bullied as a child, as I was, often, at the various schools I attended, it is better to make yourself smaller or disappear entirely. Either that or pretend that you are impervious.

None of this, of course, occurred to me at the time. It did not even occur to me in my twenties and thirties when my mantra was: 'It is better to be alone.' I learned very early that anything I loved – people, dogs, schools, houses – was taken away from me. So I decided, although not consciously, never to become too attached to anything.

To put that in therapeutic language, this state of detachment is best described as becoming 'wantless and needless'. If you adopt the position of not wanting or needing anything emotionally, you are unlikely to get hurt. To sustain that entirely, you withdraw emotionally and even physically from others, although you may show a perfectly sociable exterior when you are out in the world. It is the interior that is fiercely defended. Some people (as I did) adopt this as a solution to emotional pain, forgetting that we are communal animals, biologically and genetically determined to interact with others. The solution then becomes the problem. We not only need emotional comfort, we are programmed to seek it out, which is perhaps why I married twice. It is also, perhaps, why both marriages failed – a sort of self-fulfilling prophecy. Like the adapted child, we become the adapted adult. We engage on the exterior but remain withdrawn on the interior.

It was only as I got older that I began to understand that what I actually meant was, 'It is *easier* to be alone.' Exposing our frailties and vulnerabilities is frightening so it is easier not to do so. A part of me still believes that, even though depression showed me that shutting myself away is ruinous for my own emotional health. It is, I believe, ruinous for everybody's emotional health and I know I am happier when I am connected to other people. Even so, to this day, when I am low, my natural default setting is to shut down and hide even though I am, by nature, gregarious. In a low mood, I still have to force myself out of the door or to answer the phone. Leaving my flat still seems difficult, if not frightening. Yet, every time I manage to answer the phone, make a call or seek out the company of friends, I am amazed at the way that my mood can lift.

Nearly every depressive I know has a similar default setting, so similar that it is given a name, 'duvet-diving'. It means hiding in bed, not answering the phone, turning down invitations and generally ignoring the world. And it is the worst possible thing that we can do for ourselves.

Another name given to it is 'isolating', a word that you hear many depressives use. Isolating in a depressive frame of mind is quite different from choosing to spend time alone, which many of us need to do in order to re-establish our equilibrium. Isolating is a fearful, threatened state of aloneness, when even the sound of the telephone feels like a terrible demand and when we rarely use the time constructively but in a restless, ineffective way or numbly, slumped in front of the television. It is a negative, alienating sense of aloneness rather than a positive and constructive state.

Another way in which depressives (or anyone else) might hide is by keeping their true needs, instincts and demands disguised by the face that they present to the world. In psychoanalytical thinking this is called 'splitting' and is when true feelings (the true self) are hidden by a mask or the false self.

We often say one thing and feel another and, as people are liable always to take us on what we say – and have no idea what we feel unless we tell them – we are in a state of almost constant frustration, not to mention confusion. Sometimes, we expect other people to be mind readers and when they fail in their clairvoyant duties we are apt to shut down even further, taking their lack of response as further evidence that they don't care.

In this state of internal conflict and pressure, cracks inevitably begin to show, often in ways that may go unrecognised, such as eating too much or too little, drinking too much, working too hard, a string of failed relationships or mild depression. If these, too, go unresolved the pressure-cooker of conflict reaches breaking point and can lead to a physical or mental breakdown.

In order to break the treaty, we have to learn to ask for and then, just as crucially, accept help. First, though, it is important to understand ourselves, and to discover what it is that we need. Habits set up over a lifetime may be hard to break but, certainly, it is easier once you have identified them.

11

Home Is Another Country

*There is no duty we so much underrate as the duty
of being happy.*

Robert Louis Stevenson

I am standing in a room in my third psychiatric hospital. The
unit I am in is part of the Addictions Treatment Programme. I
am doing time: twenty-eight days. In other words, I am in
rehab. I am being rehabilitated, turned back into a sober,
responsible human being.

I am here because I am a drunk.

I am a drunk, I think, because I learned to use alcohol to try
to crush my pain. I never used to drink so much, nor with
such deliberate, destructive savagery, before the pain came.
Before I became depressed, I had a pretty normal relationship
with alcohol. I drank to party, I drank to celebrate, I drank
after a rough day at work, I drank when I felt shy or anxious.
So does most of the world.

I also, and perhaps this is where I am different, drank
when I felt sad or low to make myself feel better. When the
mood shifted, I went right back to drinking normally but
in the process, I learned that alcohol is the best anaesthetic
in the world. If I drank, I did not feel. I did not want to
feel. So, when I was severely depressed, I drank all the
time.

I drank in the morning and in the evening. I drank in the afternoon and in the night. Pain follows no timetables.

Which would have been bad enough, except that I did not want to drink. I just wanted to feel free from pain. And I knew, in that part of my brain that was still robustly sane, that alcohol would not free me from pain, except temporarily. I knew that alcohol was a depressive, that I was taking an antidepressive pill with one hand and a bottled depressive with the other. I also knew that I was trying to kill myself. Alcoholism is a slow, ugly form of suicide.

By the time I get to rehab, I have what my psychiatrist calls 'a dual diagnosis'. I am both depressed and alcoholic. I know that if I continue to drink, I will continue to be depressed. The chemical changes wrought in the brain by alcohol will not allow the chemical changes wrought by depression to come back into balance. It is a never-ending story.

As my shrink explained, 'You have to find your way into alcoholism which means drinking sufficient amounts to develop a dependency. Why you do that is open to interpretation. But once you have developed a dependency, you have an addiction not only to alcohol but also to a pattern of behaviour. The only way out of an addiction is to stop the substance abuse, and to learn new ways of behaviour.'

I could stop for a day, a week or a month. I could stop drinking for three months or even six. Stopping is easy. Staying stopped is overwhelmingly difficult if you are drinking to stop pain.

I know that I have to stop, for ever. I have to learn new ways of behaviour. Which is how I came to be standing in a room and participating in drama therapy. Otherwise there is nothing, other than the ugly, grinding, sickening afflictions that are alcoholism and depression, that would persuade me to stand in a room with a group of adults and pretend that we were trees.

Nothing.

'Sally,' says the drama therapist, 'this week, it is your turn to play the central character in the group.'

The therapist is a loud-voiced woman, wearing layers of clothing tangled up with beads, in every sort of colour and pattern. I suppose she thinks she looks theatrical. I do not like her, but whether it is the fussy style, the person she is (bossy, abrasive, condescendingly kind) or the work she does that I do not like, I cannot say. Or perhaps it's just the mood I'm in, which is not good.

'Do I have to?' I am sullen.

'Yes. You've been avoiding it for three weeks. This is your final week. You have to.'

Fuck.

'OK,' I say.

'I want you to be the person you were when you were last truly happy.'

'Truly?' I say. 'Not just a bit, or quite, or slightly or very? Not wildly, or deeply, or hysterically happy? Just truly, truly?'

She sighs. 'Stop using words,' she says. 'Don't question. Just be. Be that person.'

And so I am. I am eight years old and I am living in Aden. The group plays different characters: my mother, my father, my two brothers, my friends. And then they make me leave the place where I was truly happy.

And I cry and I cry.

Afterwards, the therapist stops me. 'That was good,' she says, 'very productive.'

'Sure,' I say. 'It was good.'

I say it was good, but I don't think it. I think it was hateful and arch and hideously self-conscious. I'd much rather talk a blue streak about emotional pain than be forced, physically, to inhabit it, let alone act it out.

There have been times in group therapy when I have thought, if one more person talks about my inner child or theirs, I swear I'll punch them. Or I'll chuck my toys right out of the pram.

But I cannot deny, much as I would like to (and in that session of drama therapy I would have really, really liked to), that being forced to re-experience old, locked-away pain helps to release it. Not immediately, and not without effort, but little by little it recedes.

Nor did the irony of my behaviour in agreeing with something I did not feel escape me. I saw it as a well-worn paradigm of my emotional patterns. I say one thing, and I feel another. I set myself up for perpetual conflict and where there is conflict, there is pain.

They say that in order to change our behaviour, we first have to understand our behaviour. And so I have to ask myself, how did I get to be like this?

I am in Aden, when I was a child and I was happy.

I trail up the road to school, my feet sliding in the loose sand. The sun is fearsome though it is only six thirty in the morning. School is a short walk from our house, along a potholed road banked by sand.

The tarmac melts in the heat, so it is never smooth. In front of the school is a bigger road. I have to be careful here because big lorries thunder up and down it on their way to and from the army base.

I saw a dead boy on this road. He was six years old and my younger brother's best friend. A big wheel from an army lorry went over his chest and dirtied his clean white aertex shirt. I watched his mother come up the road, her arms flailing so wildly she looked as if she was drowning. She was screaming and screaming, her mouth a big, black ugly circle.

Otherwise there is no traffic to speak of, just the occasional dusty car.

My parents' car is a white Ford, with sides like fish fins and red fake leather seats. My brothers and me slide around on the bench seat in the back while Mum drives. She wears cotton shift dresses in bright colours and her silver-grey hair is fixed in a bun on top of her head.

She is not old. She is beautiful. Her hair turned grey when she was very young. I think it makes her look special even though she doesn't really like it. Mum's blue eyes are hidden away behind rhinestone-studded glasses. I love those glasses. They're pearly grey, like the inside of the oyster shells that Dad and I chip off the rocks. I like to eat oysters, standing in the sea. Dad loves oysters too. We are the oyster eaters. The others don't bother.

Dad says Aden is one of the hottest places on earth, which is why our house is built on stone pillars, lifted high up to catch the breezes that sometimes come. My parents' bedroom is the only one in the house with air conditioning. I sneak in there sometimes and put my hands against the metal ridges, feeling the cold air freeze my fingers. I don't think Aden is very hot. It seems just right to me.

I am eight. My dog, Bimbo, is half-corgi and half-sausage dog. The corgi bit of him makes the sausage part quite stout. We also have a giant tortoise, although he's not exactly ours. He lives in the garden beneath our house. Mum says he's always been there, even before us. We sit on him sometimes and try to ride him like cowboys but he is so slow that we give up quite quickly.

He once escaped the garden and went and parked himself in a garage behind a big Land Rover, which reversed over him. When we got him back, he was bleeding on the top part of his shell. It got better in the end but the bleeding part came back a lighter colour than the rest, so we always know who he is.

Our house is surrounded by high walls and palm trees. I am constantly in trouble for climbing the walls. I like to sit on top of them and watch people go by. Mum says I'm too much of a tomboy in my baggy cotton shorts, with my bare, skinny brown chest and feet. Once, I sat up there and watched a sandstorm come in, the sky turning rusty brown as the horizon filled with sand, the wind picking it up off the ground as it moved across the desert.

When it came closer, it looked like great big orange clouds were boiling up the sky and we had to go into the house and batten down the windows and doors. For ages, it rained sand but it didn't fall straight, like rain. It whipped around the house, chased by a shrieking wind. You couldn't go out and see it. The sand rubbed all your skin right off, like sandpaper, or it got in your eyes so you went blind.

Afterwards the veranda was covered with sand, pushed in drifts up against the walls. The garden looked like a beach. Mum said it was a bore, it took so much cleaning up, but my brothers and I loved it.

My younger brother, Tony, is walking up the road behind me, kicking his feet. He is six and does not want to go to school this morning. He wants to play on his bike. We have a bike-riding place in the area under the pillars in the house. The ground is made of shiny stone so it hurts if you fall off.

It took me ages to learn to ride my bike and take off the balancers. Dad kept saying it was easy, but it wasn't. Then, one day, just like magic, I took my feet off the ground and I was swooshing around the pillars and belting out into the garden. One day, my brothers strung a piece of rope between the pillars. When I rode past, they pulled it tight. It got me across the neck so I fell off my bike and hurt myself. The rope hurt my neck too. It had a thick pink graze across it.

Tony trails along behind me, his white-blond head bent as he searches for interesting things in the sand. He is cross because I said he had to go to school. Dad has already gone to the office; he leaves at six when Mum is still in her bedroom. We are not allowed to wake her in the morning, it is too early, she says. The servants give us breakfast, which we eat outside on the veranda, where it is coolest.

My older brother Mike, who is ten, is at school in England. I try to imagine him there, but I can't. He says it is cold all the time, even in the summer. I've seen the swimming pool at his school. It's surrounded by dark green bushes and big trees and there are always leaves in the water which is dark green and slimy. When we went to visit him, I put my hand in the swimming pool. It is really cold but they have to swim in it in the summer, even if it is raining.

It hardly ever rains in Aden.

I was five when Mike left, and he was seven. We stood on the balcony at the airport. The airport has a bright, sharp smell. Dad says it's the fuel from the aeroplanes. I love that smell. We watched as Mike climbed the rickety metal steps to the aeroplane. It had big propellers, which made him look really small. In the sun, his hair was shiny white and his skinny brown legs looked funny in his new, grey shorts. They are wool so they must be really scratchy. And he has to wear a jacket too, poor thing, except that he says it's called a blazer.

He did not turn around to wave, or perhaps he did and I did not see him. After he left, I sometimes used to go and sit in his bedroom. It feels lonely and sad without him. I share a room with Tony. He has the bed on the left and I have the one on the right. We keep Michael's room empty for him, for when he comes home on school holidays.

He's not the same, though. Not like he was when he lived with us. He's really quiet and pale from having no sun. Sometimes he gets cross with Tony and me for no reason. He tells us we're behaving like children. When I say, 'that's because we are,' he thumps me. He never talks about boarding school or England, even if you ask. He says we wouldn't understand.

I walk through the school gates. They're not really gates, just a gap in the wall to divide the sand outside from the gardens inside, which are cool and planted with tall palms and banana trees with huge fringed leaves and bright purple bougainvillaea. I sometimes sit there and read before school starts. Reading is the thing I like to do best in the whole world.

The school building is long and low, arranged in a big three-sided square around a smaller square of sandy earth, which is the playground, and the place where we have morning assembly. The classrooms are along each side with verandas in front of them, to shade us from the sun.

At the end is a sort of stage, where the headmaster stands for assembly. We gather in the dusty playground and sing hymns in the burning morning sun, the punched holes in our sandals slowly filling with gritty sand. Sometimes, we put on plays. I was an angel once. I wore a white robe that Mum made from a sheet and a halo made from a wire coat hanger. It dug into my shoulders.

Our desks are arranged in another square inside the classroom with our teacher, Mrs Gould, sitting at the front. Her desk is the only one in her bit of the square so she doesn't have to turn her head to see us. She never misses a thing so we are very good and quiet. Only the ceiling fans make a noise, like a rickety swoosh. I love the sound of ceiling fans. They make such a slow comforting noise. I like the way they are always there, that they never change.

I like Mrs Gould too even though she is very old and fat and wears her grey-brown hair in a bun. She wears glasses too but they're not like Mum's. They're really serious. She looks very fierce and strict but that's just the way she looks, not the way she is. She just pretends to be strict. Mum says she dotes on me. I am her pet because I'm clever and always come top of the class. I don't like to come second. I don't know why, I just don't. Mrs Gould wrote in my report, 'Sally must learn to suffer fools more gladly.'

Mum thinks that's really funny so I suppose it must be good.

We start school at six thirty and finish at twelve thirty, when we go home. It is too hot to go to school in the afternoon. That's why we start so early, so we can learn in the cool of the morning. Dad comes home at one, when we eat lunch. It is too hot for him to work too. He says if we lived in England, he would have to work all day. I can't imagine why but he says it's because it's dark in the mornings so you have to start work much later and then it takes all day to catch up. He says it's the same at English schools.

In the afternoon we usually go to the beach, to the club, which is called Goldmuir. You have to be a member because it's a special place, with guards, at the end of a long sandy beach. There are shark nets all the way around, except on the side where there are rocks. In the middle of the sea, there's a concrete platform with a diving board that you reach by climbing up a tall rusty ladder. My brothers and I like to run as fast as we can along the board and throw ourselves into the sea. The one who makes the biggest splash wins.

Dad says the shark nets are tethered all the way down to the sand on the bottom of the sea, to stop the sharks coming in and eating us. There are big red plastic balls called floats to keep the nets up. We are not allowed to play on the floats or swim too close to the nets, otherwise the sharks might get us. A shark did once eat a woman's leg but that's because she was foolish enough to go in the sea outside the club, where there are no shark nets. She wasn't even swimming, just standing in the water, but the shark got her anyway.

Dad is teaching me how to do front crawl even though I can swim like a fish underwater, but Dad says it's good to do proper strokes, on the top of the water. He says I could swim before I could walk, he says I am a water baby.

When we're tired we go and sit in the shade and drink Coca-Cola out of glass bottles. There is a bit of cork inside the cap. If you're very lucky, you find a picture of Donald Duck or Mickey Mouse hiding under the cork. My brothers and I fight over them. We eat crisps too, which they fry for us in the kitchen and serve in twists of greaseproof paper. You have to be careful when you eat them because the seagulls swoop down and snatch them out of your hands.

I like Aden. It is the third country we have lived in after Brunei, where I was born, and Brazil, where I first went to school. And we went to England too, in between, but we didn't really live there, we were on holiday from Dad's work. I think I like Aden best although I don't really remember the others very well.

I remember Brazil a bit and I quite liked my school there, the British School of Rio, except the time a boy grabbed my hand and hurt me. I had a boil on my finger; I always seemed to have boils everywhere, so I told him to be careful. We were standing in a circle, holding hands so we could sing the school song and when the teacher wasn't looking, he squeezed my hand really tight. He wouldn't let go, just kept squeezing and squeezing even when I started to cry because the boil hurt so much. I hit him with my other hand and then I ran away, into a classroom where all the desks and chairs were piled up. I got under them and crawled right into the far corner so nobody could find me.

The teachers kept calling and coming in and out of the room and then one got down on the floor and saw me, but I wouldn't come out. She couldn't fit under the desks because they're made for children so I stayed there and wouldn't move. Mum came and got me although she couldn't fit under the desks either. She had to talk to me for ages and I only came out when she said that nobody would hurt me again and that I wouldn't get told off for running away from assembly.

That was my second school in Rio, and was a grown-up school so the teacher spoke in English. At the first school, which was a nursery school, they didn't speak any language I could understand although Mum says they were talking Portuguese, which is the language they speak in Brazil. The only other language they spoke was German. I was four, I think.

All we did at nursery was blow bubbles into huge canisters filled with water, and play musical chairs. I don't know what the canisters were for because nobody could explain them to me in words that I could understand. I just know that we always seemed to be blowing bubbles.

One day, Mum didn't come to get me. I had to sit on a bench in the boiling sun and wait. We couldn't sit in the shade, because they had already locked the school with a big key. A teacher sat with me but she didn't speak in my language and I didn't speak in hers. I wanted to ask if

Mum would come but she looked like she was really cross with me, so I didn't say anything. I wanted to pee too, and I wanted to cry but the teacher was so cross I thought if I said anything she might shout at me. So I didn't do anything. I just waited.

I thought, probably, that Mum wouldn't come. I thought she had lost me and I would never get found because we were in another strange country where nobody knew my name or the language I spoke. I was so frightened I wanted to scream and cry and lie on the ground but I had to be good because I was too small to be anything else. When Mum arrived, she was crying. She said the car broke down so she got on a bus but it went the wrong way and she didn't speak the language so she couldn't ask where she was. It took her ages to realise that she was lost and then she had to find a taxi and explain to him where the school was. The teacher was nicer when Mum arrived.

Later, it wouldn't have mattered because I learned to speak Portuguese. After a few months, Mum says, I was fluent enough to chatter away like a monkey but I have forgotten it all now.

Anyway, now we have to learn Arabic at school. I can count to twenty and say hello and Allah be with you and a few other things. I don't know why we have to learn it; we never seem to speak it, even to the shopkeepers.

Sometimes we go 'Home' to England. Or, at least that's what Mum and Dad call it. 'We're going Home,' they say, sounding excited. I don't understand why they call it that. Home is here; England is just a place we visit.

I hate England. It is grey and cold and the houses are very small and stuck to one another with no space in between. We go on leave, which is the word for Dad's holiday from work. It's then that we can see our relatives who are my grand-parents and my aunts and uncles and cousins.

I like to see my grandparents but I hate having to go to school in England. It's dark and cold and the buildings are grey and damp and the other children hate me. Or that's the way they act. They make a big space around my desk and pretend they can't understand anything I say. And they say I'm a funny colour because I'm so brown. Mum says it's not for very long, just for a few weeks, but I don't see why we have to go at all. She says it's so our education doesn't suffer which is stupid because we don't learn anything. They read all the wrong books.

It's nice to have telly though. We don't have that in Aden. Once I saw my grandfather being killed on telly. We were in the street, watching it in a shop window, our hands and noses pressed right against the glass because we'd never really seen telly before and it was always exciting when there was one turned on. And in the shop, there were hundreds of tellies lined up in a big row, not just the one. My grandfather was on all of them at once, being stabbed with a big knife. Dad says it wasn't real, that he was only acting because that's his job, but we set up such a caterwauling that he had to take us to my grandfather's flat, to prove it.

We've only just met him, although Mum says we met him before but I was too little to remember. He is very handsome and has blue eyes that twinkle. After he said hello, he put me on his shiny brown leather shoes and danced around the room with me standing on his feet and he sang, 'Tiptoe Through The Tulips', which is his favourite song. He gave us sweets too, Smarties and Rowntree's Fruit Pastilles. The sweets in England are better than in Aden. In Aden the chocolate is hard and covered in white marks because it's frozen and unfrozen then frozen and unfrozen again.

I don't care if the chocolate is hard in Aden. I'd never eat chocolate again in my life if it meant I didn't have to go to an English school. Nobody likes Tony and me. They say we're weird because of the way we speak and the things we talk about. I told one girl about the shark nets and she told everyone that we lived in a zoo and that our parents must be monkeys. They call us names, too, like dirty Arab and push us hard in the playground, when the teacher isn't looking, so we fall over and graze our legs. They say I'm a show-off because I know things and can do joined-up writing. So I've stopped. I write like them now, making a big mess in my book with lots of capital letters and blotches. Mrs Gould would be very cross.

They say I'm stupid too, which is very confusing. 'Stupid, stupid,' they chant in the playground. It's not my fault I don't know what they're talking about. They go on about people I've never heard of, who are on the telly, which I've never seen, or they talk about books I've never read. The books are English books and they're different from the ones we get at home. So how could I have read them? You're only stupid if you don't know something when you're supposed to have learned it.

I don't like being called names or being punched so at break I go and hide in the lavatories, which are all the way outside in a separate building. I don't know why. They're smelly and freezing cold. The walls are all slimy with damp and the floors are made of concrete, which gets slippery. But if I sit with my feet pulled up on the wooden seat, they can't see me if they look under the gap in the door. And if they can't see me, they won't hit me. I feel sick sitting there but that's because the teacher makes us drink warm, sour milk, which comes in little bottles with a straw. For our health, the teacher says.

We don't have milk in Aden except the sort that comes in cardboard boxes marked LONG LIFE in big red letters. When I was little, I used to think that if we drank Long Life milk then we would live for ever, but Dad said it wasn't the case. Which was a good thing because it tasted disgusting. Anyway, I think my health is perfectly all right. I hate milk.

I am always really happy when we go home.

12

Emotional Memory

Only by acceptance of the past will you alter its meaning.

T. S. Eliot

In my mind, it was an idyllic childhood; at least until I was nine and we went to England where I was to half-live for the rest of my childhood. I say half-live because to me England *was* boarding school, a place we rarely left, so England as a country was quite unfamiliar to me. So unfamiliar, that I still get its geography confused. I never felt that those years at boarding school in England were in any sense a life. They were simply periods of time that had to be endured. Nor was there ever again during my childhood a place that I called home, at least in any profound sense of belonging; the place where my parents lived was just somewhere that we returned to from time to time. After Aden, I never quite felt that I belonged anywhere. I still miss it, although I know it is the memory that I miss, rather than the place.

I didn't go to boarding school straight away. Dad had been posted to Oman, but there were no facilities for families in the desert so my mother stayed in England while Shell, the company my dad worked for, built some houses. It took two years so I stayed to keep her company while Tony went off to join Michael at his school. I was sent to the local primary.

I hated it. I hated the school, I hated England, I hated my dad being away and I hated being without my brother Tony to whom I had been very close. We had shared a bedroom and a life for nine years and, suddenly, he was gone. Michael was long gone, having left home when I was five. That was the last time the three of us ever lived together, except on holidays from school and I don't, for some reason, count them. They were interludes, magic fragments of happiness in a bleak school year, rather than anything resembling a life.

Mum was not happy either. She was always tired and often miserable, trying to cope with buying a house and setting up home in England. In my father's absence, she had to deal with all of the financial practicalities, something for which she had never really been prepared and which, even to my child's eyes, she obviously found exhausting and difficult.

I suppose she must have been lonely too with her husband away and both her boys at school. Like me, she had few friends in England. Like me, she had left all her friends behind, in Aden. But she, at least, was used to England. I was not. The sudden shock of my life changing beyond comprehension made me feel that my happy childhood had suddenly and abruptly ended. The sun, in every sense, disappeared behind a bank of grey cloud.

The local primary was miserable, housed in a squat and sullen redbrick building and backed by a vast expanse of freezing, windswept fields. Or, at least, it seemed to me that they were freezing but to a colonial child, raised in the Far East, South America and Arabia, everything seems cold. Even an English summer is cold.

As usual, I spent the first few months hiding in the girls' lavatories, a low-slung outhouse reeking of damp and Jeyes disinfectant. I seemed always to be shivering in those cubicles, knees pulled to my chest.

Children hate difference. And my difference was obvious as soon as I opened my mouth. I had none of the right cultural references. I had never lived in England and still thought of

Aden as home. Whenever I mentioned home, I talked about Aden. At least, I did, until I learned to keep my mouth shut. I'd missed nine years of television, so I had almost nothing to say, no means of joining in a playground conversation. I could swim like a fish, count in fluent Arabic and read a book in two hours. Other than that I had almost no social skills. I was plainly weird.

Nor was I planning to hang around the area, so there wasn't much future in being my friend. No other child was going to boarding school, let alone a school a hundred miles away. And my new home, as soon as I was allowed to make my escape, would be in Oman, Arabia.

Some of the kids were perfectly nice but they are not, of course, the ones who I remember. It is the gang of girls I recall, the ones who waited for me on the way home and dragged me off my bike, hitting and punching me or pulling my hair.

I said nothing to anyone until my mother was brushing my hair and it came out in handfuls. 'What's this?' she said.

I said that it was just a little fight. I never told her about the rest, kept the worst of it from her in that curious, protective way that children do. And I felt, too, a deep sense of that shame that bullied children (or adults) always feel. I also knew that Mum was powerless to do anything about the situation other than tell the teacher, which, I knew, would make everything worse. The discipline at the school was almost non-existent; we were often left to our own devices.

It did not seem to occur to my mother that I might be having a difficult time. She offered me no advice or sympathy and, taking my tune from her, I expected none myself. It was just another thing to get through. I knew, too, that in the midst of such anarchy, it would have been lunacy to draw any attention to myself. I had quite enough of the wrong sort already.

The bullying stopped eventually but I made no friends. I have no idea what I did with myself, or how I occupied my time. It is all a blank. I don't remember a face, let alone a name, from the two years I spent in that place. This, I think, was the beginning of a sense of disconnection that has remained with me for most of my life.

As a child I was absurdly jealous of other children who lived their whole lives in the same house, surrounded by the same friends and going to the same school. I say, absurdly, because they thought I was absurd to want such a thing. They thought that sort of life very dull. To me, it sounded like paradise. I could find nobody who understood how I felt, until I met Sarah, when I was sixteen. It is perhaps no surprise that my closest friend, who is the daughter of a diplomat, had a childhood similar to my own.

Sarah's word for that sense of disconnection is 'homesickness'. It is a good description, a vast broad-ranging word that loops endlessly across provenance and identity, settling nowhere. She suffers from it too. Sometimes, if she is low and I ask her what it is that's bothering her, she will simply say, 'Oh, just homesickness' and I'll know immediately how she feels, an unsettling unease and unrest and an inarticulate yearning for who knows what? Home, I suppose.

A part of my depression lies, I think, in my unanswered question: Where is home? I feel a sense, always, of trying to find my way back to a place that doesn't exist. The cliché that is invariably offered up is always, 'Home is where the heart is'. The simple answer is that my heart is where my daughter is. That is where it most profoundly lives. But my daughter must, as children must, go off into the world and find her own way. And if my heart goes off with my daughter, then where does that leave me?

Our childhood experiences and the sense of belonging that they root in us are important, but they are not everything. Sarah, despite having a childhood similar to my own, does not suffer from depression. We have quite different natures. Her family is very different too, as was her schooling. And while I see in her emotional patterns a legacy of a peripatetic childhood that is as familiar as my own, they are neither destructive nor overwhelming.

In other words, a disrupted childhood does not in itself precipitate severe depression. It may contribute to it by establishing deep insecurities and feelings of disconnection, but it is not the cause. Nor, usually, is any one event, or set of events. It seems more likely (and there are many, wildly differing, theories about this) that childhood, innate character, life events and a particular fragility of chemistry all conspire.

A journey through depression and the causes of depression is in some ways like the unravelling of a mystery story. It may, at first, not even be obvious to us that our present distress has a direct lineage to the past. We may respond to a particular sort of person or characteristic incredibly badly and have no idea why that person should affect us. Or a situation that is, on the surface, entirely benign, can inspire a response that is completely at odds with the matter in hand. These are what therapists and psychiatrists call triggers; they trigger some deep pain or long forgotten memory and provoke a reaction that often bewilders us.

If we can discover the triggers, we may be able to defuse them. We can never avoid them. They are always going to be present, if only because life will always be filled with incidents that cause us pain. To avoid them altogether would be to avoid life itself, which seems to me just another form of depression.

We can, instead, confront them and put them into context. For most of us, those triggers were put in place during childhood and the feelings they invoke in us are childlike, rather than childish. To our adult selves they appear hopelessly out of proportion to the actual situation. But they are, nonetheless, real.

I may remember few details of that English primary school but one incident remains vivid in my mind. My mother had arranged to pick me up from school and was late. By the time she arrived, I was completely incoherent with grief. At first, she tried to console me, but when I would not settle, she told me that I was being ridiculous, that she was only ten minutes late because she had been stuck in traffic. She grew very angry but I could not explain why I was so upset. It did seem such a small thing to be upset about. I could not even explain it to myself. It was only later that I understood the connection back to that time in Brazil, when I was four years old, and I thought that she had gone for ever.

Even as an adult, I still get absurdly, inappropriately, upset when people are late. I feel, in every sense of the word, abandoned; a feeling that expresses itself in blind panic and the threat of imminent tears – an absurd response in an adult. While, these days, I am better able to reason with myself when somebody isn't on time and temper my response, I have not conquered it entirely. A vague distress will linger with me for days.

It is what neuroscientists call 'emotional memory'. Researchers at Duke University Center for Cognitive Neuroscience have found evidence for a self-reinforcing memory loop, in which the brain's emotional centre triggers the memory centre, which in turn further enhances activity in the memory centre. In a scientific paper published about the findings, they explained that, 'an emotional cue could trigger recall of the event, which would then loop back to a re-experiencing of the event. Or, remembering the event may trigger the emotional reaction associated with the event, which in turn could trigger more intense recall.'

It is the first study of its kind using neuroimaging in human brains and provides clear evidence that the brain's emotional centre, called the amygdala, interacts with memory-related brain regions during the formation of emotional memories. They are hoping that their insights can contribute to an understanding of the role that the neural mechanisms underlying emotional memory formation play in post-traumatic stress disorder and depression.

So, perhaps I have a faulty trigger in my memory system. One like this: Every time I go to an airport, I feel an overwhelming urge to cry and feel a terrible, black sense of despair. It makes no sense. I am an adult. I love adventures and exploring new places and different cultures. I love foreignness and strangeness, which make me feel immediately at home, perhaps for obvious reasons. I love the smell of camel dung and urine, the dusty heat and noise of African villages, the car horns and chaos of Indian cities.

I even love flying, enjoy the ritual of airports, the sharply acrid smell of aeroplane fuel, the shimmer of runway lights, the no-man's land of transit lounges. In my earlier career, first as a fashion writer on *Vogue* and the *Observer* and then as the editor of *Elle*, I was forever jumping on and off planes to Milan, Paris and New York and other far-flung destinations. It was work that I loved; these were trips I loved to take. Yet, even when I am going to a place that I long to see, I always feel a dreadful sense of despair. My throat closes until I can hardly speak or breathe and I feel perpetually close to tears.

It was only when I tracked it back that I understood it has to do with an old, but, for me, terrible, reality. It means the end of the school holidays, leaving the light and warmth of Africa or Arabia and my parents' house and flying back to England, and that cold, dark and unlovely boarding school I hated so much.

And while I still feel tearful at an airport, I have lost that awful sense of dread. I am able to reason with myself until the feeling goes. It's harder than it sounds. I have to literally remind myself that I am no longer a child, perpetually being moved from country to country, school to school, house to house; a situation over which I had no power and in which I had no choice.

But when I feel that feeling again it is, I now know, a feeling pretty much like depression.

13

What We Resist Persists

Sometimes I lie awake at night and think, 'Where have I gone wrong?' Then a voice says to me, 'This is going to take more than one night.'

Charles M. Schulz

Two years after we returned to England, my mother went out to Oman to join my father and I was sent to an English boarding school where 750 girls were treated much as I imagine a farmer might treat battery hens, fed and housed with cold, humourless efficiency and with only one end product in mind: our education.

Just like those battery hens, we were weighed as soon as the new term started and four weeks before it ended. This was presumably because it was the beginning of awareness of anorexia but the treatment for weight loss was punishing in itself.

One term I did lose far too much weight. I was a teenager, growing fast and the food was so vile as to be inedible. I was also desperately unhappy. When they weighed me towards the end of the term, I was far too thin. I couldn't possibly be sent home in that state. What would my parents say? So, for a week, I was forced to take all my meals in the sanatorium where they could watch me. If you refused to eat, they simply held your nose, shovelled the food into your mouth and held it shut so you were forced to swallow. I soon learned to eat.

The sanatorium, anyway, was not a place to linger. It was certainly not a place in which to be ill or seek comfort. It was staffed by a matron who took any illness as a personal affront and dealt with it as briskly and sharply as possible. She did not, either, believe that a girl was sick unless her thermometer told her so and I am still in the habit of believing that I cannot possibly be ill unless I have a high temperature to prove it. And the temperature of depression is, of course, low.

I was sufficiently clever to do well, at least in exam results, and sufficiently bright to cloak inward disrespect with an outward cloak of obedience so was rarely in trouble. As for the rest, I was good at sport, captain of this and that, and good, too, at making myself liked. Popularity, as I learned very early in life, is a useful defence against bullying, of which there was a great deal. The bullying left no marks; or at least not of a physical nature. Teenage girls are mistresses of the most insidious forms of emotional manipulation and torture, the worst of which is the practice known as 'Being Sent to Coventry.'

Coventry, rather like depression, is a cold, unforgiving place; lonely, silent and dead. When you are sent to Coventry, nobody speaks to you or even acknowledges you. It is as if you don't exist, as if you are dead. It can go on for hours, or days, or weeks. For me, it went on for two weeks, which, in a boarding school from which there is no escape and not even a moment's respite, is the most extraordinary torture.

To this day, I have no idea why. The girl who led the offensive would give no reason. Perhaps she simply did not like me. You can say that it does not matter, that it is long gone. But it left its marks, the most serious of which is my mistrust of human nature and its unpredictabilities.

I said nothing to anyone. There was nobody to complain to, other than the teaching staff, who dealt with bullies with heavy-handed interference. My situation, anyway, was too isolated and vulnerable. My parents were thousands of miles away, so my letters home took at least five days to arrive and then another five for an answer to appear.

In any case a member of staff checked our letters, presumably for signs of unhappiness that could then be addressed. Instead, the practice served only to make us more than ever secretive and contained. What stiff, formal little letters they must have been. As for the telephone, long-distance calls were events attached only to births and deaths. It was the days when you still had to book a call, to somewhere as foreign as Oman, three hours in advance.

I did once protest about something that was bothering me in a letter smuggled past the checking system but succeeded only in upsetting my parents so badly that I never tried it again.

I remember opening the reply from my mother, remember exactly where I was standing, on the path just outside the dining room. I remember the smell of fried bacon and burnt toast. We had just finished breakfast. Letters were always handed out after breakfast. For a child at boarding school whose parents live abroad, that is the best day of the interminable week. The letter from home day.

In the letter, my mother said that I had upset my father terribly. He had opened the letter while she was away. She wrote that I should never distress him like that again, that it was not fair.

I read the letter and then I threw it in the bushes by the side of the path. And I thought, I'm on my own.

It sounds dramatic and, to my childish mind, it was. I was thirteen but it was as if I made an absolute decision that I had to do everything alone, that I could rely only on myself. It has taken me years to unlearn that lesson. Emotional self-sufficiency might be useful in some ways but it is useless when it comes to good relationships.

My mother cannot remember the letter, or writing it. She felt accused when, in the worst of my depression and in trying to untangle some of the reasons for my misery, I asked her about it. She grew angry and tearful.

'That never happened,' she said. 'Show me the letter. If I wrote a letter like that, then show it to me.'

And that's the trouble with trying to untangle the possible reasons for pain. Emotional pain is subjective, and so is memory. Did it happen? Is it real? Did I make it up? It is real to me and perhaps that's all that matters. For many years, I did not ask for help because I expected my pleas to be rejected. This was most apparent when I was struggling with depression and the final descent into breakdown. I could not, rather than would not, ask for help. When confronted by any severe emotional difficulty, I shut up and shut down.

It was not just that one incident, of course, but an accumulation across my childhood and is simply a detail in a greater picture of a family in which difficult feelings are never discussed. I doubt we're alone in this. If my experience in a psychiatric unit, which actively encourages all and every expression of emotion, and seeing the struggle people have in saying how they really feel is anything to go by (and I think it is) then I know my family is in no way unique.

After five long years, I finally found the courage to ask my parents to take me away from that boarding school and let me go to a kinder place; which they did, to a sixth-form college where I also boarded and where I was very happy. It was also where I met Sarah, who has been one of the great gifts that life has given me.

So it was not boarding school itself that I hated so much as that particular school. Nor is being sent away to boarding school a cause of depression – many people are perfectly happy. For others, it may be a precipitating factor. However, one therapist told me that out of her clients, eighty per cent were sent away to boarding schools. All bear quite severe emotional scars.

There was an added reason for my silence. I always felt I should be grateful. My childhood in all its various countries was, in many ways, a privileged existence. We lived in large and often beautiful houses. We had servants. We travelled the world. The ex-patriot life can be astonishingly glamorous although it can, equally, be wretched. Nobody mentions the wretchedness.

And there's another reason to feel grateful. I was privileged enough to be given an expensive, private education paid for by my father's company. We could not have afforded it otherwise. And if we were sent away to boarding school, it was for practical reasons. There were no decent schools in the countries where we lived. By sending us away to school, my parents were only doing what was best for us. Besides, what were the options?

All this was drummed into me during my childhood and I understood the reasons to be grateful. It's just I never actually felt them. I just felt wretched and could not say so, or why.

Before I had a breakdown, I used to believe that misery was something to be left in the past, that there was nothing to be gained from going back over it. Which is why, from the minute I escaped that school, I swore I would never have any contact with it again. And I never have, despite the letters that periodically arrive from people I knew there, who track me down at whatever newspaper or magazine my name happens to appear in. As I have no good memories to share, I prefer not to say anything at all. The letters go in the bin; the emails go unanswered. Not out of malice nor even any memory of any of those girls I was at school with; I can scarcely remember their names or their faces. I recall that most were pleasant and friendly. I have no argument with them. It is the emotions that I associate with them that I find impossible to tolerate.

As for the school, I never mention the place, never acknowledge I even know of it, let alone spent five years there. Just one memory is apt to make me miserable so, until severe depression forced me to confront my demons, I kept my face turned resolutely to the future and believed I had succeeded in wiping most of that time from my mind. 'It happened,' I thought. 'It's over. Deal with it.'

Which would have been fine and is the way that most people deal with past unhappiness except that for me, well into my thirties, even the words boarding school were apt to send me into immediate distress. When Jonathan said, simply in passing, that one day Molly might like to go to boarding school, I dissolved in such a storm of tears that he was at first astonished, and then deeply worried.

Once I had calmed down I simply said that I hated my school and wanted no more mention of boarding schools. I didn't dwell on my tears or even think about them and I suspect that had I not become so severely depressed, I would never have gone in for any self-examination.

To be brutally honest, were it not for the insistent clamour that sometimes still rages at my throat or the dark and desperate moods that periodically drag me down I would, even after endless hours of therapy (during which I became adept at leading therapists down every dark alley except the one that troubled me the most: that school) happily leave the memories of that place well alone.

Which is, of course, entirely self-defeating. I am the one paying for therapy. I am the one for whose benefit it is performed so such contrariness is simple self-sabotage. It was not the therapists I was leading down dark alleys, but myself.

This is why therapy is so terribly difficult. Or, at least, good therapy. Good therapy is incredibly hard work. In order to truly engage with it, you first have to truly engage with yourself. But why bother? Only because, at some point in our lives, unresolved pain is likely to kneecap us and at times and in ways that we least expect.

It was the psychotherapist Carl Rogers who first used the line, 'what we resist, will persist'. You can keep difficult emotions at bay for a very long time, even for a lifetime but for most of us, at some point in our lives, they will demand to be heard. Usually, it takes some cataclysmic event – the breakdown of a relationship, the death of someone we love, a career that goes suddenly, brutally wrong – for us to feel our own pain.

We might have felt it, a little, before. It manifests itself in all sorts of ways from headaches to inexplicable back pain, to stomach ulcers or drinking too much, to getting blasted on drugs, eating too much or too little. Every addiction is a manifestation of emotional distress. Nobody becomes an alcoholic or a binge eater because they love alcohol or food, they simply use excess alcohol or food to dull the pain that they are unable to express in words.

Finally, when everything else fails to soothe us, when the drink or the food or the shopping or the sex stop making us feel better, then come the tears and overwhelming despair, anxiety or depression. Most of this, of course, is unconscious. What does seem to be true is that patterns of destructive or negative thinking stop us from recovering from depression. And staying recovered. If those behaviours or patterns of thought have their roots in childhood, or the family, then they must be worth examining and challenging.

14

The Elephant in the Room

Everybody knows how to raise children, except the people who have them.

P. J. O'Rourke

Our family depression can, I think, be traced to my mother and before her, I suspect, to her father, my grandfather. Had I not been searching for the genetic roots of my depression, as well as that of my brothers, I would never have come across a type of depression known as dysthymia, a chronic condition that can wreak havoc on a person's life and happiness.

There are the diagnostic criteria, as set out by the World Health Organisation:

A chronic depression of mood which does not currently fulfil the criteria for recurrent depressive disorder. The balance between phases of mild depression and periods of comparative normality is very variable. Sufferers usually have periods of days or weeks when they describe themselves as well, but most of the time (often for months at a time) they feel tired and depressed; everything is an effort and nothing is enjoyed. They brood and complain, sleep badly and feel inadequate, but are usually able to cope with the basic demands of everyday life.

It is an almost precise portrait of my mother. Her discontent has always been obvious in a tightly wound tension, constant insomnia and an apparently insurmountable fatigue. The demands of her life sometimes seem too much for her to bear, and I remember spending much of those two years when I was nine and we lived together in England, fetching and carrying for her, worrying about her and generally trying to cheer her up.

The effects of dysthymia are not confined to the sufferer; as with every depressive disorder, it affects all those around it. As a family, we have always tiptoed around my mother as if treading on eggshells. If she is happy, the atmosphere is good and the rest of the family is happy. If she is unhappy, we all suffer.

My mother is funny, lively, extremely clever and intensely social. When she is well it is almost impossible to recognise the creature that she can become and who, anyway, she tends to keep confined to the privacy of her own home. Few of her friends would recognise this portrait of her but the presence of those outside her immediate family seems to act on her like a tonic and she is able to throw off her mood, at least for a couple of hours. She is best, always, in company.

An article in the February 2005 issue of the *Harvard Mental Health Letter*, a newsletter issued by Harvard Medical School describes dysthymia thus:

> The Greek word dysthymia means 'bad state of mind' or 'ill humour'. As one of the two chief forms of clinical depression, it usually has fewer or less serious symptoms than major depression but lasts longer. Dysthymia is a serious disorder. It is not 'minor' depression, and it is not a condition intermediate between severe clinical depression and depression in the casual colloquial sense. In some cases it is more disabling than major depression.
>
> Like major depression, dysthymia has roots in genetic susceptibility, neurochemical imbalances, childhood and

adult stress and trauma, and social circumstances, especially isolation and the unavailability of help.

Dysthymia runs in families and probably has a heredi-tary component. The rate of depression in the families of people with dysthymia is as high as fifty per cent for the early onset form of the disorder. There are few twin or adoption studies, so it's uncertain how much of this family connection is genetic.

As the Harvard Mental Health description suggests, it is difficult to see whether my mother's depression is an inherited predisposition, the result of a lonely and disrupted childhood or of a troublesome marriage exacerbated by social isolation in the many (often difficult) countries in which my parents lived. Perhaps, as in the case of most depressive disorders, it is all of the above.

My mother was an only child whose parents worked in the theatre so were travelling for much of the time and living in digs. It was unsuitable for a small child so she was packed off to live with her aunts, who ran a nursing home for the elderly, in which she spent most of her young life. My mother, who rarely even mentions her childhood, once said, in a rare moment of candour, that she didn't have a mother until she was eleven, or at least not a mother who was in any sense present.

Of the two maiden aunts, the elder was a dominant character, the younger a weak, almost childlike figure who was often bullied by her older sister. The younger confided in my mother, herself only a child, seeking her out for comfort and a place to unload her troubles. It must have been a lonely, not to say alarming, existence for a small child, deprived of her parents and under the care of two adults, neither of whom had any experience of children and one of whom was scarcely an adult herself.

Then there were the war years, evacuation and a boarding school. Her parents adored her, but they adored each other too, often to the exclusion of anyone else. I had seen this first hand, having spent a great deal of time with them during holidays from my boarding school. While they were always welcoming, they also seemed faintly surprised to find somebody else in their midst. It must have been doubly difficult to be their child, conscious of their intense focus on each other but never quite included and often sent away for long periods of time. Perhaps this is why my mother has always demanded singular amounts of love and attention from those around her.

Then there was her married life, trailing around the world after my father, living in alien and often difficult cultures, particularly for women, her children sent away to school in another country. My mother's lively intelligence never suited the coffee mornings that dominate ex-patriots' wives days.

My mother was also, and I think this is particularly important for a woman of her independent nature and intelligence, unable to work because there was no work for women in the countries to which my father was posted. She was part of that generation of women who were expected to be entirely dependent on their husbands; their confidence so diminished that they often became frightened by the demands of the wider world and hid that fear behind a stubborn and defensive domesticity. I know I would have hated it and I am so like my mother, I cannot believe it did not do her harm.

Neither did my mother find the solace and comfort she needed in marriage. My parents have endured a troubled and sometimes frankly unhappy relationship, but are still together after fifty-two years. In that they are no different from many other couples of their generation who stayed together despite an obvious incompatibility. Age has mellowed them and they are perhaps happier than they have ever been. Whether that is an argument for staying in a difficult marriage, I really don't know.

I do know that their unhappiness had a profound impact on me and on my younger brother, Tony, who spent the early part of his adult life convinced that he would never marry or have children because he could not tolerate the possibility of the misery that would inevitably follow.

Happily, he did marry and have children. He has, in effect, broken the treaty although it has not always been easy for him. So has Michael. Then again, they were less connected to my mother who used me as her confidante and, too often, as the dumping ground for her disappointment and bitterness with my father. Perhaps she mistook me for an adult, not understanding that in the presence of our parents, we are always children. I listened, for hours, to her dislike of him and her desire, never actually carried out, to leave him. If ever I suggested that she should leave, she would either tell me that I didn't understand, or find some reason why it would be impossible.

I love my father very much, and found it increasingly difficult to listen to my mother's litany of his failings. I love my mother too, and felt sorry for and sad about her unhappiness. I was torn, and the only resolution I could see was to walk away from both of them but I could not do that either. For better, or for worse, they are my parents.

It is not, I fully believe, my mother's fault. She has never had any help with her emotions or her depression and lived through a period of history when any analysis of feelings was not considered useful. She is aware that she gets depressed, but does not know how to deal with it or, even, how severe depression can become. When I telephoned her to say that I had just been diagnosed with severe clinical depression and was to be admitted to a mental hospital, her first response was to say, 'I'm so depressed, I need the bed next to you.'

When I recounted that remark to a therapist, she shivered in protest, as she did when I said that my mother came to visit me only once, and briefly, in three psychiatric units. My father did not come at all. This might seem astonishing, and when I look at it dispassionately, I feel quite astonished myself, but I know it was not out of indifference, it was because they would have thought it better to leave me to the experts.

Some people say, 'Oh, it's just their generation,' but there were plenty of elderly people visiting their sons and daughters. I said nothing to them at the time because it seemed to me that there was nothing to say; it was merely symptomatic of the emotional distance that exists in my family as well as the stigma that creates an impenetrable barrier around those who suffer from mental illness.

My family's apparent lack of concern as well as the fear and secrecy surrounding a stay in a mental hospital made me feel inexpressibly lonely and, of course, only made my condition worse. And it was not just family. One of my closest friends, closer than a brother, failed to send even a card, let alone visit. This is a man who, when I had flu, sent fleets of cars carrying orange juice, magazines, flowers and grapes to my bedside because he could not be there himself. Yet, after I left the psychiatric unit, he was bewildered to be met by tears and anger at his absence. 'But I thought that was what I was supposed to do,' he said, himself in tears. 'I thought I was supposed to leave you alone.'

Why? In which other illness are we supposed to leave people alone? This is an aside, I know, but it may be important for anyone who does not know what to do when a friend or loved one is in a mental hospital. Go and visit them, unless they are too ill to see people or have expressly said that they don't want visitors. The nursing staff will tell you if that is the case. Send them something, whether it is love, flowers or a card. Let them know that you care, and that they matter. Don't wait to be asked. The depressive is in no state to make that sort of demand. They scarcely know their own mind.

As for my mother, her inability to express her true feelings has, over the years, caused her great unhappiness, resulting in a constant, simmering frustration and an irritation that she tends to vent on my father. It is extraordinarily painful to watch. My father, as many men before him have done, simply withdraws and becomes yet more silent. It is not in his emotional make-up to take such things personally, which, of course, manifests in indifference and only makes my mother's behaviour worse. She wants a reaction, even a negative one, and the frustrated need to get a response blinds her to her own escalating and sometimes cruel behaviour.

Similar wars of attrition are being fought, even now, in countless houses across the land. My parents are far from unusual. As a child who loves both their parents, it is heartbreaking to watch but it is the fate of many children, whatever their age, caught up in an unhappy marriage. Loyalties are torn to breaking point and children, for whatever reason – and there are many theories about this – will always feel responsibility for their parents' happiness. It is, in brutally biological terms, in their best interests. A child must depend on its parents – it has no choice – so it will deny and internalise any difficulties by withdrawing and shutting down. Either that or it will become difficult, or wayward or actively aggressive. Anything to get the attention of its parents, to distract them from the hostility, overt or otherwise, that they are waging on each other.

If a parent is too absorbed in their own problems or misery, they have little time for their child's demands. Their own needs come first. Their own emotions are paramount so their tensions and arguments are played out in full view of their children. Self-absorption is a powerful thing; it blinds us to all manner of destructive behaviour – even towards those we love the most.

The worst, and most profound impact of my parent's unhappiness with each other was on my understanding of relationships. If you are raised in an atmosphere of tense and sometimes poisonous silence, or witness a relationship in which two adults rarely touch or kiss, you are unlikely to learn how to have a good relationship yourself. Or, even, to know what a good, intimate relationship might look like. As a result, I have always felt it is better to be alone and at the same time, I long for connection. It is not a happy place to be and if depression is precipitated by stressors, then one of the greatest we can endure is the breakdown of our intimate relationships. Most research into the effect of unhappy marriages on children focuses on the impact of divorce, assuming, somewhat pre-cipitously, that all marital unhappiness ends in divorce. There are fewer studies of the effect on children of long-term, chronic and often unspoken marital misery that continues over dec-ades, but those that do exist are pretty conclusive.

A study by E. Mark Cummings, a professor of psychology at the University of Notre Dame, Indiana, examined the impact of parental conflict on children's future behaviour. It found that the manner in which parents handle everyday marital conflicts has a significant effect on how secure their children feel, and, in turn, significantly affects their future emotional adjustment. Destructive forms of marital conflict – such as personal insults, defensiveness, marital withdrawal, sadness or fear – set in motion events that later led to emotional insecurity and maladjustment in children, includ-ing depression, anxiety and behavioural problems.

According to research done by Alan Booth and Paul Amato at Penn State University, marital conflict among continuously married parents was associated with less contact and greater emotional distance between parents and their adult children, irrespective of whether the parents' marriage had ended in divorce. Although not previously studied, this finding sug-gests that even children with continuously married, rather than divorced, parents can feel caught between the two. Moreover, growing up with discordant parents is linked with elevated levels of psychological distress, even after children have left the parental home.

We can leave the last word on this to Freud. Who else?

If there are quarrels between the parents or if their mar-riage is unhappy, the ground will be prepared in their

children for the severest predisposition to a disturbance of
sexual development or to neurotic illness

My mother's irritation with and disappointment in my father
has a source, even if it is not one that we understood as we
were growing up. Although he has never been officially
diagnosed, it seems almost certain that he has Asperger's
syndrome. This condition, also known as high-functioning
autism, was not officially recognised until the early nineties,
although it was described in medical literature in 1944 by
Hans Asperger. It has become yet more public since the
publication of the best-selling novel, *The Curious Incident
of the Dog in the Night-Time* by Mark Haddon, in which the
main character, a young boy, suffers from Asperger's. Its
sufferers are predominantly male and the spectrum of the
condition ranges from very mild to severe in its manifestation.

The recentness of its discovery explains why my father,
who is now in his eighties, was oblivious to the condition. He
only became aware of it when my nephew, Michael's son,
was diagnosed and, in order to better understand the condition affecting his grandson, read a textbook on the syndrome.
He pointed out that he recognised himself on every page. And
we recognised him. Michael, himself aware that he also has
distinct characteristics of Asperger's, is convinced that my
father is affected.

It has always been apparent that there was something very
different about my dad. It was just that until recently, we did
not know what. The most pronounced characteristics of the
syndrome are social discomfort to the point of avoidance of
any situation involving unfamiliar people or places, repetitive
behaviour patterns and extreme difficulty in looking somebody in the eye. As children, we used to put my father's odd
manner down to an almost pathological shyness. Even normal
interactions, which the rest of us take for granted, are difficult.

There is also a possible link between Asperger's and
depression. According to the Autism Research Institute,

researchers believe that Asperger's syndrome is, 'probably hereditary because many families report having an "odd" relative or two. In addition, depression and bipolar disorder are often reported in those with Asperger's syndrome as well as in family members.'

The other, and most difficult characteristic of Asperger's syndrome is the distinct absence of what we call normal emotions or attitudes. Among its described behaviours are,

> Difficulty understanding others' feelings. Pedantic, formal style of speaking; often called 'little professor', verbose. Extreme difficulty reading and/or interpreting social cues. Socially and emotionally inappropriate responses. Literal interpretation of language. Difficulty comprehending implied meanings.

While I always felt valued for my ability and loved in every practical way, I never felt in any way understood by my father. And I never felt that I understood him and, to extrapolate from there I never felt that I understood men or male behaviour. This is what, according to every piece of research, little girls use their fathers for; as a sort of test case.

My brothers weren't much help either in that they both disappeared to school when I was very young. Perhaps it's no wonder that I didn't understand relationships either, or how to have them, as two failed marriages bear testimony. I am still astonished when men behave kindly towards me, in an emotional rather than a practical sense, and find it difficult to reveal any emotional fears or weaknesses, not out of any fear of ridicule but because I always feel that it will be met with either blank incomprehension or indifference. I have no such difficulties with my female friends.

That is my father's legacy to me. Or, rather, the legacy of the condition from which he suffers. I'm sure, too, that it is the legacy of every child growing up with an Asperger's parent although there has been very little documented or written about this. Modern research seems almost exclusively concerned with theories about dealing with an Asperger's child but as the research around the condition is still, in every sense, in its infancy, this is perhaps not surprising.

I love my father, very much. He is a kind man, supremely well intentioned in every respect. His nature is, in every way, good. But I would despair, sometimes, of his behaviour. And so I would watch him with a mixture of love and hopelessness, wanting him to be in charge, to take control or to show some empathy and understanding. I also, in my mother's footsteps, felt blind irritation. Why could he not behave like normal men?

This, of course, was at its worst when I was a teenager, wanting some lead or direction and wanting, more importantly, some emotional support and understanding. There is not, in my father, an inability to love. On the contrary. There is, instead, an inability to empathise. That might seem like a small distinction but in my emotional terrain, it is huge. I am aware of a constant sense of frustration, a nagging undertow of feeling perpetually misunderstood and the belief that my deeper and most important feelings will always be rejected or ignored. As my mother has a similar emotional blindness to my father, through her own undiagnosed depression, this was doubly enforced.

In a wider context, a child who feels ignored or misunderstood turns that message against themselves. It becomes, *I have no right to feel the way that I do*. And an analyst will, inevitably, take that to yet another level. A child whose deeper feelings are constantly minimised, challenged or simply ignored, ends up believing, *I have no right to be the way that I am. I reject myself*.

Depression, some thinkers believe, is a rejection of the self.

John Bowlby, psychotherapist and the originator of attachment theory, puts it this way, 'Whether a child or adult is in a state of insecurity, anxiety or distress is determined in large part by the accessibility or responsiveness of his principal attachment figure.'

This responsiveness or what, these days, we might call unconditional positive regard is the quality that children actively need in order to flourish. Certainly, it's the quality that lays the blueprint for an emotionally healthy adult. A lack of it or a skewed weakness is known as attachment disorder and all sorts of emotional conditions from depression to addiction are ascribed to its presence.

I can look at my parents' responses, today, and track their ghostly echoes back to my childhood. Their responses to me as an adult have changed very little from their responses to me as a child, which in many ways is how they still, inevitably, regard me. That's why our own parents' behaviour can trigger responses in us, as adults, that seem, in adult terms, to be wildly inappropriate. They are inculcated, hardwired, if you like, into our personal belief systems. They become the scripts according to which we lead our lives. And they are very difficult, without conscious effort, to change, which is where the hard work of therapy comes in.

My father, years after the event, remains baffled by Jonathan's and my decision to end our marriage. At the time, he was plainly disbelieving. Our continuing friendship confused him more, not less. When I said that we separated because we were very unhappy, he said, 'What does unhappiness have to do with it?'

He was not being provocative. It is, for him, a perfectly logical question. While he understands the more obvious emotions such as grief or happiness, he does not get the spaces in between, the delicate nuances of unhappiness or happiness, the body language and unspoken behaviour that make up at least eighty per cent of communication. Emotions such as unhappiness, isolation, lack of intimacy, growing apart; all these may as well be a foreign language.

Before I knew that my dad had Asperger's, I used to think that he simply didn't care. I grew used to it, eventually, by ceasing to hope that he would ever engage with me emotionally, but there is in that very hopelessness a huge well of loneliness. It was not that I thought that he did not love me because he showed me that he did, in all sorts of practical ways. It was simply that I knew that he did not know me, and furthermore did not appear to want to. He took no interest in me that was not, at its heart, purely pragmatic; knew nothing of my hopes or dreams, my fears or difficulties. Such conversations as we had were brief, emotionless exchanges; we dealt in facts not feelings.

He is apt to have an impact, to more humorous effect, on other people too. All my life, my father has behaved in quite astonishingly tactless ways, at least according to normal social conventions. If a guest at a dinner party at his house turns down a pudding on the grounds that they have put on weight recently, he will simply agree with them.

'I've got so fat,' they cry, in mock despair.

'Yes, you have,' he says, eyeing the expanse of their stomach.

He takes them at their word and is perplexed by the nuances of language and behaviour that dictate that he should disagree with them when what they say is so self-evidently true.

But, just as most social behaviour is learned, so the person with Asperger's will gradually learn to deal with the puzzling antics of human beings. This, certainly, is the case with Dad. He has mellowed and become easier as he has aged, but he has had eighty years to become familiar with our ways. I say 'our' not in a pejorative way but because it is, I suspect, like arriving on earth and only speaking Martian.

Soon after I became ill, a therapist asked me what my relationship was like with my father. I found I could not answer her. I could say, 'I love him and he loves me,' but more than that was impossible. Before I was ill, I had never sat down alone with my father and talked to him about anything of importance. And when I say, never, I don't mean it as a dramatic exaggeration. I mean, never, not once. So I called my father and asked him to come and visit me, I said that I

needed to talk to him because I did not know who he was. I
was crying.

There was a long silence. I could almost hear his mind
attempting to compute this strange and, in our family,
positively bizarre request. Eventually he said, 'I am your
father and I love you.'

Which is, as I said, what I had always known. The only
thing about him I had always known. There is also, in that
statement, all the beautiful logic and simplicity of the Asper-
gic mind.

So he came to lunch with me, by himself (in itself an
extraordinary event), as he was to do for many weeks afterwards. I was too ill to leave my flat by then so Dad made the
journey to London by train. I would watch him walking
slowly up the road to my flat, wearing his flat tweed cap and
clutching (always) a bunch of flowers. The sight of him made
me cry. He looked so near, so dear and familiar and yet I
knew from long experience just how far away he actually
was.

Over those lunches, I tried to get to know him by asking
him a series of questions.

First, I asked him how he would describe himself.

This is what he said.

'I am a man who has no imagination.'

He did not mean that he has no creative imagination,
although he hasn't. He meant that he lacks the ability to
imagine how other people might feel and without imagination, there can be no empathy. If you cannot imagine another
person's pain, you are unlikely to feel any sympathy for it.

He said, 'I don't understand what it is that people talk
about. I have never, for example, understood jokes. When
somebody tells a joke, I watch everybody really carefully.
And when they laugh, I laugh too.'

This does not mean that he does not have a sense of
humour. He does, but it is always formed around a play
on words – which is a particular characteristic of Asperger's.

Jokes, as he says, are lost on him. So are abstract concepts such as despair. I had never told my parents that during my most severe period of depression, I tried to kill myself. I wrote about it, in a newspaper, instead.

Here are the opening lines of that newspaper article, published in the *Daily Telegraph*.

Exactly one year ago today, I tried to kill myself. Fortunately (or unfortunately, as I felt at the time), I am blessed with an iron constitution. At 3.20 a.m., I woke up. Through some sick irony (who says the heavens don't have a sense of humour?), it was the same time, to the minute, that I had been waking for a year before I was finally diagnosed with clinical depression.

It went on in a similarly candid (some might say brutal) vein but, after he read the article, the only thing my father said was that he thought it was a fine piece of writing, and that he was pleased to see that I was getting work again. He did not ask me how I had felt about trying to kill myself, about the illness or even about the ways in which I was coping. He said nothing at all about the actual subject in hand.

Some people might think that odd. I simply think it is my dad. Since my illness and the time we spent together, we have become closer. He telephones me without being prompted. We see each other often. We do the crossword together. I don't confide in him because to do so would only frustrate me and revive the terrible certainty I have felt since I was a child that my dad is simply a mirage; the closer you get to him, the further he recedes.

My father was not a normal father if normal means leading his children confidently, emotionally as well as practically, into and through the ways of the world. Put that together with my mother's inclination to depression and it has meant, I think, that my brothers and I each stumbled into the world in our own ways. We are travellers with no sure guides; a pattern only heightened by our peripatetic and disrupted childhood growing up in so many different countries.

I think, though, that my parents, like most parents, did the best that they could, so in looking back at our relationship, I don't mean to imply blame. Blame is the least helpful and most destructive of all the emotions. It solves nothing. What is needed is acceptance and understanding. If I am to be free of depression, I need to be aware of the unpleasant truths that took me there in the first place. If I can understand the origins of my responses and the ways in which they are flawed or detrimental to my happiness, I might stand a better chance of changing them. The truth, as the saying goes, will set you free.

Alice Miller, psychoanalyst and the author of *The Drama of Being a Child* puts it best when she describes the uses of analysing the past and the formative experiences of our childhoods:

> It cannot give us back our lost childhood, nor can it change the past facts. No one can heal by maintaining or fostering illusion. The paradise of preambivalent harmony, for which so many patients hope, is unattainable. But the experience of one's own truth, and the postambivalent knowledge of it, make it possible to return to one's own world of feelings at an adult level – without paradise, but with the ability to mourn. And this ability does, indeed, give us back our vitality.

15

Who Am I?

Ah, yes, vitality – the very opposite of depression. It is the life force, the energy that makes us care about our own existence and enables us to struggle on through life, even when it is difficult. It is that, rather than the loss of abstracts such as happiness or contentment that is the true marker of the illness.

The only saving grace of the acute, catatonic stage of severe depression is that we are no longer self-conscious enough to care. We no longer have any consciousness of self. We don't know who we are. We are as lost to ourselves as we are to you. Once out of that phase, we are as conscious as you are of our behaviour, and fairly powerless to do anything about it.

The terrible truth about depression, and the part of its nature that terrifies me the most, is that it appears to operate beyond reason; feelings happen to you for no apparent cause. Or rather, there is usually an initial cause, a 'trigger' as they say in therapeutic circles, but in severe depression the feelings of sadness, grief, loneliness and despair continue long after the situation has resolved itself. It is as if depression has a life of its own, which is perhaps why so many sufferers refer to it as a living thing, as some sort of demon or beast.

Trying to appeal to us as the people we used to be, or referring to some character trait that we once possessed is also liable to send us into despair. When I was still quite unwell but attempting to patch together some semblance of a life, I went to a party. It was an annual event at Christmas given by close friends and I had promised that I would attend, even though I was scared beyond measure. I had always loved it, a relaxed affair filled with good humour.

In my previous incarnation I was a party creature par excellence. Perhaps they thought I still was. Perhaps I thought I still was. I don't know. I do know that some part of me believed that if I could only recreate the girl who used to love parties, I could recapture myself.

So I went. It took me hours to get ready; hours spent getting dressed, only to undress again. Most of that time was spent in tears, not through any profound sense of self-pity but because I could not match myself to the person I had become. Every garment I put on looked odd to me. I could not find a fit between my inner and my outer self. Even wearing my most familiar clothes, I looked like a stranger.

In the end I decided on a pair of black trousers, black high-heeled boots and a simple but nondescript jacket; the dress, you might say, of anonymity, of no particular type or persuasion.

At the party, for an hour or so, I managed perfectly well. I talked, I listened, I laughed but all the time I was conscious that I was watching myself. 'See,' I seemed to be saying to myself, 'you can do this. You can join in with life. You can talk and walk and pass yourself off as Sally.'

Then I found myself face-to-face with somebody I don't know terribly well, but who I had, professionally at least, been very familiar with. We talked for a while and then she said, 'Are you all right?'

I said that I was.

She said, 'It's just that you seem so nervous and agitated. You used to be so calm.'

She went on like this for some time, marvelling at the character change in me until I was forced to admit that I had been ill with depression. 'But you're all right now,' she said in the bright, dismissive tone of somebody who doesn't want their mood sapped by any talk of illness.

It was then that I knew that I wasn't, how profoundly I was not all right, so I went and found a close friend and asked him to drive me home.

'What is it? What's happened?' he kept asking as I sobbed, incoherently, all the way back to my flat.

'I used to be,' I kept repeating. 'I used to be. Don't you see? I tried so hard and I couldn't be me. I'll never be me again. I'll never regain myself.'

He was as distressed as I was but I could see that, as hard as he tried, he had no idea what I was talking about.

'You are you,' he kept repeating. 'Of course you're you. You're just a bit down, that's all.'

'Would me have left a party early and cried all the way home because I am no longer me?'

'No. Yes. I don't know,' he said, with a sigh before sinking into a baffled silence.

Later, he called. 'Are you feeling better?'

I wanted to say, better than what? But I didn't. His only wish for me was happiness. So I said, 'Yes, thank you. I'm feeling much better.' And all the time I was saying it I was wondering what would be the best way to kill myself.

I couldn't stand being me, or the person I had become, but I did not know how I could get back to being myself. And that, I think, is why some depressives take their own lives, and why their friends and family are so perplexed when they do. 'But he seemed so much better. He said he was fine. I know he's been depressed but he seemed to have pulled out of it. He went to a party. The last time we spoke, he said he was feeling better.'

You see, we want to be better, we want to be ourselves, and it is not through any lack of trying that we fail. But we do fail, because we are deep inside an illness. And it is that failure, and that struggle, that sends us into a despair so terrible that we would rather not exist.

It is the glass wall that separates us from life, from ourselves, that is so truly frightening in depression. It is a terrible sense of our own overwhelming reality, a reality that we know has nothing to do with the reality that we once knew. And from which we think we will never escape. It is like living in a parallel universe but a universe so devoid of familiar signs or life that we are adrift, lost.

Sometimes, somebody can reach through that glass wall and pull us back. Sarah called me after the party to see how I was. She had noticed my sudden disappearance. I told her what had happened, about the 'used to be'.

She was furious, angrier than I had ever heard her. 'Stupid woman. What an idiotic thing to say. She knows you've been really ill. Of course you're not the same at the moment. All I can say is, she *used to be* quite intelligent.'

I laughed. It was not so much what Sarah said, as that she understood. She took my reality and put it with her own. And by doing so, she gave me a hand back into life.

There is a notion that depression is a positive event, that it is not so much a question of a breakdown as a breakthrough to a freer, less fractured sense of self. While this is comforting, it is too often an easy, romanticised interpretation of an original idea from the psychiatrist R. D. Laing who said, 'Madness need not all be breakdown. It may also be breakthrough. It is potential liberation and renewal as well as enslavement and existential death.'

I think Laing is right, or can be right, but the danger here is in misinterpreting his idea and thinking that major depression is simply a brief interlude, a short, sharp transformation that shocks us into a new and positive state of being. A matter, say, of a couple of difficult months.

The idea carries, too, definite echoes of morality, of a 'good' or 'bad' state, which sends us right back to the idea that depression is some sort of moral weakness or dangerous character flaw.

It implies that the very experience of severe depression somehow makes us better people, that with it come great dollops of compassion, wisdom, kindness and general self-improvement. No gain without pain, and all that.

This is even worse when it is taken into the arena of other mental or emotional illnesses such as alcoholism, where the recovered alcoholic is sometimes referred to as the 'reformed' alcoholic, as if the person in question merely needs to see the error of his or her ways. This happens so often that there is a phrase in the recovery movement that states: 'We are not bad people trying to be good. We are sick people trying to get better.'

Mental illness is not a question of good or bad, or even before and after character makeovers – as anybody who has ever experienced it knows. Depression may force us to reconsider our thinking, our behaviour and our very identities but it is not a transformation that happens overnight – or even one that necessarily happens at all. Nor is that 'potential liberation' that Laing describes without its own pain and anguish. It takes a long time to change, sometimes a lifetime, and requires intensely hard work.

I know that's not an attractive thought in a culture that demands instant and immediate results but it's the truth. Anyone – therapist, shrink, doctor or healer – who claims otherwise, is either a misguided fool or a liar. Every one of us who has ever been sick knows the urgent desire to be better, right here, right now. Nobody wants that more than the depressive locked into a state of intolerable mental and emotional pain.

Laing's breakthrough can and does happen. There can, post-depression be, 'a sense of renewal'. I know I'm not the person I used to be. I'm not better or worse but I am more awake, more conscious if you like. I'm more aware of the texture of my days, the light and the dark that shades them. I waste less time, in worry, in fear, in anger, in pleasing people I don't like and don't wish to like. I spend more time with people I love and doing the things that I love such as gardening, reading, hanging out with friends. Work now takes second place. I don't mean that I work any less hard but success or even failure have lost the importance they once had. If I mess up, I mess up. I try to remember to have, as somebody once said to me, 'a human experience rather than a perfect experience'.

I have learned, too, to take life less personally. That sounds odd, I know, for what is my life if it is not personal? Well, it is simply life, for a start, and learning to look at it in a new way, or ways, is one of the keys not simply to unlocking depression but keeping it at bay.

It is by breaking old habits (also known as 'old behaviour' or 'old thinking') and instilling new ones that we change the way we think. And one of those old habits might be a sort of ingrained cynicism, a refusal to try new things or ideas simply because we think, at least from the outside looking in, that they are ridiculous, or embarrassing, or both.

Cynicism, or a closed mind, is a refuge depressives can't afford to have. It may, even, be what got us there in the first place. In my entirely subjective research into what makes happiness, or freedom from depression, I'd say that the single most effective habit is an open and receptive mind.

16

The Second Loony Bin

Depression is melancholy minus its charms.

Susan Sontag

Tom drove me to the mental hospital. I don't mean that he drove me via love to madness, although part of that is true, but that he put me in his car and took me there for my second stay. It was here that I met Kate, and Susie and Nigel, whose friendship was to become invaluable.

It had been eight months since I left the first hospital. This time, I asked my psychiatrist to admit me. The bleakness of my mood was unrelenting. I was in pain, physically, either from the effects of depression or the side-effects of the antidepressants – or perhaps both – and suffering emotionally from the black violence of my mood. The only times I did not feel pain were when I was asleep, knocked out by pills, or drunk.

By then I was playing with my medication, as so many depressives do. The high dose of antidepressants I was taking seemed to have no effect but I discovered that if I took a tranquilliser (or two, sometimes three) on top of a bottle of wine (a good French white burgundy was my drug of choice) I could achieve a state of relative peace. I measured out the wine in increments and never more than two bottles in a day; a lot, I know, in any normal life, but my life was not normal.

It was then that my alcohol dependency really kicked off. I did not drink for the taste. It became my anaesthetic, the only thing that came close to relieving the terrible stranglehold at my throat. To put it bluntly, I liked to be mildly but consistently drunk all day, every day.

I found that a steady stream of alcohol together with Valium or Xanax, whatever my psychiatrist prescribed, taken slowly, could ease me through the blackness of my days and into the night when I took a sleeping pill and found complete oblivion, at least for a few hours. I loved my sleeping pills; they were the only moments of peace I could find during that wretched year when my depression was at its worst.

If someone had taken them away, as one well-intentioned GP threatened to do, and removed those few hours of unconsciousness (and my psychiatrist was too clever, or too understanding of my mood and character, to do any such thing, although lesser men might have tried) I would certainly have killed myself. As it was, they were my passport to sanity or the only sort of sanity that I could manage at that time. If I knew that the night would bring me sweet oblivion, I could just about make it through the day.

It was a good system, in that I knew it worked. It was a bad system in that I knew that I would die, and in not too long a time, perhaps a few years, as a result of the quantities of alcohol and prescription drugs I was consuming daily. I confronted my death with grim ambivalence. If I died, I won because I was free from pain. If I died, depression won because it was the cause of the pain from which I wished to be free. I could not decide whom I would prefer to see as the victor.

Nor could I square all this with the person I used to be, with the life I used to love and which now seemed like some lovely reverie I once had dreamed. Just as my daughter was a lovely reverie, so blue and gold and sweetly innocent that I was mortally afraid that, just by being alive, I would infect her with my darkness. But if I died, I would leave the stain of my death on her long after I had ceased, physically, to exist. I had done enough reading to understand the terrible effects of a parent's suicide on a child and be fully aware of the heightened incidence of future mental disorder it imposes on children, including depression.

The last thing I wanted to do was inflict the horror of this illness on my beloved child.

The last thing I wanted to do was to stay alive.

So what to do?

It was in this mood that I lay on my sofa and watched 9/11 played out on the tiny screen of my portable television. I felt nothing, neither horror nor outrage. It seemed to me inevitable that such things would happen in the world. It was that lack of moral outrage and absence of any feeling that, more than anything else, convinced me that I had to do something to ease the terrible grip depression had on me. I was so lost in my own world that I had ceased to have compassion or feeling for any other. If the sight of bodies dropping from a burning building did not horrify me, that absence of feeling did.

The next day, I called my psychiatrist and asked him to admit me to hospital. I also asked Tom to come and sit with me while I waited for a vacant room – not as easy to find as it might sound. Even private psychiatric units are woefully over-subscribed, which says much about the mental health of this nation.

A word about Tom here. We were still seeing each other, although our relationship was erratic and more highly charged than was comfortable, or even tolerable. He had by then separated from his partner who had, some months before, discovered our affair and was justifiably furious, even though as she herself admitted, their relationship had been dead for years.

I felt badly about it. I had betrayed her, and was wretched with guilt and shame; emotions that I could do nothing about because I was, in every respect, in the wrong. That did not change my feelings for Tom; it just made them more complicated and uncomfortable. Nor did the fact that we were both free mean that we were free to settle into a relationship or to love each other well. A good relationship requires more than simple availability.

I loved him, absolutely. If there is such a thing as a complete, all-embracing love for another person who is not our child and is not a part of us, then I felt it for Tom. He was my intimate in every sense. But love goes wrong. Sometimes, it goes so badly wrong even when it is infinitely right, that the pain is catastrophic. And so it was with Tom and me. There were children involved and he put his children, rightly, above all else, above himself and above me. He had known the burden of an absent father and was determined that his children should not suffer in the same way. His unhappiness and his own feelings did not, as he put it, matter. And neither, by extension, did mine.

But strong emotion and need has a habit of making itself felt, even when every right and rational part of us is pushing it away. There are brief glimpses of time when we think we might be happy, when we allow ourselves to feel hope. And then, just as quickly, we realise that we were mistaken and the failure of that hope is more terrible than had it never existed at all.

It was in this way (he was by then fighting as hard for custody of his children as I was fighting severe depression) that we crashed through that year; a most terrible year, for both of us. We loved and fought, were kind and hurt each other, came together and fell apart. We could not be together and we could not stay away from each other. I don't mean that in any great romantic sense. It was not romantic. It was ugly and bruising and underneath it all was the recognition that we loved each other and recognised some unswerving connection but could not find a way to manage it. There was very little bliss. It was, in its own particular way, hell.

That ruinous love affair did not cause my depression,

although it was one of the reasons why it continued, inasmuch as the constant re-experience of hope and loss and profound disappointment is a good enough reason for depression.

I felt, that year, as if my heart broke over and over again. Our inability to sort out or even to embrace the mess that surrounded us and the weeks or months when Tom disappeared, physically as well as emotionally, into his own misery seemed to lock into some part of me that was already fragile, that part where I felt a sense of profound abandonment, perhaps, or emphasised my unswerving belief that the people I love most will never respond to my unhappiness. I was, by then, too ill to be able to reach out to him or to do anything about the pain that he was so obviously suffering, so felt more than ever helpless and hopeless.

While difficult relationships can cause intolerable pain, to ascribe to a love affair the entire cause and continuation of depression is to profoundly misunderstand the illness. Once severe depression has a hold, it is unshakeable until it has run its course or that course has been diverted by treatment. There were times, weeks and even months, when I thought that Tom and I would be together, and happily. That had no effect at all on the severity of my depression. It carried on, regardless and relentless. It did not lift when he was present and nor did it suddenly return when he left. My mood might have changed. The depression did not. But then you would not expect any other illness to lift according to the person who is standing in front of you, however happy they might make you feel.

As we waited for a vacant hospital room, we lay on my bed at home and Tom read to me from the book *On Liberty*, by the nineteenth-century philosopher and political economist John Stuart Mill; a particular passion of his at the time. As a teenager, inflamed by social inequities and the rights of women, I too had loved John Stuart Mill, so it seemed right and familiar that Tom should be reading his words to me. I remember the sound of his voice and my head pillowed on his chest and the irony, which did not escape me, of listening to Tom read about liberty as I waited for a call from the loony bin.

This time, rather than being treated in a psychiatric unit in a general hospital, I was admitted to a dedicated mental hospital. When the call came, we loaded a few possessions into Tom's old VW Beetle and drove the short way to the hospital in silence. Tom carried my case through the smart reception and into the shabby corridors that lay behind it and I felt the sharp click of the metal security doors lock securely behind me.

We stood in the empty room that was to become my home, at least for a while. It held a single bed with a green and brown striped cover, a so-called easy chair covered in worn green nylon that had scratched wooden arms, and a vanity unit of cheap wood veneer that sat squarely below a mirror, stuck firmly to the wall. The window was barred and locked into place, allowing barely two inches of air.

We stared at each other.

'It could be worse,' I said, meaning the room.

Tom shook his head sharply and looked away but not before I saw the expression on his face and I knew that it couldn't. It couldn't possibly be worse. A psychiatrist appeared to give me an initial assessment and I saw, through Tom's eyes, the shocking gravity of my situation. I had not, until that moment, truly thought about where I was and why. I was in a mental hospital because I could not manage to stay outside of one and alive, in any meaningful sense.

Tom left soon after.

The first evening, Molly came to visit me wearing her school uniform, and that innocent grey pinafore and red and white gingham shirt looked so out of place under the harsh fluorescent strip lights of the sad green hospital corridors that, had I had the energy and strength, I would have bundled her up and scooped her right out of the door. Instead, I diverted both of us by taking her down to the canteen to have supper, which was served at six o'clock.

I was hoping for pizza or burger and chips, but there was not much she wanted to eat, except white rolls and butter. The catering staff seemed particularly taken with Quorn, that chalky vegetarian substitute for meat. There was curried Quorn, Quorn sausages and Quorn casserole and I remember wondering if there was some weird connection between meat substitutes and mental illness.

Across the room, which was decorated in bright chintz with white painted bamboo furniture like some cheap gastro-pub, a table of people discussed me in that obtrusive way that people have when they are trying to be discreet. As I buttered Molly's rolls, I was tempted to stop and write my diagnosis, *Severe Clinical Depression*, in large black letters on a paper napkin and attach it to my forehead together with a list of my medications. I was by then enough of an old timer to know there are only two pieces of information that are of passionate interest to inmates of a psychiatric unit. 'What are you in for?' with its resonance of prison and long sentences and 'What have they put you on?'

Later, a doctor (medical rather than psychiatric) came and gave me a routine physical check-up. This is usual, for in some cases, depression has a physical cause. Depressed people are also less likely to take care of themselves so are more likely to be suffering from malnutrition or some other condition that may exacerbate their illness. Many of them, too, have been abusing alcohol, with its attendant physical damage.

As the doctor went about his work, he asked me why I was in hospital.

'I have severe depression.'

'And why do you think that is?'

Because I enjoy it? 'I have no idea.'

I was slightly taken aback. It is not usual for medical

doctors to embark on psychiatric questions, even in a mental hospital. But this particular doctor seemed intent on blurring the disciplines.

'You must have some.'

I mumbled something about a marriage breakdown.

He had his face very close to mine, he was checking my heartbeat with a stethoscope at the time. He said, 'Do you hate men?'

At first, I thought I had misheard him, so I asked him to repeat himself. He came out with the same, trite phrase. I was so angry, I was tempted to hit him but I knew the consequences on my mental health record. 'Don't be a fucking idiot,' I said, and burst into tears, more out of fury than anything else.

Wearing a smug, knowing expression, he tucked his stethoscope back into his pocket.

My mother was there at the time, the only time she was ever present when I was in hospital.

'Don't upset yourself,' she pleaded, after he had left.

'I am not upsetting myself,' I said, sobbing. 'I am being upset by somebody else.'

My mother left soon after.

Later, I wondered if the doctor was actually a patient who had nicked a stethoscope.

I was lucky, inasmuch as I was able to be fairly active. I felt bleak despair, could not eat, read or sleep and was constantly preoccupied with death and dying, but I could get up, get dressed, walk and talk.

Across the hallway, there was someone who could do none of those things. She lay immobile, head covered by a sheet, her inert body forming a long hump like a dune of heavy, wet sand moulded to a single bed. Her open door, through which you could see her terrible immobility, was guarded day and night by a nurse who sat in a grey plastic chair that squeaked as she bent to pick up another back issue of *Hello!* from the pile of magazines at her feet. Her mind was on Posh and Becks, but her eyes were on suicide.

I never did find out the patient's name. I knew only that every few hours or so, she would get out of bed and throw herself with thunderous force against the walls, bruising herself badly and cracking her head against the plaster. And then they would pick her up and put her back into bed. And so it went on.

Suicide attempts in psychiatric units are, not surprisingly, frequent and the desperation of the suicidal is, in the old sense of the word, pathetic. The cutlery is plastic and so are the cups in order to avoid serious injury (broken china makes too effective a sharp edge to be allowed) but that does not stop people sawing at their wrists with a barely serrated plastic knife. When I was there, a woman soaked her bed pillows in water then climbed into a full bath and held them over her face. When the staff found her, she was very cold, with skin like a prune. She was also alive and inconsolable at the thought. Another gouged bloody holes in her wrists with a pair of eyebrow tweezers. There was nothing to be done about the glass light bulbs and most of us in there wondered why it was that they were not used more often, either as blades or ground up and eaten.

The hospital was divided into floors, according to particular conditions. I was on the ground floor, with the depressives – 'the saddos' as we were known – as well as those suffering from severe anxiety disorders, or both, as depression is often accompanied by severe anxiety. On the floor above us, there were more saddos, depression being the most prevalent of the mental illnesses, and above that was another floor containing the sectioned patients, put there against their will because they were too sick, too violent or simply too unwilling to be admitted voluntarily. On the top floor was the detox unit, for alcoholics and drug addicts ('alkies and druggies'), who were often moved down to be with the saddos, once they had cleaned up. Then there was the eating disorders unit across the road, containing mainly teenage girls but some older, long-term anorexics and bulimics.

All of us, with the exception of the sectioned patients (or 'sections' as they were known) ate together in the canteen. Most conditions clustered at tables together, saddo with saddo, alkie with druggie and the anorexics with a nurse, to supervise their eating. The talk was always of medication (depressives sound like they've swallowed medical textbooks whole) or therapy, with particular attention given to the inadequacies, real or imagined, of each therapist.

It was like being back at school; the therapists, like teachers, were each given nicknames, none of them flattering. But that's what happens when the balance of power is catastrophically disrupted; when you are incapable of fending for yourself or staying alive and feel powerless to do it in any adult sense, you slip easily into the role of the dependant.

It was not long after I had been admitted, perhaps the second day, when I was confronted as I helped myself to a plate of food.

'Hello,' he said, in a tone so knowingly familiar that I stopped in my tracks.

'Hello,' I said.

He peered down at me. He was very tall, with black curly hair hiding most of his face.

'I know you.'

This is always a tricky situation in a mental hospital, particularly when the person in question is skeletally thin and wearing full black leathers and multiple piercings. I had no recollection of him but my memory, at that time, was not at its best. Did he know me or was I part of some virtual reality playing in his head?

'Of course,' I said, because it seemed simpler to agree.

'What are you in for?'

'Depression. You?'

'Drugs,' he said, as if I would have guessed for sure. 'You know. The old days.'

I tried to place him. Fashion? Magazines? Fleet Street? Nothing about him was familiar. I shrugged. 'Well, they got us both, in one way or another.'

'They sure did.' He raised a benevolent hand. 'Be well,' he said and faded away.

'Who was that?' Nigel asked.

'I have no idea.'

'Consorting with the druggies already,' he teased.

'No, I mean I really have no idea. Absolutely none. But he knows me. Or, he thinks he does.'

'He's Thin Lizzy,' said Nigel. 'Or he thinks he is.'

We are standing on a cobbled mews street in London. It is ten thirty at night and a faint drizzle makes the pavements shine. I am wearing a nightdress and a pair of flip-flops. According to Nigel, I wore flip-flops all the time, mostly unsuitably he says, but I don't remember. They were jewelled, and my toenails were painted red. I remember the painted toenails. I had developed a fixation with my hands and feet, believing that if they were perfectly manicured and painted, then I still had some semblance of control. I chose to ignore the fact that I couldn't manage the parts in between. I had worked in or around fashion for twenty years but had so lost any connection to or understanding of myself, that I no longer knew how to get dressed. Getting dressed requires an identity I seemed to have lost or, at any rate, mislaid.

Standing in the mews in flip-flops in the rain, I realise that most of us are out of our heads on drugs. Or, rather, more out of our heads than usual. Our medication is always handed out at nine thirty precisely, so we are an hour into our dose. There's a faint buzzing in my ears from the sleeping pills I have taken. Max dosage, or so the nurse who gave them to me said.

'Now you'll sleep,' she pronounced cheerfully.

That was before the fire alarm sounded and the entire intake of the hospital spilled out into the back street. Some, the most serious cases, had to be carried, bundled in blankets.

One man is propped in a wheelchair, head lolling, spittle dribbling across his cheek.

Around him, people talk excitedly, voices high-pitched and hyperactive. Most smoke furiously. It looks like some mad rave, a warehouse pyjama party. A phalanx of nurses stands further up the street, arms crossed like bouncers, although they are there to keep us penned into the mews, not to keep us out.

A woman is shouting. She is bone thin, with transparently white skin and wild red hair and is wearing a ripped lace negligee under a battered old leather jacket.

'My fucking psychiatrist fucking sectioned me,' she yells, at no one in particular. 'I said to him, "What the fuck are you doing, fucker?" I'm not mad. How dare you section me? Don't you fucking know who I fucking am? I'm fucking Janis Joplin, you fucker!'

And she starts to sing, her voice rising over the wail of sirens as the fire brigade arrive. As Joplin imitations go, it's not bad but everyone ignores her.

A voice says, 'Sally?'

I turn around. A sweet-faced woman is staring at me. She is young and pretty although the bloat of alcohol is in her face. She must only be in her thirties, and is hugging a Gap hooded top over striped men's pyjamas. For a moment, I can't place her.

'It's me,' she says. 'Lily.'

I do know her. She's a fellow writer.

'Hello,' I say. I don't ask her how she is. In the loony bin, you learn not to ask questions like that.

'What are you in for?' she says.

'Depression. You?'

'I'm with the alkies, top floor. They put me in here, occasionally, to dry out. Then I go and do it all over again.' She pulls a face. 'I drive everyone mad. Have you got any money?'

I look down at my nightdress and flip-flops and my empty,

bare hands. They look half dead under the neon of the street lights. 'No.'

'Pity. The pub up the road's still open. We could get a swift one in before closing time.'

A man behind us takes off, starts running up the road, whooping loudly. The great escape. The phalanx of nurses edge together nervously.

'He's got the right idea,' Lily says, watching his progress towards the pub.

Halfway up the road the man stops, his arms held wide, then swoops back towards us like a deranged bird.

'Got any money?' Lily says to him.

'It's a blast,' he says, panting. 'You should try it. It's like *freedom*!'

'Have you got any money?' Lily says.

'Silly bitch,' he says, then all energy seems to leave his wire-thin body and he flops down on to the wet pavement. 'Do you think they'll let us back in soon?' he whines plaintively. 'I'm tired.'

Lily turns abruptly and disappears into the crowd. I hear her voice, trailing high above the noise. 'Anybody got any money?'

It is the last time I see her. Two years later, I hear from some mutual friends that she is dead from an accidental overdose, complicated by excessive alcohol. I am sad, but not surprised.

A nurse appears, framed in the lit doorway. 'Back to bed, everyone,' he says. 'Excitement's over.'

We shuffle back in to the building like obedient children. Apparently some madman set fire to his bed. Or a pile of magazines. Or a letter he took exception to. The stories vary.

There are two more fire drills that week. Neither are false alarms.

Tom comes to see me every night, after the six o'clock meal. We lie on the hard single bed, arms around each other. I kiss him and he kisses me back, and then he pulls away.

'Too weird,' he says. We lie together, not talking much. I don't know what he's thinking. I don't ask and he doesn't say. I try to tell him something about my day, the routine that we slip into as easily as a warm bath. It is comforting to be told where to go and what to do, and even what to think, when you haven't the strength to decide for yourself. It is hard, though, to explain that to somebody who still carries the smell of the outside world, sharp and clear and tearingly familiar, so I don't.

Tom never stays long. I feel his eagerness to be gone, even as he arrives. I don't blame him. It's not a place to linger, unless you have to.

I have begun to make friends among my fellow patients. There are around thirty of us depressives but, even though I listen to their stories in group, most of them remain as opaque to me as they, presumably, do to themselves.

One of the friends I make is Andy, who is suicidal. He was admitted after stabbing himself six times in the stomach, with a kitchen knife. He was discovered, early in the morning, lying under a bush on an empty stretch of common ground, quietly bleeding to death. He cannot remember how he got there or, even, really why. They took him to hospital and stitched together his innards and then sent him here, to have his head examined. His head is shaved, or perhaps it is bald, and he has a bullish neck and a belly on him that must, or so one can only hope, have cushioned some of the severity of the blows.

'Did it hurt?' I say.

He rolls his eyes. 'Of course it fucking well hurt. And only a loony would ask that question.'

Despite his appearance, he is a gentle man and a graphic designer by trade. Business is bad. It's an unforgiving profession and Andy feels, more than anything, unforgiven. Not just by his work, but by everything.

He is inquisitive and makes friends easily, almost too determined to be liked, and is not in the least disconcerted by his surroundings. He seems, more than that, to enjoy them. Some people do. After the lonely hell of mental illness, a hospital with all its rules and regulations can seem like a safe haven.

He's not one of the smokers, although he hangs out with them. They gather outside my room, which is right at the end of the corridor, tucked away on its own. There is a table, a cluster of chairs and two overflowing ashtrays and, at any given time, three or four people smoking furiously. I don't know why we need a smoking area, as we're allowed to smoke in our rooms. I encounter the smokers every time I step out of my room to go and make a cup of tea in the small kitchen up the corridor.

'Sorry, sorry.' Kate flaps her arms furiously to dispel the smoke, but only manages to shoo it straight through the open door into my room. Not that it will make much difference. My room is already thick with smoke.

Kate is big and loud and glamorous with dark hair, streaked with tawny blonde, and hazel, cat's eyes. She wears hoodies and track pants 'the only thing that'll fit my fat ass' and white trainers with fluorescent stripes. And false nails, 'these are perfect, the best, I'll tell you where to get them done, if you like' and lots of jewellery. She works in advertising. It seems the wrong job for somebody with a crippling anxiety disorder. Not that you'd credit it now.

'You wouldn't recognise her as the same person who arrived here,' Nigel says later. 'She hardly spoke, and kept her arms wrapped tightly around herself and her head right down. And she wore these spooky glasses, very narrow and severe. We were all completely terrified of her.'

Kate is laughing at something that Susie has said. 'Silly cow.' The two are inseparable, bound together by their mutual diagnosis of a severe anxiety disorder. 'Sorry about the smoking,' she says again, flapping her arms inconsequentially in the air.

'It's fine,' I say. 'No problem.'

Andy says, 'We're having a party. Would you like some birthday cake?'

I shake my head. I've been crying for hours. I'm not in the mood to face people.

'Bad day?' Kate says.

I shake my head again, not trusting myself to speak, and start walking up the corridor.

'Catch you later,' Kate calls.

We meet again in group therapy and bond in Negative Automatic Thoughts. This is one of the strands of Cognitive Behavioural Therapy (CBT), the form of therapy used most often in psychiatric units and by the NHS. This is partly a financial decision as CBT is thought to be effective after ten sessions, rather than the ten years, or more, usually devoted to Freudian-based analysis.

Unlike analysis, CBT pays only a nodding reference to the past and concentrates instead on solving present problems. One of those, or so it is thought, is that depressives hold to a rigid pattern of negative thinking which leads us to act in self-defeating ways. The central tenet of CBT is that thoughts beget behaviour – hence its name, *cognitive*, as in thoughts, and *behavioural*, as in actions.

In essence, it consists of a number of repetitive exercises designed to identify and then challenge those negative thought patterns and put fresh ways of thinking and behaviour in their place. It is designed as a course of exercises; it has a beginning, a middle and an end, so by its particular nature it is possible to assess results empirically, a virtue that no other form of therapy (which is by nature, unstructured; wandering through childhood, stopping off at adolescence, coming into adulthood and meandering back to childhood again) can lay claim to. And, because hospitals and health services like to see results, or evidence-based programmes and because it is time-limited, it has become the most highly regarded and therefore most popular form of therapy on offer. In many local health services, it is the only form of therapy available.

Its greatest virtue is in the treatment of anxiety disorders, which are more susceptible than many other emotional disorders to the sort of logic that CBT proposes. Most anxiety is based on faulty thinking, or misplaced fears, and CBT exercises can both challenge and then dislodge those fears if used consistently. It is also magnificently good at addressing phobias, which, as one psychiatrist put it, 'have to be bored into submission.'

It is less effective, and this is simply a personal view, in the treatment of severe depression or, at least, a depression that has no obvious, single cause. In the case of a reactive depression, which, as the name suggests, is a depression caused by a reaction to an event, it tends to be more effective. But in depression as pathology, it seems only capable of chipping away at the solid block of frozen feelings, or lack of feelings characterised by the black hole of which so many sufferers speak.

Part of the strategy of CBT is in investing, absolutely, in the belief that emotions are simply thoughts in action. A thought begets an emotion, and not the other way around. I'm not sure that I entirely believe that. Some emotions are inarticulate, they are without words or language. They seem to come from some primitive, pre-verbal base. Memories rely on language to exist, they form a narrative, a continuous loop running in our heads. Without words, memories cannot exist. Or, at least, we cannot access them through our minds. We may, however, be able to access them with our bodies, which perhaps explains the remarkable physicality of emotions – a knot in the stomach, a pain in the neck.

Or it may be that these physical emotions are memories lodged at a time when we were infants and pre-verbal, when words did not exist. This is some of the thinking that goes into analytical therapy, and why it concentrates so emphatically on the first two years of life in an attempt to try to access the subconscious, or unconscious. Now neuroscientists are beginning to discover that perhaps those early thinkers were not as misguided as modern opinion tends to believe. The brain is not, as had been previously thought, fixed, but subtly plastic; so abuse in the early years, or even a failure of mother–child bonding, can cause certain areas of the brain to fail to develop, or to develop abnormally. Inarticulate emotions also go some way towards explaining post-traumatic disorder. When events are too horrific to verbalise or too terrifying to stitch into the verbal narrative of memories, they become lodged in the body and manifest in shaking, sweating and flashbacks.

I don't know if that's true, although it makes a sort of sense. It seems to me that nobody understands the genesis of emotions, ungovernable or not, although neuroscientists are beginning to take ever greater strides in understanding the workings of the human mind. Perhaps before too long we shall see the emergence of new forms of therapy.

Right now, we're stuck within the limits of our understanding, which is how I come to be sitting in a group of people examining my Negative Automatic Thoughts.

First, the therapist says, we must banish imperatives from our heads. No 'musts' or 'oughts' or 'shoulds' are allowed. Words such as these keep us stuck in negative thinking. So we are instructed to replace, 'I *must* get better' with, 'I am *going to try* to get better'.

Or, how about, 'I *should* love my mother' with, 'I am *going to try* to get along better with my mother'.

I put up my hand.

The therapist smiles encouragingly. 'Yes, Sally?'

'Isn't banning the use of imperatives in itself an imperative? We *must* not use imperatives. We *must* not say should.'

'No, not really, not in the way that we use it.'

I catch sight of Kate. A broad grin has settled on her face. She senses trouble.

I say, 'In what way do we not use it?'

A tiny frown of irritation knits itself above the therapist's eyes. 'Shall we deal with this later, Sally?'

I shrug. I am not being contrary. I prefer to fully understand a method before I can engage with it. Kate's eyes roll expressively and I catch, just for a moment, a glimpse of who she is. She's the bad girl who always sits at the back of the class. And I'm the annoying one who likes to challenge authority. Both of which, as it turns out later, are true.

A little later, the therapist assigns us a task. CBT is filled with tasks, or exercises. There's homework too, or written work, none of which I do. Not because I think that CBT is a waste of time. For some people, it works and it works well. People like Kate and Susie, for example, for whom it worked magnificently. At the time, I was unable to read or write so it was of little use to me. Nor could I engage with it, in part because of the logic it prescribes, which seems to me too limited and prosaic. It assumes that life is logical, when all my evidence shows that it is not. It also assumes that my thoughts, or my mind, are logical, which is assuredly not the case.

The therapist asks us to imagine something, an activity, which we hate most to do. I have two. They are driving (about which I had a full-blooded phobia for ten years) and public speaking. Both of them seem to me to be eminently sensible things to be afraid of. One may kill you or somebody else, which seems a good enough reason to dislike it, and the other forces you into full sight of crowds of people, a situation I have never enjoyed.

'Sally, what's the thing you most hate doing?' asks the therapist.

'Public speaking. I'd as soon have tacks put through my eyes.'

She winces slightly. 'An interesting choice of words.'

'But descriptive.'

'What would happen if I made you do it now?'

'I would shake. My voice would tremble. The palms of my hands would grow clammy. I might feel as if I was going to faint.'

'And that would frighten you?'

'Yes, of course. Those are all physical symptoms of fear.'

'What frightens you exactly?'

'That those things would happen.'

'And what would people think of you?'

'That I'm afraid.'

'And why is that bad?'

'We all avoid fear. None of us like it.'

'Would people thinking you are afraid make you feel like less of a person, like a bad person?'

'No. It would make me feel like a frightened person.'

'And you prefer not to be seen in that way?'

'Of course.'

'Why?'

'Because it makes me vulnerable.'

'And you think vulnerability is bad?'

'No, it's fine in its place. But public speaking is not its place.'

'Why not?'

I am trying, really I am and I can see where she is trying to lead me. It's just that I don't believe that the route is valid.

'Authority is necessary in public speaking if you are to be in any way convincing.'

'And you don't think that you have it?'

'No, I think that I am frightened of public speaking. That has nothing to do with authority. It has to do with fear of other people.'

'Why are you afraid of other people? Do you think that they dislike you?'

'No, I think that a crowd of people can be frightening because they can be unpredictable.'

She tries another tack. 'What would feel so bad about shaking and your hands growing clammy?'

'It would feel uncomfortable.'

'Would it make you a feel like bad person, for feeling that way?'

'No, it would make me feel bad. There's a difference.'

I know what she wants me to say, but I just can't do it. I'd like to help her out. She's trying to help me to challenge my automatic negative thoughts. She believes that at the base of every depressive is a person who feels bad about him- or herself. She is trying to challenge that negative belief. Which might work, if I did feel bad about myself. But I don't. I don't suffer from low self-esteem. I suffer from blank, alienating despair. There's a difference but it's one that too often gets blurred in group therapeutic practice or in a one size fits all prescription, such as CBT.

She makes me read a poem out loud, in front of the group.

I do.

She claps her hands excitedly, like a child. There is something endearing about her pleasure. 'But that was wonderful. You read that beautifully. How did it feel?'

'Terrible.'

Her face falls and, momentarily, I feel sorry. 'I didn't say that I couldn't do it,' I explain. 'I said that I didn't like to do it.'

'But you can do it. Doesn't that give you a sense of achievement and make you feel better about yourself?'

'No.'

Later, Kate says to me. 'You're difficult. I like that.'

I say that I'm not trying to be difficult. I am trying to understand.

She gives me a hug. 'You think too much.'

Nigel is, if anything, even worse than I am. In group, he bats away words like flies. It is how I notice him in the first place. He wears a navy hoodie and black combat trousers, scuffed at the hems. He hunches down in his chair, arms crossed, legs crossed. I watch him trying to join in with the sincerity that

CBT demands. He can't do it although he tries, a lot harder than I do. After a while, we start to bat off each other, which does neither of us any good – at least, not in any therapeutic sense. We enjoy ourselves in another, equally therapeutic way, by becoming allies and, later, friends.

Then, one day, it is just three of us in a group session. Me, Nigel and a man called Michael who, like us, is suffering from suicidal depression.

The session begins. Nigel and I, as usual, are chucking around ideas and words. Core concepts, as they are known in CBT. We are enjoying ourselves. Michael says hardly a word, although we try to encourage him to join in.

After a while, the therapist says, 'Michael, how do you feel?'

Michael shakes his head slowly. 'I feel bad. Really bad. I don't understand it and I can't use words like these two can. I don't know enough words, or words like the ones they use. So all I'm going to say is that I feel bad.'

Nigel and I look at each other, ashamed. Michael's right. We tell Michael that he's right, that we are both just bored, or trying to avoid the real, the central issue of why we are there. Which is that we feel bad. No other words, really, are necessary. And then we all start to talk, to actually say the way that we feel. It makes us all feel better.

I don't mean to dismiss CBT entirely. It has its uses, the most profound of which is that it teaches us to challenge negative thoughts and to question why they might exist in the first place. As a tool, it is useful, but thinking is just one aspect of what makes us depressed, or human. I worry too, about the assurances that are given, that CBT 'works' in a limited time frame, that we are 'cured' and that our most destructive thought processes can be altered in a matter of hours. Recovery is not like that. It is slow and stumbling; a profound understanding of oneself, of the impulses and emotions that drive us, comes in fits and starts. Then again, one should not blame CBT for that. The ability to feel right in our own skins can sometimes take a lifetime to achieve, if it is achieved at all.

The best therapy seems to me to lie in being understood, or in sharing with another human being our most unmanageable emotions. The central idea that we are all fragile, faulty and flawed in some way, that no single one of us is exempt from difficult feelings is, for me, the most reassuring form of therapy, and the best and most precious communication of them all.

17

Travels Through Therapy

One must learn to love oneself with a wholesome and healthy love, so that one can bear to be with oneself and need not roam.

Friedrich Nietzsche

I feel lonely. I have many, and good, friends and still I feel lonely.

A therapist once said, 'When I look at you, I think you may be the loneliest person I have ever met.'

I was astonished. It was perhaps the only interesting thing that particular therapist ever said to me, but it was not that which astonished me or got my attention. I was astonished because I thought I hid it so well. At the time, I was neck deep in depression and addiction, both of which are sometimes called diseases of loneliness. So perhaps it was not surprising. More surprising was that, in more general terms, I think that he was right. I am conscious, often, of a deep-seated sense of loneliness. It has been present since I was a child. I know I am not alone in this. Many depressives suffer from it but it is rarely analysed or discussed, even in group therapy. CBT, for example, would try to challenge it by establishing the facts and using them to challenge the notion of loneliness.

Here are the facts: I have a child, who I love well; a man, who I love well; a house; a cat; a family who loves me; many friends; a successful career. Those are the facts. My loneliness has nothing to do with reality. It is, instead, some existentialist yearning for meaning, for sense or connection.

When I was depressed, I thought I had found the reason for my loneliness. I thought, of course I feel lonely. I feel lonely because I cannot function, at least not in any effective or meaningful way. Is function then the opposite of depression; is function the very meaning of life? Or is it perhaps the meaning that gives life? My battle is not in finding out how to function, my battle is in finding a point to functioning. Or in finding, in other words, what is the point of me. Perhaps that's what depression is, then. It is losing the point of oneself. If so, how does one rediscover it? Forget rediscover. How does one discover it at all?

These are my questions and they are not best served by CBT, which might teach me how to function more happily and effectively but it does not teach me what the point of functioning well (or badly) is in the first place. Perhaps there is no point? Perhaps there is only acceptance that there is no point. Perhaps that's the point. Perhaps our expectations are simply set too high and Freud had it right when he said, 'Much will be gained if we succeed in transforming your hysterical misery into common unhappiness.'

I have always rather disliked the notion of hysteria when applied to mental illness, perhaps because of its modern connotation of exaggeration. I have always rather disliked Freud too, although not as a thinker. Some of his thoughts are good. What I dislike about him is his legacy, the frigid practice of psychoanalytical psychotherapy, but perhaps he should not be blamed for that.

It may have been different lying on the great man's couch in Vienna, rather than sitting on a shiny green sofa in a bland room in North London. Perhaps he might have smiled, in an avuncular way, or exuded some personal charm or magnetism. Perhaps he might have said 'hello' as I entered the room instead of bestowing a chilly little nod or presenting me with a face so wiped of expression that I felt as if I had somehow entered the wrong door.

This is the modern face of analysis, which most people think of as therapy. I know I did. Before I finally understood the extraordinary life-enhancing benefits of good therapy (or therapy that was good for me) I stumbled through (or should that be past?) four different therapists, all of whom practised in the psychoanalytical school. One left me standing in the rain for five minutes, because I had arrived too early. She didn't answer the doorbell despite being there and, from what I could see, unoccupied. Nor, once she finally allowed me in, did she offer me a cup of hot coffee or even a towel. Such touches of simple humanity supposedly interfere with the therapeutic process.

In the psychoanalytical culture, this is normal behaviour. The analyst behaves as a blank screen, inferring from your response your primary areas of emotional damage. Now, I am not good in no-speak situations at the best of times. I am worse when expected to leak my wounded heart across someone's sofa.

I know people who have been going to see a therapist for years, with no obvious benefit. This is partly because they do not know what therapy really is, or the difference between good therapy and bad. Nor do they know that they have a choice. Apathy, fear, resignation and misplaced good manners keep a lot of people in thrall to bad therapy.

So does pain. We want to be fixed and we don't know how to do it ourselves. Self-regulation goes against the culture in which we live, which is to hand all our power and responsibility over to experts. Most of us know so little about therapy we don't dare question it. To be honest, we don't even know the questions. As a result, there are few other service industries (and therapy is one, make no mistake) where we happily hand over money for negligible results. This is partly because of the pseudo-scientific, medical cloak in which therapy is shrouded, but it is more to do with the stigma around mental disorders, which stops them, and the successful treatment for them, being discussed with any vigour or transparency.

I was once furiously reprimanded by an acquaintance for mentioning that a mutual friend was in therapy. My friend is perfectly open about this himself but I was told that such matters should not be mentioned in public. I countered by asking, if he had cancer, should it not be mentioned that he was consulting an oncologist? No, that was fine. There is a difference, apparently, between seeking help for your physical or your emotional health or even just talking about it.

Even the basics are little understood. When I was ill, if I ever mentioned that I saw both a psychotherapist and a psychiatrist, people were apt to look confused. Why both? Because my psychiatrist monitored the levels of chemicals in my head and adjusted my medication accordingly, while my therapist monitored the levels of distress in my head and adjusted my therapy accordingly. One is a drug cure, the other a talking cure. Therapists, having no medical training, are not allowed to prescribe drugs. Psychiatrists are allowed to talk but as most approach the human mind at a fairly high empirical level, I wouldn't recommend most of them as counsellors of the heart.

Then there's the accompanying jargon – denial, resistance, transference, projection, boundaries, issues, core beliefs – which is apt to make the average person feel like a stranger in an even stranger land.

There are also personal issues. At one psychiatric unit, the leading therapist constantly put me down, telling me I was too clever, too intellectual, that I used fancy words like armour. I'm a writer, I said, that's what I do. My head is always filled with words. He was relentless. In the end, I gave up speaking, retreating still further into myself. My sense of loneliness and isolation increased. As a child, I was bullied for showing any cleverness. When I pointed that out, and said to him that he was making me feel more rejected rather than less, his reply was that he was 'breaking down my intellectual defences, so I could really feel the feelings.'

I understood his method, but not his manner. Many of us are capable of overruling our hearts with our heads, of denying feelings that can literally make us sick. I also knew that this was personal. He did not feel sufficiently clever himself; he was playing out his own insecurities by undermining those he thought might challenge his authority. And the therapeutic environment, filled as it is with fragile souls, gave him full permission. Anyone who thinks that every therapist checks their prejudices and neuroses at the door before they enter a room, needs their head examined. The best do, but some don't.

Then there is the pill versus talk debate. One therapist told me that I might get better without medication, but I would never get better without therapy. Yet another was downright hostile to my taking any antidepressant medication, maintaining that chemicals mask the pain so the real issues underlying the depression would never be confronted.

This attitude is completely irresponsible. If you give a healthy person antidepressants, they have no impact other than drug-induced side-effects. Antidepressants do not mask or take away pain – that's the Disney version – they simply bring the brain back into some sort of focus. Without that focus, it is impossible to engage in therapy at all. Therapists themselves disagree, often quite violently, on such issues. Many embrace medication as a necessary part of recovery, others embrace a whole slew of spiritual practices such as meditation, yoga or a Twelve Step programme – which another branch mock. A CBT therapist may be highly dismissive of psychoanalytical psychotherapy, rejecting the form as outdated, expensive and time-heavy. Still more condemn CBT as short-term intervention, or a temporary sticking-plaster. Little wonder the average person finds it difficult to get their head around the subject. I tried, really I did. When

I was at my most ill and trapped in the heart of severe depression, for over a year I attended therapy religiously, twice a week, in order to analyse the causes of and reasons for my unhappiness. I was told I would not get better otherwise.

I was assigned a therapist by my psychiatrist. Let's call her Margaret. She was large, with long dark hair and a liking for colourful full skirts, smock dresses and shawls. There was an air of self-conscious vanity about her; here was a woman who was not happy in her own skin. So why, I wondered, did she think she could make me feel happy in mine? But she was kind and well intentioned, determined to do good and be of help to her patients, and had a motherly air of comfort about her. She was intelligent, too, and well read in her particular field, although her mind was not original or surprising. She cared about me, and my distress.

I could not stand her.

I went to see her, every Monday and every Thursday, not out of pleasure or even a sense of duty, but out of pure desperation. I knew that I had to have therapy in order to get well. I had been told as much, in no uncertain terms. The best treatment for depression is medication and therapy, in combination. Nobody, though, told me which particular therapy might work for me. It was just 'therapy' just as a therapist was simply a therapist, a person who practised a particular skill or discipline, rather than another human being with whom you might engage – or not.

And, because I knew no other way and I was not, at that time, capable of making up my mind because I had no mind to speak of, I kept going back, week after painful week. The cost ran into thousands of pounds. I don't mind that. Money is there to be spent, or be wasted. Time is not. I can't get it back. That I do mind.

'We must try,' Margaret was fond of saying, 'to contain you.' In other words, we must try to contain the pain that is threatening to swamp you, to overwhelm you so badly that you can bear it no longer and want to take your own life.

'Do you feel more contained now?' she would ask at the end of a session, eyes bright with anticipation.

'Yes,' I would say, even though it was not, for me, a finite position. I might feel less contained, or more contained, but I never once felt the comfort of the safety that word implied.

It didn't help that I loathed the process. It irritated and pained me and, eventually, I behaved so thoroughly badly that Margaret must, surely, have come to hate her sessions with me as much as I did. Most of the time I was angry, irritated by a methodology that seemed to me to make no sense.

The relationship model, which Margaret kept banging on about, literally drove me mad. 'What relationship?' I asked, week in, week out. I knew nothing about her. There was no dialogue. She refused to answer a question. How, then, could we have a relationship? This impersonal approach, in the analytic tradition, supposedly allows the therapist to gauge and address your emotional responses. The relationship model simply means that the therapist extrapolates from the 'relationship in the room' (the way in which you react to a therapist during a session) a direct interpretation of your conduct in the world. If my conduct in that room bore any relation to my conduct in the world, Margaret should have assumed that I was a madwoman, given to shouting at blameless strangers.

'What relationship?' I kept asking. 'We don't have a relationship. I know nothing about you. You know everything about me. The balance of power is completely unequal. How can that possibly be the basis for a relationship?'

'Does it upset you,' she said, 'when you get angry with me?'

'No. That's what I pay you for. Does it upset you when I get angry with you?'

She did not answer me.

What little I knew of her, and most was gathered through body language, mannerisms, dress and all the other silent methods of communication, made me believe that we had absolutely nothing in common, other than my illness. Almost nothing she said interested me, or pulled me up short enough to make me think she might have a better take on life. Had I met her in the outside world, in the relationship outside the room, I would have had absolutely nothing to say to her.

I continued with it because I believed it would make me better. I believed she had a particular training in the conditions of the mind, and I did not. I carried on because I did not know what else to do.

It was only later that I understood that it did not have to feel so alien or so cold and that a therapist is simply another expert who we consult when we are ill. And who, just like any other expert, if we are not happy with the results, we leave. As a depressive, I am not interested in either sympathy or theory. I am only interested in getting better. And that, as far as I am concerned, should be the one and only golden rule. If you do not like a therapist, if you are not getting results, then leave. Go and find another.

I know that this, for somebody in the throes of severe depression, seems intolerably difficult, but I cannot urge you enough to try or ask friends or family to help you. The best therapists usually come by personal recommendation so it's worth asking anyone you can think of. This, of course, requires you to be open about your illness, but there is no shame in trying to make yourself well. If you were searching for any other sort of specialist, it would be natural to ask around. Why should therapy be any different? Keep trying until you find somebody who you are comfortable with and who, after a session, allows you at least a brief moment of respite.

I felt no respite.

One day, without intending to, I stopped therapy.

I had been in the room for only a few minutes.

'How are you feeling?' Margaret asked.

'Terrible.'

'Why do you think that is?'

I told her that my period was due, so I was hormonal, irritable and physically tired. I had also stopped drinking having become aware that my alcohol consumption was reaching danger levels. I was detoxing, or going through alcohol withdrawal, and, given the amounts I had been drinking, I was feeling very bad.

'But what's underneath all that?' she said.

'There's nothing underneath it,' I said irritably. 'I've just told you that I'm hormonal and detoxing. I feel like shit. That's all.'

'But what's underneath it?' she asked again.

At first, I thought she was joking. And then I realised that she was serious. According to her training in psychoanalysis, nothing could, or should, be accepted at face or even reasonable value. And I knew that I couldn't stay in that room a moment longer. That, if I was mad, ignoring two perfectly rational physiological reasons was madder still. And so I got up and said, 'I'm sorry, I can't do this any longer.' And I walked out of the room.

Her voice followed me down the stairs. 'Sally? Sally!? Where are you going?'

I didn't reply. I just kept walking. I felt free, in control, for the first time since I had become depressed.

She called me later. 'What was all that about?'

I couldn't be bothered to give excuses so I said what I knew to be true. 'I hate it. I don't want to do it a minute longer.'

'Then don't,' she said.

I abandoned therapy for a year after that. Not only did I abandon it, I was hostile to the very idea of it. I loathed it, thought it was the preserve of middle-aged, middle-class, middle-brow do-gooders, most of whom had been through a personal crisis of their own which, with a little training, became a qualification for fixing other people's pain.

I still believe that some of that is true. Anyone can set up as a therapist and, often, anyone does. Therapy should be far

more widely regulated. Its lack of regulation is both dangerous and symptomatic of the myopia we, as a society, have
around mental illness. We know so little about the workings
of the mind that we assume that anybody who has studied it,
however passingly, has all the answers. This is simply not so.

Good therapy is about connection – helping somebody to
connect back into life. That's a rare enough commodity in the
human race so there's absolutely no reason why we should
believe that therapists have the monopoly on it. A great
therapist is both a great teacher and a healer – someone with
wisdom and perspective. They also need to be a great role
model. In order to trust them and to learn, you have to want
at least some of what they have. A course in therapy doesn't
give someone that. Life does, or a great gene pool. Who
knows?

What most of us do know is that we sense when it is not
present. Unfortunately, confused as we are about therapy and
the mystery in which it is shrouded, we ignore those very
instincts.

It is something I still regret. The failure of my initial
attempts at therapy drove me even deeper into depression.
I thought that I was beyond help and beyond hope, that I was
incurable. At the same time, I was struggling with my medication, which seemed to have no discernible effect on the
blackness in my head but, instead, made me so physically ill
that I could scarcely function.

I finally found a therapist, Elizabeth, who gave me enough
strength and hope to believe that there was life after depression and that, one day, I might experience happiness again.
She turned up at a retreat, in the depths of the country, where
I had gone in a desperate effort to soothe my still violent
depression with meditation, acupuncture and yoga. With
everything and anything except therapy. When we met I
was belligerent and hostile to all and every form of it.

The first thing she did was to make me laugh. She talked
back. She was irreverent, cynical, funny, warm and, above all,

human. She did not practise psychoanalytical therapy, but a combination of different forms including person-centred therapy, transactional analysis and relationship therapy. Many therapists train in more than one form of therapy, slowly adding to their knowledge of the field (which is constantly changing) over the years.

Now that I know a little more about therapy, I realise that I have no personal favourite form. I have only favourite therapists, practitioners who combine the disciplines of therapy with a wisdom and humanity that I might want to own.

Such was the case with Elizabeth. On the retreat, I discovered that she lived and worked in London. I asked if I could see her, once a week, for a two-hour session. I like my therapy in large uninterrupted chunks, although some people find that too gruelling and prefer the usual fifty-minute session. All I know is that two hours works for me.

And so I embarked on the final phase of therapy, which lasted for nearly two years. In the end, Elizabeth sacked me. 'I don't think I should take your money any more,' she said.

'Don't you like it?'

'I love it! It buys me great shoes but I think that you're emotionally healthy enough to go out there, on your own. Try it, see how it feels without a safety net. Life is for living, Sally. There's no other way of doing it.'

It is one of the marks of a great therapist, to know when to stop.

'You can always come back, if you need to.'

I did. Once.

18

Withdrawal

Hell is empty, and all the devils are here.

William Shakespeare

I left the second hospital as precipitously as I had the first, and for the same reason: lack of insurance. This time, I was in tears.

'We can't let something as stupid as money stop you from getting better,' Sarah said. 'If we find you some, do you want to stay?'

'No, because I'll have to pay it back later and I can't work. And if I can't work, how can I pay it back? Then I'll spend the whole time worrying about it and trying to work and beating myself up because I can't even read at the moment, let alone write. I can't make sense of the patterns on the page.'

'You don't have to pay us back.'

'I do. I could never be happy until I did. You know I hate feeling beholden to anyone.'

Sarah laughed ruefully. 'Yes.'

'But thank you.'

There was a silence. 'What are you going to do?'

'I'll go home.'

'I don't think you should be by yourself at the moment. Come and stay with us.'

'No, but thank you. I'd rather be at home. It's the only place I feel safe.'

'Will you be all right?'

'I'll be fine.'

A long sigh. 'OK. But call me.'

'Yes, of course.'

I was not fine. I was, if anything, worse. But I had people now, who understood. The only time I left my flat was to see my therapist or my psychiatrist or if Kate or Andy or Susie or Nigel, all of whom left hospital soon after I did, dragged me out. The medication I was taking was so strong it made me shake constantly, but when you're among friends who are also shaking from their medication, it comes to seem almost normal.

'Oh, that,' Nigel said, as I spilled my drink. 'That's nothing. I have to lower my head to my glass and lap it up, like a dog.'

We were in a bar, somewhere in the East End of London. Me, Nigel, Andy, Susie and Kate. It was our first, and only, night out.

It was so dark, none of us could see.

'Fuck,' Kate said, tripping over a stool. 'I haven't got my glasses on.'

'Where's Susie?'

'I think she got lost on the way back from the loo.'

'Oh, well,' somebody said.

'She'll turn up,' said somebody else.

'I couldn't get out of the loo,' Susie said, when eventually she turned up. 'The door didn't make any sense. And the loo kept flushing, all by itself. Nearly gave me a fucking heart attack.'

Nigel laughed. 'Poor you. Just the thing for panic disorder.'

The music was so loud that none of us could hear each other, and we all got headaches, so quite soon we had to go home.

My feet hurt so much from wearing high heels for the first time in months that I had to take off my shoes and walk barefoot through the dark, frozen streets. 'At least you're not wearing flip-flops,' Nigel said.

We had a party, The Loonies Work Christmas Party, as it was known. None of us was working, because none of us could. Nigel and Andy both owned their own companies ('or what's left of them,' as Nigel said), and the others were on sick leave. Jonathan and I had sold the family house, so I had enough money put away to live off, if I was careful.

'Everyone else has a work party,' Kate said. 'So why shouldn't we? We're working hard at not being mad.'

I cooked chicken, with all the trimmings. I delved into my fashion past, and my wardrobe, and produced a black Jasper Conran jersey top, a black Betty Jackson satin skirt and Helmut Lang leather boots. There, I thought, I've got dressed. I'm normal. Then I went and spoiled it all by putting on so much mascara that my eyes stuck together from the heat of the oven and the potatoes were burned beyond repair. Nigel told me my eyes looked like demented spiders.

Susie turned up three hours late, because she'd got lost. I kept her lunch warm, in the oven.

'Lovely,' she said, eyeing the plate of sticky, congealed food and lighting a cigarette. We all got completely drunk, even Kate who didn't normally drink and Susie, who only seemed to be drinking tea. There were presents, of course. Nigel gave me a book, a 1950s hardback edition of Angela Brazil's *The Naughtiest Girl In School*.

Kate had a row with Andy, Susie kept shouting at herself for being such a loser and getting lost on the Tube and I had a row with Nigel because, as I said, he was always laughing at me.

'He laughs at everybody,' Kate pointed out.

'You should watch that,' Andy said. 'Humour is denial.'

'Oh, fuck off,' everyone chorused and Susie fell asleep, curled around Bert the cat.

We all agreed that it had been a very good Christmas party.

*   *   *

Tom came, and Tom went. He was living in a rented flat, which he hated, but it was all he could afford. It was next to a railway line and square, like a box, with three tiny bedrooms. He was fighting for the right to see his children. It took all of his money, and most of his sanity.

'When I was twenty,' he said, 'I owned my own house. I seem to be doing life the wrong way around.'

'We both do,' I said, thinking of the first days of our affair and the pubs and street corners, where we had kissed and fumbled like teenagers. I missed them. Now, I just felt old.

We kept our relationship a secret, because of his children. Or, he kept it a secret and so, by default, did I. When he was with them, he wouldn't answer the phone or speak to me. It was as if I didn't exist, which only added to my already pronounced sense of unreality. We never discussed his refusal to acknowledge our relationship, or the kids, or his situation or mine, or the future.

'I can't see a future,' he said. 'My position is completely precarious. What is there to discuss?'

'We could make a plan.'

'The kids are in pieces.'

We couldn't make a plan.

He always came to see me at my flat. We always went straight to bed. We were as passionate about each other as we had been when we first met. We lived in separate bubbles; our time together, our lives apart.

After a while, I began to feel like a hooker.

'We should go out sometimes,' I said, knowing why we didn't. If we went out, we would have to acknowledge reality. 'We always stay in.'

'I like it here.' He put his arms around me. 'We have everything we need.'

Everything, except the truth. It drove me mad.

The shaking grew worse. It started, every morning, an hour after I took my medication, Venlafaxine, also known by the brand name of Effexor. Prescribed dosages are typically in the range of 75–225 mgs per day, but higher dosages are some-times used for the treatment of severe or treatment-resistant depression. I was taking 300 mgs and felt so physically ill that some days, I could not leave my flat. My vision was blurred so I found it hard to judge distances. I also shook so badly that crossing a road became an act of fierce concentration as I tried to factor in how far away a car was with how fast I could walk, shakily, to the pavement on the far side. It seemed to take an eternity and my heart pounded so badly, I was sure that it would leap out of my chest.

I stopped drinking, again. Alcohol made the shaking worse and I was determined to at least try to give the medication a chance. Going to see my psychiatrist or my therapist, who both worked out of the same building a short Tube ride away, took all of my energy. The Tube station, which also served as a mainline national train station, was filled with people who shoved past me as I stood, stock-still and shaking, willing myself to take another step. The escalator, one of the deepest in London, seemed to drop like a precipice beneath my feet. I clung on to the handrail, dizzy with vertigo, convinced that I would fall, as people clattered past me down the sharp, corrugated metal steps. There was a time when I used to run down those steps, two at a time, or casually push past tourists. It seemed to me then that it belonged to another life, another Sally.

'I think I'm being poisoned,' I said to my psychiatrist. 'My body can't handle these drugs. I shake all the time. I get dizzy. I can't see properly. Sometimes, it's so bad I think I'm going to go into convulsions.'

My psychiatrist frowned. 'Venlafaxine is the best antide-pressant for resistant depression. We've tried three others and none of them seemed to agree with you.'

'I hate it. Perhaps I should stop taking it.'

'I'm concerned that you may experience a drop in mood.'

'I'm not sure that I could go any lower.'

'It's not advisable.'

I had grown to hate my psychiatrist. Or, 'that cunt' as Nigel pointed out he had come to be known. I swore a lot when I was very ill. I have no idea why. Anger was a strong and constant feature of my depression. I was, literally, in a bad mood. I felt my psychiatrist never listened to me, that he pumped me full of drugs according to whatever new research he had read. I felt like I was a guinea pig, not a human being. He had a habit too, of answering his phone when he was with another patient. 'This will have to be brief, I'm with somebody,' is what he always said.

Finally, I could stand it no longer. 'If you're with somebody, why are you answering the phone?'

Long pause. 'I'm a busy man.'

Yes, busy pissing off two depressives, instead of just one.

My psychiatrist was speaking. 'If we try another SSRI, it means you have to withdraw from the present one, and wait while the new one takes effect, which is usually anything up to six weeks. Do you think you can handle that?'

I buried my face in my hands. 'No.'

'How about ECT. Have you thought about that any more?'

'No and no.'

I was still not sleeping, at least not past four hours a night. I had not had a full night's sleep for nearly two years.

'Let's try you on rohypnol, which is also known as the date rape drug. Be careful. It's very strong. It can also be associated with short-term memory loss, if used in combination with alcohol.'

I remember being excited, the first night I took the drug. I thought, if I can sleep, perhaps my mind will get back into order.

It kept me awake.

I felt worse. The treatment seemed more violent than the illness.

My hands shook so badly, I could barely hold a pen. For a week, I practised writing a signature, but could manage nothing that looked even vaguely like my own. I had bills I needed to pay, cheques I had to write.

I called Jonathan. 'I need your help.'

'What's happened?'

'I can't pay my bills.'

'I'll lend you some money.'

'No, I have money but I can't write a cheque. My hands shake too much. Can you come over and pay my bills for me?'

'Sure,' he said, sounding baffled.

'Oh dear,' he said, when he arrived. I was deathly pale and my teeth were chattering uncontrollably. I was in my dressing gown but kept my arms wrapped tightly around myself to stop the shaking. If it got too bad, I fell over. I didn't want anybody to see that. 'What's wrong with you?'

'I think it's the drugs.'

'Perhaps you should change them.'

'There's nothing left to change them to.'

'There must be.'

'There isn't.' I was too tired to explain the intricacies of psychopharmacology. Besides, if you haven't been there yourself, it is impossible to understand.

'There must be,' he said again.

'If you could pay all these,' I said, showing him the bills laid out on the table, 'and tell me how much I owe you, I'll give you a cheque. I think I can manage to sign one.'

It was after he left that despair began to set in. True despair. I sat alone in my flat, unable to control the shakiness in either my body or my mind and I thought, I can't go on like this. I can't go on.

Then I thought, I have to. I have to find out about these drugs I'm taking. I turned on my dusty computer and went on to the Internet. This is what I found.

Venlafaxine
Common side-effects
Nausea
Dizziness
Sleepiness
Insomnia
Vertigo
Dry mouth
Sexual dysfunction
Sweating
Vivid dreams
Increased blood pressure
Electric shock-like sensations
Increased anxiety towards the start of treatment

Less common to rare side-effects
Drowsiness
Allergic skin reactions
External bleeding
Serious bone marrow damage
Hepatitis
Irregular heartbeat
Increased serum cholesterol
Tardive dyskinesia
Difficulty swallowing
Psychosis
Hostility
Gas or stomach pain
Abnormal vision
Nervousness, agitation or increased anxiety
Panic attacks
Depressed feelings
Suicidal thoughts, suicidal ideation
Confusion
Neuroleptic malignant syndrome
Loss of appetite

Constipation
Tremors
Pancreatitis
Seizure
Activation of mania/hypomania.

In pre-launch drug trials, nineteen per cent of the people taking Venlafaxine gave up because they could not tolerate the side-effects.

I stopped taking the pills. This is the worst possible thing you can do although I did not understand, until I did it, quite how bad it could be. You should discontinue any antidepressant slowly, a fraction at a time. Every box of SSRIs carries a warning. Every medical textbook tells you so. Every psychiatrist will advise you never to stop abruptly. So will I.

Don't do it.

At the time, I was in no mood to listen.

I called my psychiatrist. He said, 'It'll have to be brief. I'm with somebody.'

'I want to stop my medication. I intend to stop, as of tomorrow morning, which means I took my last dose this morning.'

'It is severely contraindicated.'

I said, 'I've already told you that I feel poisoned. I hate them. I'm shaking so much I'm starting to convulse.'

'Come and see me and we'll talk about it.'

'I don't want to take another pill. I think that if I take another pill, I'll die.'

'That's very unlikely but if you stop abruptly, you may go into discontinuation syndrome. You could have a relapse.'

'A relapse?'

'Of mood.'

I laughed.

He sighed. 'If you really want to stop taking them, cut down to 200 milligrams from the 300 you're on. But no more than that. That's far more than you should. And let me know how you get on.'

'OK.'

The next morning, I went cold turkey. I knew that I might face a worsening of depression. I had no idea that I would have to face an extreme physical withdrawal. I had been told that SSRIs are not addictive. That, as I discovered, is quite wrong. Any drug that creates a dependency is addictive. Any medicine that creates withdrawal that extreme should be classified as a class A drug.

Hell is too kind a word.

I'll leave the description to the Internet which is these days filled with postings about the terrifying consequences of coming off antidepressants. Here is the most lucid, from Wikipedia, and, interestingly, the emphases are not my own. Sadly, it was not available when I discontinued the drug. If it had been, I might have felt a little better, knowing that I was not alone. As it was, I simply felt that I was becoming even madder.

Venlafaxine, also known as Effexor, may cause potentially severe withdrawal symptoms upon sudden discontinuation (the recommended discontinuation is a drop of 37.5 mgs per week; sudden stops are usually advised only in emergencies). These have a tendency to be significantly stronger than the withdrawal effects of other antidepressants but are similar in nature to those of SSRIs such as Paxil or Seroxat. Discontinuation effects may include *irritability, hostility, headache, nausea, fatigue, dysphoria and the fairly unique 'brain-shivers'*. Symptoms may include a feeling of spinning, similar to drunken 'bed spins'; patients may experience spinning in two different directions, often felt between the area of the head above the nose and below the nose. This feeling of spinning is associated with severe nausea and disorientation. Rarer withdrawal symptoms include *shaking legs, tremor, vertigo, dizziness and par-*

esthesia. Other non-specific mental symptoms may include *impaired concentration, bizarre dreams, agitation and suicidal thoughts.* Missing even a single dose can also induce discontinuation effects in some patients including minor *psychosis.*

Antidepressant withdrawal effects do not indicate addiction, but are rather the results of the brain attempting to reach neurochemical stability after an abrupt change. These can be minimised or avoided by tapering off of the medication over a period of weeks.

The distinction between 'withdrawal' effects and addiction may be nothing less than semantics to make a distinction between a prescribed antidepressant and illicit drugs, as addicts also suffer withdrawal effects when trying to stop taking an illicit drug. This is in the vein of the use of the term 'self-medicating' to feel good as a euphemism for addiction.

Studies by Wyeth, the manufacturers of Venlafaxine, and others have reported occasional cases of withdrawal symptoms severe enough to require permanent use. In some of these cases, successful discontinuation was eventually achieved by the addition of fluoxetine (Prozac), which was later discontinued itself without difficulty. It is important for patients to be aware of these risks so their choice to take this drug is balanced against the severity of potential side-effects. A petition to Wyeth, signed by more than 11,000 patients as of June 2006, argues that disclosure regarding the side-effects and efficacy is neither full nor accurate and asks Wyeth to improve the Effexor documentation for patients and medical professionals.

A week later, I went to see my psychiatrist.
'How are you?'
My back felt like it had been broken. Electric shocks were running across my face. Every time I heard a loud noise, my body jumped in sympathetic response, as if the startle reflex

was wrongly wired. My head, arms and legs hurt. My vision went in and out of focus so walking had become a serious problem. I had terrifying nightmares, when or if I finally fell asleep. I shook all over. I could not eat, because of the extreme nausea. I was hostile, paranoid and very, very angry.

'Terrible,' I said. 'I stopped the medication.'

He looked, momentarily, horrified. 'All of it?'

'Yes, even the sleeping pills.'

'That was most unwise. Then I should think you are feeling ill.'

'You never listen. I told you how I was feeling on Venlafaxine. I told you I felt I was being poisoned. I told you I was shaking uncontrollably. And all you did was precisely nothing.'

'I didn't tell you to stop taking your medication. I told you it was a very bad idea and to reduce it, if you must. Venlafaxine is an excellent drug. People tolerate it very well. It's helped millions of people, including patients of mine.'

I handed him a thick pile of paper, articles printed off the Internet about the adverse reactions that people suffer with Venlafaxine. It is a journalist's most tiresome habit. All medical practitioners hate it.

'This is for you. It's about the people who don't tolerate it, who it doesn't help.'

He put the papers to one side without looking at them.

That gesture infuriated me. It had taken all my strength to research the drug and why, perhaps, I was feeling the way that I did, and he simply ignored my efforts. 'You're supposed to be a doctor and listen to your patients. Instead, you behave like the patronising male scientist confronted by the hopelessly deluded madwoman. I have been telling you the truth, my truth, and you can't even listen.'

'You're being irrational, Sally.'

'Don't fucking tell me what I'm being. What's rational about a psychiatrist who can't listen? A psychiatrist who answers his phone when he's with a patient? What if I was suicidal? What if the patient you were with was suicidal? How is that supposed to make us both feel? That you care? That you're not interested if we kill ourselves? And you're supposed to be a doctor of the head?'

My psychiatrist closed his eyes. I could see him counting slowly to ten. Or, perhaps, a hundred. He opened his eyes. 'We appear to have a breakdown in communication. Would you rather see another psychiatrist?'

'Yes.'

'In the meantime, I would like you to take a very small dose of an SSRI, to see if we can relieve the pain. You are in severe withdrawal. It might help.'

It didn't. A tiny dose of SSRI brought on such severe diarrhoea one hour after taking the pill, that I was trapped in the bathroom for three hours. I managed it for five days, and then I gave up. I called my psychiatrist.

'That sounds very unpleasant. Can you manage to come and see me? I'd like to talk to you.'

I went.

'How are you?'

'Very close to suicide.'

'I'm sorry.'

I shrugged, 'Me too. And I'm sorry I shouted. I was unforgivably rude but I was, in non-psychiatric parlance, beside myself.'

'I meant that I was sorry that I didn't listen to you. You're right. I believe you were at grade A toxicity.'

'Being poisoned, you mean?'

'If you like, although we would not phrase it in that way.' He went on. 'I've recently set up a new practice. I've taken too much on. After our . . .' he hesitated, 'conversation, I've halved my workload so I have more time for my patients. And I called another psychiatrist, to see if she could take you on. Unfortunately, her books are filled but I could try somebody else if you like. In the meantime, because I really think you need to be under proper care, would you like to go on seeing me?'

I looked at his mobile, which was lying on the desk.

'Is your mobile switched off?'

He smiled. 'Yes.'

'I really don't want another psychiatrist. I just want to get better.'

'I know.'

I switched to another drug, Amitriptyline, part of the older family of antidepressants known as tricyclics. Some people find them hard to tolerate. So did I, but they were better than Venlafaxine. The side-effects are unpleasant and include dizziness, blurred vision, shortness of breath, severe constipation, weight gain and all the usual pleasantries of psychopharmacological drugs. They are also fairly sedating, which helped with the insomnia and, at the right dose, are analgesic, which helped with the pain from SSRI discontinuation syndrome from which I suffered, very badly, for another three months and less badly for a year.

Every twenty minutes, I would have to lie on the floor for five minutes, to stop the world spinning around or jerking, abruptly, out of focus, and to try to control the pain. My back still felt as if it was broken, and I suffered from intense flu-like aches in my arms and legs. As I stared up at the ceiling, I wondered how my life could have collapsed into such utter disintegration.

I am a believer in alternative medicine, particularly since conventional medicine had done so little to help me, so I took myself off to see an acupuncturist, who said he could help me through the withdrawal. I would arrive, my whole body twitching. It was as if my skin had been turned inside-out, leaving the nerves exposed. Any loud, or even not so loud, noise would make me jump, then I'd break out into a sweat as electrical impulses shot through my system. According to my psychiatrist (himself a believer in alternative therapies), withdrawal from the drugs had sent the sympathetic nervous system, which regulates the fight or flight mechanism, into overdrive.

'I'm just going to put a needle in your back,' the acupuncturist said. 'You may feel an odd sensation.'

My whole body lifted off the bed, electric currents shot through my arms, legs, back and head. 'What the fuck was that?' I yelled.

'That's where the drug is lodged, in the spine. It will help the body to speed up withdrawal but it's rather a severe treatment. We can't do it very often, at the most, every two weeks.'

By the time I left the acupuncturist, my body had settled. I could walk down a street without jumping out of my skin, or feeling as if I was about to faint from shock. The effects lasted for about three days but bit by little bit, the drug began to leave my system.

I was unlucky in having such a severe adverse reaction to Venlafaxine. I am unlucky in not being able to tolerate antidepressants. I use the word unlucky carefully. It is a lottery. I was one of the losers. There are winners – those in whom the drug creates an effective remission – but there are no sure or safe bets. There is no way of knowing how somebody might respond or react to a drug, before they take it. The only way of knowing is in the doing. Unfortunately, that takes time. Unfortunately, and in a spirit of grotesque irony, the side-effects of the drugs mimic the illness they are treating. Even more unfortunately, that leads psychiatrists and doctors to believe it is simply the illness reasserting itself and to dismiss the concerns of the patients they are treating. In all the law suits against drug companies with regard to suicides caused by an adverse reaction to an SSRI, the defence is always that it is the illness and not the drug that is at fault.

I know how it feels to be told that it's all in your mind.

It drives you mad.

19

The Beginning of the End

In a real dark night of the soul, it is always three
o'clock in the morning, day after day.

F. Scott Fitzgerald

New Year came. Tom and I spent it together. We were plainly, lyrically happy. And plainly, undeniably drunk.

'Will you stop disappearing,' I said. 'And can we be together now?'

He kissed me. 'Yes, I'll stop disappearing and we can be together now.'

We did not mention reality. Reality, on that New Year's Eve, seemed like another country.

I decided that I would be better. I would leave depression in the old year, where it belonged. I put my flat on the market. It was beautiful but to me it felt like a prison, a place I had come to hate. Depression had seeped into its walls like a chill, grey mist. When I put my hand to the surfaces, they felt damp. Nobody else could feel it. But I could.

The first person who came to see the flat put in an offer. I accepted.

A friend, Lulu, called.

'How are you?'

'I'm fine.'

She sounded amused. 'Fine as in the weather? How are you really?'

I laughed, taken aback.

She said, 'I heard you hadn't been well. I wondered if there was anything I could do to help.'

'That's kind of you but I'm—. Well, I'm trying to get my life back on track.'

'It's hard, isn't it?'

Something in her voice, a note of complete understanding, pulled me up short. We had known each other for years, although not terribly well. Our kids were friends so our relationship had always revolved around them. I knew, though, that she had battled depression and recalled, distantly, that she had once had a problem with alcohol.

'Yes. I think I may—. I don't know why I'm telling you this, but I think I may have a problem with alcohol.'

Her voice did not skip a beat. 'Let's have lunch.'

Before I left the flat to meet her, I drank a bottle of wine to give me the courage to say what I knew to be true but that I found hard to admit, even to myself. 'I have a problem with alcohol.'

She looked lovely, in a flowered dress of silk crêpe de Chine and a turquoise cashmere cardigan. Her cheeks were pink, her mouth painted a perfect red. As I bent to kiss her, she smelled of roses and clean, fresh air. Her eyes were clear and sparkling. I couldn't believe she knew how I felt. I couldn't believe she'd ever had a drink, let alone a problem and so I said nothing.

We chatted inconsequentially, about mutual friends, her business, our children, the property market.

Suddenly she said, 'Tell me about drinking too much.'

I shrugged. 'I drink too much, end of story.'

'Shall I tell you about my drinking? Would that help?'

'If you like.' I was awkward, unused to somebody being so open about drinking. I kept mine a secret, even from my closest friends. I liked to drink alone. That way, I could drink as much as I liked. That way, I was the only witness to my shame. And I was ashamed. Alcohol does that to you.

Lulu said, 'Every night, I promised myself that I wouldn't drink the next day and every morning, when I woke up, I promised myself that I wouldn't drink that day. As I left the house to go to work, I promised myself, again, that I wouldn't drink that day. As I stepped into the off-licence, I pretended that two miniature bottles of vodka didn't really count as a drink. If I drank them on my way to work, it would level me out sufficiently to get through the morning. Any more, and I'd be a wreck. Once I had drunk them, I swore that I'd never drink again.'

I said nothing. Those promises were familiar territory. I had made them myself, countless times.

'I'd get through the rest of the day somehow, but my mind was always fixed on alcohol. Perhaps if I just had one drink, after that I could stop completely. Just one couldn't hurt, could it? Then I would decide that, no, I would be good. I would go home, have a bath, make myself something nice to eat and have an early night so I'd be fresh for work the next day.'

She looked at me, her eyes clear.

'I knew that was what I was going to do. But I still stopped at the off-licence and bought myself a bottle of wine and got straight into bed without washing or eating and I drank until I passed out.' She grimaced at the memory. 'I don't even like the taste of alcohol.'

Nor did I. In fact, I'd come to hate it. But I loved the effect, the way it stopped the pain, stopped me feeling.

She said, as if reading my mind, 'I drank to change the way that I feel.'

I wanted, right then, to change the way that I felt, or how she was making me feel. Even thinking about it made me want a drink. What could be the harm in having one drink, to make me feel better? Perhaps she didn't know what she was talking about. After all, it wasn't as if she had been drinking that much. I knew people who drank far more and they didn't think they had a problem. 'It doesn't sound too much, a bottle of wine and two miniatures a day.'

'It's not how much you drink. It's how you drink. And why.'

'I only drink because of the depression. If it wasn't there, I wouldn't drink,' I laughed nervously. 'Or I wouldn't drink so much.'

'I know. I'm a depressive. Manic, actually. Bipolar. It gives you a real thirst.'

I laughed.

'Seriously, though, a drink doesn't make it better. It only makes it worse. How much are you drinking?'

'A bottle of wine, perhaps two a day.'

'Can you stop?'

'Yes, no,' I sighed. 'I don't know.'

I thought of my psychiatrist. 'You must stop drinking, Sally. You're not giving yourself a chance. You're taking antidepressants with one hand and a depressant with the other. You'll never get better if you keep drinking.'

I sighed. 'No. Well, I find it hard to stop. But I'm not an alcoholic.'

Lulu's smile curved. 'What's an alcoholic?'

'Someone who sleeps on a park bench? Who passes out? Who gets violent? Who can't hold down a job?'

Lulu's smile curved even higher. 'I am an alcoholic.'

I looked down at my hands.

Her voice was gentle. 'Sal, I know exactly how you feel. I tried doing it on my own too, and it doesn't work. We need help. We cannot do it on our own.'

'But you look so well, and happy.'

'I go to AA. It works, I promise you. Why don't you come to a meeting and see what you think? I'll look after you. It's not scary. It's only the thought of it that's scary.'

I shook my head. 'I don't know. Maybe I can stop on my own. I've done it before.'

Lulu got up and hugged me. 'We've all done it before. We've done it so many times we're sick and tired of feeling sick and tired. We all think we can do it on our own. It's just that we don't have to. We don't have to be alone.'

I nodded. For some reason, I wanted to cry. 'OK.'

'I have to go now. Call me,' she said, and I watched her walk up the road, her flowered silk skirt swinging.

I bought a bottle of wine on the way home. I drank it and then I went out and bought another. I drank that until I stopped feeling anything at all.

Tom started to disappear again. I felt him slipping further and further away from me. I wanted him back, wanted the intimacy we used to share so easily. I felt as if we were standing on either side of a huge chasm, both unhappy, both unable to reach the other. I started to blame him for destroying the thing that we had. It never occurred to me to blame myself. I was the one reaching out. He was the one who was refusing to take my hand.

He sent me an email.

Darling,

I find myself slipping into old patterns of behaviour that I know have upset and confused you in the past. My solution, to withdraw and regroup, just exacerbates things but I don't know what else to do sometimes.

The source of it all is my anger with myself, I suppose, which makes it hard for me to accept or return affection. I'm sorry.

xxx

I started to drink a little harder. My loneliness grew, until it seemed unbearable. I was never going to get out of this place, was never going to be able to connect. Everything was in pieces, and I could see no way out.

The person who had put in an offer on the flat wanted to move very fast. Could we complete in four weeks?

'He's fallen in love with it. He says it's perfect.'

I thought of the damp walls, running with tears. But they were my walls and my tears.

'I don't have anywhere to go.'

'I'll help you look,' the estate agent said.

'OK, but it must have a garden.'

'In the meantime, can you get on to your solicitor so we can start the ball rolling?'

'Of course.' I didn't have a solicitor. Panic rose, acrid in my throat. I had to find a solicitor, and somewhere to live.

'Four weeks?' I said.

'You can always rent.'

'That means moving twice.'

'He's come in on the asking price. In the present market, it's a great deal. I'm not sure you'll get another offer like this. You might have to drop ten thousand and that's going to cover rented accommodation, and more.'

I sighed. 'OK.'

When I put down the phone, I felt very tired and very alone.

'My name's Sally, and I'm an alcoholic.'

The words stuck in my throat. Fifty people were looking at me.

'Hi Sally,' they chorused. 'Welcome.'

Lulu, who was sitting next to me, squeezed my hand. 'Well done,' she whispered.

I sank lower in my seat. 'Everyone's looking at me.'

'They always do that with a newcomer. They want to remember your face, so they can help you.'

'Oh, God.'

I was sitting in an AA meeting because I knew that my drinking was out of control. I could pretend to my friends that I did not drink too much, because I kept most of my drinking a secret by drinking alone. I could pretend to myself that a bottle or two of wine a day was not excessive. But I could no longer pretend that I could stop drinking for more than a couple of weeks. I always went back to it and that failure, together with the knowledge of what I was doing to my brain, made me feel worse than ever. The guilt and the shame were appalling and, every time I felt them, I simply wanted another drink. I was trapped in a vicious circle. So I called Lulu and asked her to take me to a meeting.

We sat in an old church hall, on moulded grey plastic seats arranged in a semicircle to face a low table. Behind that sat two people, a man and a woman. The woman was young, with long straight shiny hair and a wide smile. She wore skinny jeans and a leather jacket and a red cashmere scarf, which she kept winding and rewinding around her neck. 'It's fucking cold in here,' she said. 'Is anyone else fucking cold?' Then she clapped her hand to her mouth. 'Fuck,' she said, 'sorry. I gave up swearing last week.'

The man sitting next to her, who was wearing a black baseball cap pushed low over his eyes, patted her gently on the back. 'A day at a time,' he said, grinning.

'More like a minute,' she said. 'OK, everyone, welcome to the Monday night meeting of Alcoholics Anonymous. My name's Sarah and I'm an alcoholic.'

'Hi Sarah.'

Sarah said, 'The format of this meeting is that the speaker will share his strength, hope and experience for fifteen to twenty minutes and then there'll be hands raised for sharing until the last fifteen minutes when we'll slow the meeting down for anyone in their early days to come in and share. It was suggested to us that we sit back and relax and listen to the similarities, and not the differences. And now it gives me great pleasure to introduce our speaker, Chris.'

'My name's Chris and I'm an alcoholic.'

'Hi Chris.'

Chris leaned back in his chair and threaded his hands over his chest. 'Yeah, hi,' he said, affably. 'I have to tell you that this was not my idea. It was never my idea to end up sitting in a church hall with a bunch of drunks. It was never my idea to be a drunk. I wasn't a blackout drunk. I never went to prison or lost my job or lost my house or ended up in any of those places that alcohol took so many of us to. I was a high-class drunk, I wasn't like you.'

He grinned. 'I was special and different, or so I thought. It took me a long time to understand that a drunk is a drunk. It doesn't matter where they come from. It only matters where alcohol takes them, which is to the bottom of a bottle, staring into the abyss.'

A few people nodded, some yawned. Others had their eyes shut but I could tell, from the quality of attention, that everyone was listening.

Chris shrugged. 'I drank for a simple reason. I wanted to stop the pain. My pain was, you know, heroic. Nobody else could understand my pain. That's why I drank. I couldn't connect with other people. I looked fine on the outside, life and soul and all that, but on the inside, man I was a mess. I didn't tell anyone, I thought I could fix it myself. But I couldn't and the place it took me was where I always knew I was going to end up, on my own. In the last few years of my drinking, it was just me and a bottle. I didn't answer the phone, I didn't go out, I just sat on a sofa with the TV on and,' he shrugged, 'I drank. I was looking for the solution in a bottle and we all know what a shit answer that is. But I wouldn't be told. I thought I was better than that. I thought I was special and different because nobody could understand my pain. It was only when I got to these rooms that I understood that I wasn't special or different or that my pain wasn't special or different. It was, like . . .,' he stretched the word out for emphasis, 'normal.'

A few people laughed.

I didn't. I knew what he was talking about. They say in AA that you don't hear what you want to hear. You only hear what you need to hear. It takes you a while to understand that. It takes you a little longer to be honest enough to admit it and even longer to accept it.

'How was that?' Lulu said afterwards.

'It was – interesting.'

'Interesting good? Or interesting as in, I don't know what to say so I'm just going to say that to shut you up?'

'The latter.'

'Don't worry. It gets easier.'

'Sure.'

'What are you going to do now?'

I just wanted to get out of there, to get home and be on my own. To try to stop the pain that nobody else understood. Except they did which, somehow, made it worse. Now, I had no excuse. Now, I really wanted a drink.

'I'm going to go home and have an early night.'

'Will you be all right?'

'Sure.' I was going to have a drink. Just one glass of wine. That couldn't do any harm. Just to stop the feeling in the pit of my stomach.

She gave me a quick, scented hug. 'Of course you are.' And then she said, as if she could read my mind, 'Try not to have a drink. Remember, it's the first drink that does the damage.'

'Sure. I'll be fine.'

I turned away, but not before I caught her look of patient affection. Inwardly, I winced. She understood. 'Look after yourself,' she said.

I bought a bottle of wine on my way home and drank myself to sleep.

*   *   *

Tom said, 'I don't understand what it is you want. I can't seem to make you happy.'

'You do make me happy.'

'So why are you so unhappy?'

'I don't know. Depression, I guess. I'm lonely. You make me feel so lonely.'

He shifted away, a quick exasperated movement. 'Why? You have an interesting life. You've got hundreds of friends. I don't see what I have to do with this.'

'You keep disappearing.'

'I have stuff to do, you know? I'm up to here with it, with the kids and work and legal stuff.'

'I know. I'm sorry.'

'I don't want you to be sorry. Me being busy is not personal. It's just the way it has to be at the moment. At New Year, you said you were happy. I thought we were both happy.'

'We are happy. It's just that we seem to keep going around in circles.'

Tom sat down abruptly and buried his head in his hands. 'You always seem to want to be somewhere and I don't understand where it is you want to go. There *is* no end point. Life is a series of circles, that's all it is. We never get to a place where we can say, here it is, this is the place I am happy. The minute you get there, it's gone. That's the nature of life, to go round and round.'

I looked at his bent head. I knew that I wanted too much of him. I wanted him to take away my pain. I did not know, back then, that nobody can take away another person's pain. It is not in their power. I wanted to be rescued from myself.

I put my hand on his back. 'Yes, you're right. I'm sorry. So, would you like to go round in circles with me?'

He sighed. 'Yes.' Then he stood up and wrapped his arms around me. 'Yes, of course I would.'

'I love you.'

His arms tightened. 'I love you too.'

I couldn't find a flat. There was nowhere I wanted to live, nowhere I wanted to be. I didn't even want to be in my own skin. With every call from the estate agent, every letter from the solicitor, I felt the darkness moving in.

'I can't do this,' I said to Nigel.

'Then don't. Call the whole thing off.'

'I can't. I promised.'

'You'll make yourself ill again. I don't understand why you wanted to move house in the first place. It's the worst thing we, as depressives, can do.'

'A fresh start. A new beginning.'

Nigel laughed. 'We've only just got out of the hospital. That's enough of a new beginning. You were suicidal, remember? Right now, the most important thing is to feel safe and being in your lovely cosy flat is going to make you feel safe, not selling it and moving into some ghastly rented place. Call them. Tell them you're too ill to sell right now.'

'I'm too tired.'

'Then I'll call them.'

'No, I'll do it.'

They were not pleased. Nor was I. All my plans for a new beginning seemed to be lying in tatters at my feet. I was never going to get out of this place. I didn't mean my flat. I meant that other place. My head.

I hit Tom.

I have never hit anyone in my life, before or since. I thought I was incapable of violence.

I slapped him hard across the face, a gesture so filled with need and passion and disappointment and anger and complicated love that it shook me to my centre.

It shook him too. I could see it in his face.

We had lost each other.
'I'm going,' he said.

He sent me an email.

I'm sorry to make you unhappy but I don't have room in
my heart to give you what you want.

The pain was so bad I thought it would kill me.

20

Suicide, the Last Goodbye

An individual in despair despairs over something
. . . In despairing over something, he really despair
over himself, and now he wants to get rid of
himself. Consequently, to despair over something is
still not despair proper . . . To despair over oneself,
in despair to will to be rid of oneself – this is the
formula for all despair.

Søren Kierkegaard

The first time I tried to kill myself, it was not so much a trying for death as an abandoning of all pretence that I had, or any longer wanted, a life. I simply gathered together all the pills that were close at hand and took them. I didn't count them, didn't even look to see what they were, I just swallowed them. So, when I woke again, I wasn't too much surprised, just accepted my being alive with a kind of weary resignation.

I felt neither pleasure nor pain. In truth, I felt hardly anything at all, not fear or wonder or any sort of horror at my own actions. I simply felt that, as the taking of unscientific quantities of pills hadn't succeeded in killing me, that I might as well carry on with the grim business of being alive. I was a burden that I had to tolerate, at least until the agony of staying alive became too much to bear at which time, I thought, I would simply try a little harder to die.

I told nobody, not out of shame but because I believed that it was nobody else's business. I still believe that suicide is personal. I know this is not a popular view, just as I understand the suffering of family and friends after somebody has taken their own life. But I also know the suffering of the person who takes their own life. I know how, literally, unbearable living can become.

The second time I tried to die, a few months later, I felt something. It was relief. As I took the pills, I remember thinking, with absolute clarity, 'Thank God it's all over.' I had tried, very hard, for two years, to stay alive. I had carried on when all I wanted was to be dead. I had stayed alive for other people. I never stayed alive for myself. I cannot begin to describe the intensity of that effort.

I counted out the pills, having looked up the number required for a fatal overdose on the Internet. I trebled the dose and, almost as an afterthought, added my usual, nightly sleeping pills, just to be sure I would sleep. I remember thinking, even as I took my sleeping pills, that it was surely madness to take pills to make me sleep when I had just taken pills to make me die.

I smiled at my own foolishness, as I swallowed the pills. I smiled, thinking that at last, I was going to be free.

When I woke up, I did feel horror; not a moral horror that I had tried to kill myself but an irritable horror at my body for letting me down by insisting on staying alive. I also felt panic, as I appeared to be paralysed from the waist down. The panic was not so much that I was terrified I would be paralysed, although that was surely bad enough, but panic at the thought that now I would be unable to prevent anyone from locking me up. I would be unable to get more pills to do the job properly. Then there was panic at the thought of having to explain myself to all the people who would no doubt line up in front of my paralysed self and want to tell me all the good reasons why I should stay alive.

And then there was my daughter. I had sunk so low that I could not even stay alive for my dearest, darling, beloved Molly. I know the accusations of selfishness. I aim them at myself, often. I find it very hard to forgive myself. But forgive, I had to, if I was to find any sort of peace.

It was Molly herself who brought me that. When she was twelve, we were watching the film, *About a Boy*, in which the heavily depressed mother is carted off to hospital following a suicide attempt.

'What's wrong with her?' Molly said.

'She's suffering from depression.'

'Like you were?' she said.

'Yes.'

'Did you try and kill yourself?'

Now, I could have lied or I could have told the truth. I am not entirely comfortable inhabiting the no-man's land known as a white lie. The truth seems preferable in any situation and, in particular, with my daughter who, generous and pragmatic creature that she is, finds dishonesty baffling. Also, my suicide attempt is a matter of public record as I wrote about it in a national newspaper and, while Molly hadn't read it, I knew that one day, she might. At the time, I had not even thought about writing this book, so it was not a consideration. I have always attempted to describe to her, within the language acceptable to a child, the nature of depressive illness and suicide is part of that nature. So I said that, yes, I had.

'Well, I'm glad you didn't,' she said, scooted over and gave me a kiss, then went back to watching the movie.

A few months later, we were sitting in my bed one morning, having a cup of tea and a chat, as we like to do. Molly suddenly said, 'Promise me that you won't try and kill yourself again.'

I looked at her. 'I can't promise that because if I do promise and break my promise, I'll let you down twice. Besides, suicide is part of depression and I'm not depressed now but I can't promise that I won't get depressed again. It's the nature of the illness that it can sometimes come back.'

She thought about this for a while. 'OK,' she said. 'Then promise me you'll try.'

I did. I promised her that I would try very, very hard; so a large part of my bid to stay well is in order never to have to break a promise to my daughter.

Molly was not with me when I took those pills. She was with her father. Even in my blackest moment, I had that much sense. I also had the sense to know that nobody would find me for three days. In that way I could have been said to have planned my death, but in no other. I left no note, put none of my affairs in order. I did, though, tidy the flat and do the washing up. I don't know why except that I have never liked other people having to clear up my mess. It didn't occur to me that I was the mess that other people would have to clear up.

I woke at three twenty, my insomnia hour; my waking nightmare. I was desperate for a pee. I swung my legs out of bed. They collapsed under me. I hit the ground hard.

'What's happened to my legs?' I said, out loud. There was nobody there to answer.

'What's happened?'

And then I remembered. The pills. How many did I take? How much vodka did I drink?

I tried to crawl but my knees buckled under me. My legs would not work. I wanted to pee so badly I thought I would bust but there was no way I was going to piss on my own bedroom floor. I lifted myself on to my elbows and crawled down the corridor. It took hours, or so it seemed to me.

As I dragged my paralysed body down that corridor I thought, I have handled this badly, with consummate lack of grace. Just like I've handled everything else.

I hated myself.

I wasn't dead.

Fuck.

I didn't call the emergency services. I was too humiliated. I was humiliated and ashamed, both of the impulse and by the result. I wanted to go on the Internet, to check the drug profile and see what the chances of paralysis were, but I did not have the strength.

How much vodka had I drunk? I could not remember. I dragged myself to the kitchen and pulled the bottle from the fridge. There was, at most, one glass missing.

Was that good or was that bad? If I had drunk the whole bottle, would I now be dead?

Perhaps.

I took the bottle and dragged myself back to bed, crying in despair and frustration. I drank straight from the bottle and then passed out.

My dreams were filled with my child, her mute reproachful face.

How could I have done it? How could I have let her down so?

How could I be such a bad mother?

How could I still be alive?

How could I not be dead?

How could I go on?

How could I?

How could you, Sally? How fucking could you?

I moved in and out of consciousness. Awake or asleep, Molly stayed with me. She would not let me go.

A little later, I tried to get out of bed again to get a drink of water. My legs collapsed under me.

I thought, you are an unfit mother.

Ha ha.

I thought, Nigel would have laughed. He did laugh, when I told him. He did not scold, or turn his head away in fear or disgust. He laughed and then he hugged me. In microcosm it's that old saying, if you don't laugh, you cry. In hospital, when we met, we did both – it's just we rarely inhabited the place between. Suicide is not funny, of course. But making jokes about it is our way of taking the horror out of something that is very close to us and which, ordinarily, we are not allowed to talk about, let alone make light of.

He came and got me, sat me in his kitchen and cooked me food I could not eat, then put me to bed in his spare room. He put an ashtray by the bed for the cigarettes I smoked through the interminable nights.

Nigel smoked at night too. 'It's *marvellous*, like smoking behind the bike shed for grown-ups. We can call out to each other when we feel bored.'

'I really must give up smoking,' I sighed.

He laughed. 'Yes, you wouldn't want to cut your life short.'

He didn't hide my pills. In fact, he collected the rest of them from the table beside my bed. I felt humiliated enough already, without being treated like a child as well. He knew exactly how I felt. He knew that if I was going to die, I would do it; without his help or his hindrance.

The next day, I went home.

'Stay,' he said. 'It's probably better if you're not alone, at least for the next few days. Or maybe it's better if I'm not alone.'

He's a depressive. He prefers to be on his own. I knew he was being kind.

The only other person I told, other than Sarah, of course, was my therapist, Margaret who I was still seeing at the time, and only because I felt that I should.

She was outraged. 'I can't believe you sat here for an hour without telling me. And then, just as you're walking out of the door, you drop it into the conversation as casually as if you're talking about the weather.'

I didn't tell her because I loathed the fuss I knew she'd make. The demands, the questions, the explanations.

'It's over,' I said. 'And I'm still here. There's nothing more to say.'

'I think we should talk about it.'

'No,' I said. 'No.'

What more was there to say? I wanted to die. I'd told her that often enough. And now I had tried to die, and it hadn't worked.

'We must try to contain you,' she said.

I laughed. A woman in a purple smock was going to try to contain me. How absurd. Her belief in the method, her earnestness was touching. Or it would have been, if I had cared enough to feel touched. A failed suicide attempt is dangerous. It destroys inhibitions, cuts through the guidelines that keep us tethered to behaviour, to sanity, to life. What certainty could she offer me that was bigger than death? What *containment*?

Margaret immediately called my psychiatrist, who called me. 'I understand that you're not feeling very happy.'

'No,' I said.

'What did you take?'

I told him.

'Yes, they're highly sedative. I expect you're feeling very tired. Are you sleeping a lot?'

'I was, in the first few days.'

'It might be a good idea if you came to see me. I thought your mood might crash, when you came off the medication.'

'It wasn't coming off the medication,' I said. 'It was the failure of the medication, or any other medication to bring me back to myself. I am not myself. I will never be myself again. That's the despair.'

He was silent for a moment. I knew his head was busy, considering different medications. I was a problem that needed to be solved, a chemical imbalance that needed to be put right. 'Perhaps we can sort something out that will suit you better.'

Like a new head?

'OK,' I said.

That's why I like psychiatrists. No despair too great, no madness too impenetrable. Later, I realised he had never asked me why I had tried to kill myself.

He understood why.

I was grateful for that.

Killing oneself is, anyway, a misnomer. We don't kill ourselves. We are simply defeated by the long, hard struggle to stay alive. When somebody dies after a long illness, people are apt to say, with a note of approval, 'He fought so hard.' And they are inclined to think, about a suicide, that no fight was involved, that somebody simply gave up. This is quite wrong.

There is a theory, among the psychiatric profession, that people tend to commit suicide when they are getting better, when the acute phase of depression has passed. It is then that they have sufficient energy to take action. I don't know about that. It's not my experience but I spent very little time in the acute catatonic phase. My depression was furiously active, filled with black, loathsome despair and continued for so long that, by the time I did try to kill myself, it was because I had lost all hope of ever pulling out of it.

One day, when I was feeling particularly hopeless, Margaret said to me that I would get better.

'I know it doesn't seem possible now,' she said, 'but you will come through.'

I was sick and tired of people telling me that I would get better, when there was absolutely no evidence to prove it.

'How do you know that?' I said. 'How can you presume to tell me my reality? Your feelings are not my feelings. I have seen nothing that shows me I will get better.'

And it was true. For two years I had seen nothing, no chink of light, no sense of possibility that I would ever be well again. I was not interested in the future, I was interested (if that's a word that could possibly be applied to my furious, nihilistic despair) in the present, in the unendurable pain I felt, which was a pain that seemed to me then to be endless.

I thought at the time, and I think it still, that promising a depressive that they will get well is like telling somebody who has just broken their ankle that it will heal in three or six or nine months' time – but being able to offer them very little to relieve their present agony. In cases of severe depression, it's like giving an aspirin for a broken leg. Except that, and here's the really crucial difference, we know the given time scale within which bones heal. We know why and we know how. Nobody knows how depression heals. We don't know why and we don't know how.

But it does.

I say that at the risk of infuriating any depressive reading this book, just as Margaret infuriated me. I know how you feel. I know, terribly, how you feel. There are no time limits and there are no guarantees, but if you can just hold on through the worst of the pain, its quality will change.

Not all at once, but slowly, you will catch glimpses of the self you used to know and the life you used to have. It is important, though, to try to believe in life even at a time when belief seems impossible, even, when death seems preferable. It is important, too, to accept that severe depression is an illness of body as well as mind and that both have a profound capacity for healing. I can say that because I know, because I've been there. My irritation with Margaret was that she was speaking intellectually, not from the heart – or the soul – of experience.

What I do know, from my own experience and that of other depressives, is that severe depression and suicidal pre-occupation are absolute intimates. They are inseparable. I like the way psychiatrist John Greden, at the University of Michigan puts it: 'Suicidal thoughts are to depression what fever is to pneumonia.'

It is important that depressives understand that suicidal preoccupation is not a matter for shame or guilt. It is simply a clinical symptom of an illness. It may feel like a reality but as John Greden says, it is only a passing manifestation, like a high fever, that will, with time, abate. I knew, when my preoccupation with suicide began to diminish, that I was getting well again.

Suicide is so much a part of the illness that twenty per cent of people with severe depression will make a suicide attempt while half of those with bipolar depression may do so. Someone in a first depressive episode is particularly likely to attempt suicide while those who have been though a few episodes are less likely to do so, presumably because they have learned to live with their illness and to believe that, eventually, it will pass.

These days, I rarely think about suicide, unless I happen to be passing through one of my infrequent black holes. On days like that I cannot think, cannot feel but, above all, I cannot connect. I remember standing in my garden, a place that I love, and looking at a flower, blooming on a plant that I had grown from seed. Ordinarily, I take intense pleasure in plants and, being naturally selfish, in plants that I personally have grown, but on that particular day I looked at the flower and felt nothing, not even interest. It was a flower, an object, a thing with no power to rouse admiration or pleasure or wonder.

And I thought, this is depression, this absolute and complete lack of connection to life. At times like that suicide, or death, presses heavy on my mind. If I cannot live, cannot connect with life but am doomed, for ever, to have my face pressed against the window watching it pass me by, then why not die? What is that already, if not a living death?

I used to think that I was alone in those thoughts until I heard a man say, in group therapy, that he had spent the past week considering all the ways in which he might kill himself.

'But I know now,' he said, 'not to take my mind too seriously. It is simply AST, or Automatic Suicidal Thinking.' He paused comically. 'Doesn't everyone have that?'

These days, whenever Nigel or I are focused too much on death, we say to each other, 'Oh, that's just AST. Doesn't everyone have that?' It reduces the terror (and taboo) of our thoughts to a commonplace, a shared symptom that will pass.

If we can bring our most unmanageable thoughts into the open, we can reduce their terror. Fear grows in the dark. I used to tell nobody about my suicidal thoughts. I thought that they were too appalling, too unmentionable to be allowed. When I felt like that, I used to go to bed and stay there, unable to face the horribly changed world, waiting for my focus to shift back to normality.

Now, I do two things.

First, I tell somebody how I feel. Obviously, I choose that person carefully. Some people panic at the very word, suicide, and panic is the last thing that I need. It makes me feel ashamed of my thoughts, and shame makes me feel wretched. It makes me feel so wretched, that my preoccupation with suicide grows worse.

Secondly, I force myself to go through the ordinary, domestic motions of life. Even small achievements help, washing up a mug, throwing out a pile of newspapers. So does going for a walk, particularly first thing in the morning, which is when my depression is always at its worst. It is my black dog hour.

The effort, to get into my car and drive to a park (in London any contact with nature requires effort) can be monumental. I have driven through rush-hour traffic and early morning school runs with tears pouring down my face. I have walked every inch of three London parks, crying. I have cried in the rain and cried in sunshine; I have worn dark glasses to hide my tears and I have worn no disguise, have felt past caring. But one thing I know is true; after an hour of fast walking, I always feel better.

Research bears this out. A pilot clinical trial at the University of Texas Southwestern Medical Center, Dallas, found that adding exercise to antidepressant medications significantly reduces depressive symptoms in patients with major depressive disorders. The study involved seventeen patients with major depression. All were taking antidepressants but were still experiencing residual symptoms of depression, such as insomnia, lack of concentration, irritability, sleep problems, lack of motivation, and sadness. Participants in the study were prescribed a twelve-week aerobic exercise programme (walking, treadmill, or cycling) of at least thirty minutes daily. Each week the severity of depressive symptoms was evaluated using both clinician and patient-rated instruments. Exercise had a marked effect on reducing symptoms suggesting that exercise along with antidepressants could prove an effective strategy for the treatment of major depression.

Another study at the University of Texas Southwestern Medical Center found that thirty-minute aerobic workouts done three to five times a week cut depressive symptoms by fifty per cent in young adults while research at Duke University, North Carolina, found exercise as effective a treatment for depression as antidepressants, with fewer relapses and a higher recovery rate.

Walking has yet another benefit for me. It is as if, by going through the motion of walking, I can convince myself that I am still a part of the motion of life. When my mood is particularly low, I tell myself that the black hole, the abrupt and horrible disconnection with life will pass ('this too shall pass, this too shall pass' is my mantra as I walk). I know my despair is not real and nor is my sudden and intimate attachment to suicide real. It is a manifestation of my mind, or my illness, and it will pass.

For some, it does not pass. The overall fatality rate for depressive illness is thought to be anywhere between ten and twenty per cent, although the figure most mentioned is fifteen per cent. The fight becomes too hard and we let go. This should not be a matter for shame or stigma, nor for reproach and guilt among those we leave behind. For the depressive it is the abandoning of a long and terrifying struggle and a struggle that we feel we can never win. It is not a matter for shame, just great sorrow. It is the bitter end to a terrible illness, desperately fought.

21

The Tipping Point

As soon as you trust yourself, you will know how to live.

Johann Wolfgang von Goethe

In the months immediately following my suicide attempt, I felt that it was over. I had given up. Nobody and nothing could help me. No drug, no shrink, no hospital, no therapist, no lover, no friend. Not even death could help me.

I was on my own and the only way through I could see was to take one halting step at a time.

And so it began, the long, slow and painful road to recovery.

It took three years.

Curiously, I see suicide as the turning point, although it didn't feel like it at the time. By giving up on any expectation that anyone could help me, I took absolute responsibility for my illness and began to look for ways in which I might help myself. Here are some of the things that I did. I offer them up in the hope that they might help somebody else.

I took up yoga.

I walked for at least half an hour a day.

I tried not to isolate myself and began to see my friends, but only for a cup of tea or a quiet meal. I particularly saw my friends who are depressives both because it was soothing to be among other people who understood and also because I learned that in helping other people, I began to help myself.

I avoided any social situation that put me under pressure to perform, dress up or pretend that I was fully functional.

I accepted that I could not read or write (at least not in a way that was in any sense effective, bearing in mind that this is the way that I earn a living) and began instead to focus on the things that I could do. Most were mechanical tasks such as doing the washing up, cleaning my flat, painting a wall, restoring an old vintage chair or gardening.

I stopped trying to use energy that I did not have and accepted that going to bed in the afternoon did not mean that I was worthless. It meant that I was tired.

I watched old movies and comedies and avoided news programmes, current affairs, highly charged emotional drama, or anything that might trigger distress.

I understood that I had an illness, not a weakness.

I stopped feeling ashamed.

It was not easy. There were bad times and worse times and there were also times when, as Nigel is quick to point out, 'You were quite mad.'

As, indeed, I was.

If insanity means having no judgement or intuition, I was honestly mad. There were times when I put my faith in people in whom it was so plainly mad to have faith in they may as well have had warnings stamped on their foreheads. My usually good intuition seemed to have gone astray but when your mind is in that much disarray, all sense has fled. You are, literally, at the mercy of others. I felt, at times, that I was as innocent as a child and often seemed to find myself washed up, beached in the company of fantasists and charlatans but, somehow, I was always rescued. I will say this: there is enough goodness in this world to prevail. Or perhaps I was just lucky.

But in among the bad and the worse times, there were also moments when I felt, if not hope, then at least the glimmerings of possibility. I began to believe that, one day, I might be well again and would re-inhabit the person I call myself. But, first, I had to understand myself. I had to learn how to live again, just as somebody with a physical illness might have to learn to walk again.

It was like starting from the beginning. It took me a long time, for example, to understand, or to re-understand, why people do things. Why, in fact, they do anything at all. What is it that occupies their time? What is the point of doing?

During my long morning walks I watched people hurrying along in suits and trainers. Where was it they were going, and why were they in such haste? I simply couldn't imagine feeling such urgency. I watched others throwing a ball for a dog, picking it up, and throwing it again. Why? Where was the sense in such pointless repetition?

Finally, I accepted that essentially there is no point – the doing *is* the point, that and that life is made up of a series of actions that, repeated often enough, begin to assume a shape and a meaning all of their own. They become meaningful to us only because we attach meaning to them or because they give us an outcome that serves us in some way.

Immediately after my suicide attempt, those were the thoughts and ideas that occupied my mind. Life had ceased to have meaning but so, as well, had death. If nothing has meaning, how do you go on? In what do you trust? The defining character of severe depression was, for me, that absolute loss of trust. The healthy mind does not question every single, tiny little action. It accepts. It trusts in the process.

I started in small ways. There was meaning to the washing-up inasmuch as it meant that Molly and I had plates and knives and forks to eat with. There was meaning to walking up the road to the shops because it was there I bought the food to feed my child. There was meaning to cooking because it made food that gave my body the energy to do the washing up and go to the shops and do the cooking and eat the food that gave me the energy to . . .

I understood that it was a process and either you took part or you opted out. I had tried opting out and there I found no solution. So I took part in the process and in the taking part, I began to find meaning.

I took up yoga, at the suggestion of a friend. It had helped her through some bad times and she thought it might help me. It was also the exercise recommended by every psychiatric unit I had been in, where classes were held every morning. One of the nurses told me she had seen good results with yoga in some cases of severe depression.

So I found a class and in that simple act began to find meaning inasmuch as it got me out of the house, among people, and it made me move my body in ways that, afterwards, made it feel easier and freer. Gradually, I began to realise that it made me feel stronger, calmer and more expansive. And so I began to look forward to my yoga sessions until, gradually, I realised that when I woke up, it was something that I wanted to do every day. Slowly, I began to build up a practice. I trusted in the process, and in the outcome.

It taught me, too, about acceptance, in that in order to do yoga well, you have to accept the body just as it is with all its kinks and pains and strains and awkward bits. It taught me to be gentler with myself (something, I believe, that every depressive needs to learn) and to encourage, rather than push, my body to perform in new and unexpected ways. It taught me that it was fear, or rigid and habitual thinking, that made me believe that I would never achieve a headstand or be able to do a handstand. If our minds can hold us back, then they can push us forwards too.

Now, I can do both a headstand and a handstand with ease. Those achievements may be small in the greater scheme of things but to me they are huge. They mean something.

Yoga also helped me to understand that comparing myself to others is pointless. They can do what I cannot and I can do what they cannot, because we are all different, and unique. I cannot, for example, squat or sit back on my heels, at least, not yet, but I can sit cross-legged or in lotus position with relative ease. The person next to me may catch their heel and bring it to their head in a way that seems to me impossible, but I can turn upside down in a position that seems to them unattainable.

Yoga helped, too, to ease the pain that I was in. I had by this time understood that the throat monster was a purely somatic condition. In other words, it is emotional pain masquerading as physical distress. That did not stop it being real (it was so painful that, at times, I was in tears, and could not eat or drink) but it did mean that no amount of neck massage or soothing throat medicines had any effect. People who suffer from it tend to think that they must have advanced throat cancer, despite a battery of medical tests showing there is nothing physically wrong with them.

Yoga has the double benefit of being a gentle intervention tailored to the individual (no two yoga practices are ever the same, because no two bodies are the same) as well as a set of exercises that calm the nervous system and alleviate stress. There is a wonderful, comic American phrase, 'our issues are in our tissues'. In other words, emotions or old, unresolved feelings can cause neck pain or back ache, a nervous stomach, stiff hips or a throat monster.

I was astonished by how physically painful my depression was. Everything hurt, but in particular my throat, neck and chest while my arms and legs were often stiff and aching. I had always assumed, like most people, that depression is a neck-up condition and that my mind is somehow a completely separate entity to my body. I paid lip service to the view, 'healthy body, healthy mind', but until I became depressed, I had no idea that it worked the other way around too, 'healthy mind, healthy body'.

Experts now accept that the physical pain and suffering experienced in severe depression is real. It is not a figment of imagination or a deluded mind. A study carried out by researchers at the University of Alberta, shows that depression is a major risk factor for the onset of severe neck and lower back pain. People who suffer from depression are four times more likely to develop intense or disabling neck and lower back pain than those who are not depressed.

In a study of over 25,000 patients at fifteen primary care centres on five continents, Seattle researchers found that fifty per cent of all depressed patients worldwide report multiple unexplained physical symptoms and concluded that 'somatic symptoms are a core component of the depressive syndrome.'

In truth, the mental and physical are inseparable and it is this holistic fusion that yogis have long understood. Yoga helped to ease the pain and stiffness in my body, but it did more than that; it began to disentangle the black knots in my mind. As to why this should be, there is very little hard evidence. This is because a singular control group is impossible in yoga as there are so many variants within the 3,000-year-old discipline that it cannot be subjected to the rigid rules that Western science demands. Timothy B. McCall, medical editor of *Yoga Journal* puts it this way:

> As with any holistic endeavour, measuring the constituent parts is not the same thing as understanding the sum of those parts. Reductionist science may tell us that yoga decreases systolic blood pressure and cortisol secretion and increases lung capacity, serotonin levels, and baroreceptor sensitivity, but that doesn't begin to capture the sum total of what yoga is.

The most persuasive evidence of the benefits of hatha yoga (the physical practice of postures that also includes deep breathing exercises and meditation), and in particular pranayama (a series of deep breathing exercises), comes from the

National Institute of Mental Health and Neuroscience in India. Studies have shown a high success rate (up to seventy-three per cent) for treating depression with sudharshan kriya, a pranayama technique that involves breathing naturally through the nose and mouth in three distinct rhythms. Stephen Cope, a psychotherapist and author of *Yoga and the Quest for the True Self*, maintains that hatha yoga postures improve mood by moving energy through places in the body where feelings of grief or anger are stored. He calls hatha yoga, 'an accessible form of learning self-soothing.'

Together with walking, if there is an exercise that is helpful to someone suffering from depression, I believe it is yoga. It must, though, be done properly and with some persistence. That may seem horribly difficult when you're very ill, but yoga is such a forgiving discipline that even lying on a yoga mat and practising deep, rhythmical breathing is helpful. From there you can build up to five minutes of gentle poses and from there to ten, to twenty and so on.

Amy Weintraub is a yoga teacher who once suffered from severe depression and took up yoga in order to soothe her depression. In her book, *Yoga For Depression*, she writes passionately and convincingly (using numerous case studies) about the benefits of yoga and breathing practices. She also, like many yogis before her, stresses the importance of regular practice.

You don't take an antidepressant medication just once and expect to feel better. You take it regularly. So with yoga, to restore the body and mind to a state of well-being, you must also practise regularly. The very commitment to practise can begin to diminish depressive symptoms. Unlike taking a pill two or three times a day, when a yoga student practises once a day, she is adding the element of what psychologists call 'self-control' – the ability to be actively involved in the healing process. Self-control, not to be confused with willpower or restraint, means in this context, that you can determine your own course of action. Self-control, as in self-determination, has been shown in numerous studies to have a positive outcome in recovery from illness, including depression.

It is, though, worth seeking out a yoga teacher with whom you have an affinity, just as it is better to find a small class. The larger classes tend to be filled with people in search of that elusive 'yoga butt' or in pursuit of the body beautiful. For those of us who are in pursuit of the mind beautiful, one to one attention from a yoga teacher is crucial as is doing the postures slowly and correctly. So is abandoning the prevailing cultural belief that exercise is about competition or perfection.

There is no such thing as a perfect yoga pose; we aim for progress rather than perfection. We try to do the best that we can and it is in the trying that we discover that the best is always good enough – a useful lesson for anyone who battles depression.

22

Making Sense

What saves a man is to take a step. Then another step. It is always the same step, but you have to take it.

Antoine de Saint-Exupéry

I was practising yoga and walking every day, but the year following my suicide attempt was complicated in other and various ways. Two steps forward, one step back. A few sideways.

My father was diagnosed with prostate cancer.

'Most men die with it, rather than of it,' he said, in his matter-of-fact way as he embarked on a round of treatment. Once I had got passed the original shock of the diagnosis, I worried about him, but not profoundly. It seemed that they had caught it early and, by then, I had learned enough from therapy to concentrate on the present and on practical solutions and not to project dark imaginings into the future. My father made light of it and I took my cue from him.

I embarked on a search for a garden, having finally put my flat on the market and sold it. I knew a garden was essential to my recovery and, eventually, I found it; a tangle of weed and bramble on which I could impose some order while still respecting the structure and the life that existed deep within it.

It was, I decided, like my mind, in need of loving care and valiant restoration. The weeds and brambles of depression needed clearing. I could only hope that my mind still existed, intact, beneath them.

I had never designed a garden before but I bought graph paper and thick black pens, coloured pencils and set squares and began to lay out on paper what had lived only in my dreams. I worked around the existing trees, designing the garden to fall into shape with the symmetry it had inhabited for so long before I arrived.

It was my therapy, a way of moving forwards and of trusting in the process. Not just in my process, but in the process of life. I knew the garden would exist, although not perhaps in the state I imagined, long after I had ceased to matter, and I took great comfort from that. My distress and the enormity of my illness (which was, of course, enormous only to me) meant little against that. More than that, things that had fallen into disrepair could be made beautiful again.

Once my plans were on paper, through happy chance, I met Martin, a landscape contractor who looked at my plans and began, meticulously, to carry them out, laying paths and terraces and digging flower beds until, one freezing November day, the bare bones of my garden appeared, rising out of the mud as if by magic. It is not a huge garden, although it is big by London standards, but it does have a curiously peaceful charm and atmosphere. I sometimes think it is because it was designed and then planted with such hope. Perhaps that is fanciful but I did once say to a neurologist, as she stood in my garden, that it had played a huge part in my recovery from depression. 'Yes,' she said. 'I can see that.'

I bought a car. This is a more important statement than its casual nature might at first imply. I had not been able to drive for ten years, since the time that Molly was born, having suffered from a phobia of driving so intense it made me shake so badly I would come close to passing out. My heart would race and I would sweat until my hands slipped off the steering wheel – even in a stationary car. I was scarcely better as a passenger. It got so bad that I had to give up driving entirely and rely on Jonathan to take me everywhere. Looking back, I think the phobia may have been the first sign of impending depression. I was also very low for a year after Moll was born, although certainly not clinically depressed. Those two things make me understand that I may, even then, have been fragile in some way.

Now I was on my own. I needed a car, and I needed to be able to drive. My new flat was some distance from Jonathan, although no distance by car. Molly had to be ferried between the two of us, and taken back and forward from school. She needed to be able to rely on me. More than that, I needed to be able to rely on me. I was determined to beat the phobia, just as I was determined to overcome my own mind.

So I bought a new car using some of the money from the sale of the house, and had it delivered. I thought it might embarrass me into driving. I thought too, that by then, I might have overcome my fear.

It sat in front of my flat looking shiny and new and utterly terrifying.

It sat there for weeks.

Finally, I called a driving school, and booked some lessons.

'I have a new car which I am too frightened to drive,' I said. 'I need the calmest, and nicest, instructor in London.'

A woman said, 'Do you have a date booked for your test?'

'I passed that eighteen years ago.'

There was a long silence.

'I have a driving phobia, and a new car,' I said. 'I need help.'

'You need Geoffrey,' she said.

Two weeks later, Geoffrey appeared at my door. For a week, for three hours every day, we drove round and around the city. Then we moved outside London. We drove down the M25, up the A1, along the M1. Motorways held a particular terror for me. Even as a passenger, I had to close my eyes. Obviously, this was no longer an option. The first time I pulled out of the slow lane to overtake, Geoffrey applauded. At the end of the week, he shook my hand. 'You'll do nicely,' he said.

I discovered, again, that I love driving, rather like I discovered, once the depression had receded, that I love life. That both hold particular terrors for me has nothing to do with driving, or with life. The terrors exist in my mind. Learning to drive again went a long way to exhuming them.

That summer, just after I had moved into my new flat, my mother was taken into hospital. One of the main arteries in her thigh had become blocked. There was little, or no, blood reaching her foot, which was slowly dying. The pain was excruciating. The consultant attempted to blow open the artery but the blood clot was buried so deep that the operation failed. She had a morphine drip by her bed, but it did little to help. She could not eat, because of the pain and the nausea from the drug. This went on for six weeks while we considered, with the consultant, what could be done.

I drove up and down motorways to the hospital. Every time I saw my mother, she seemed to have shrunk a little more. By the time she left that hospital, she had lost four stone. I bought her cashmere socks, to warm her frozen toes, and massaged her foot and leg. In the operating theatre, they stuck needles in her leg and pushed balloons through her arteries. Nothing worked.

There was only one thing to be done: amputation. My mother agreed to have her toes removed. There was no hope of saving them and little chance of saving her lower leg but it was worth a try. If the first amputation did not work, she would need a second, then a third, each one moving further up her leg.

On the afternoon she agreed to the amputation of her toes, I walked out of her room and into the hospital corridor and burst into tears.

'Why are you crying?' Dad said.

'Poor Mum,' I said. There is something brutally shocking about amputation. My mother has always had very beautiful legs. I have a black and white photograph of her on my mantelpiece, taken in the 1960s, in Aden. She is dancing, wearing a silk dress and high heels. Her smile is radiant.

Dad patted me ineffectually on the shoulder, looking vaguely alarmed.

I drove home, ready to return the next day after the operation. My father called that evening, distressed and panicky. The hospital had discovered that his health insurance would not pay for the six weeks my mother had spent in hospital. It was a technical point. The insurers maintained that the procedures she had undergone did not constitute surgery. The consultant was furious, but impotent. We owed in excess of £20,000, which had to be paid the next morning.

No money. No operation.

My father said, did I have any savings? Fortunately I did, from the sale of the house I had owned with Jonathan. I had bought a smaller flat than I might otherwise have done, in order to put money aside in case I was unable to work. I did not know, at that time, if I would ever be able to write again. My concentration was still horribly awry. I could just about manage to read but still found it difficult to remember the beginning of a sentence once I had reached the end. Holding an idea, let alone a sophisticated network of thoughts in my head – in other words, meaning – was still difficult. What would happen once the money had run out, I did not know. And nor could I bear to imagine.

The next morning, I met my father at the hospital and gave him a cheque.

'This is all wrong,' he said.

Dad went to the accounts department and I went to see my mother. She was adrift in a sea of tears and pain.

'They came into my room last night and asked me who was going to pay. I said I don't know about money. My husband handles that. I told them to ask him. Imagine asking for money from somebody who is about to have a foot amputated.'

Yes, imagine.

Once Mum had been taken down to theatre, I drove Dad home. On the way, we stopped at a pub for lunch.

'If it doesn't work, she'll have to go to the NHS hospital for the next operation,' he said fretfully. 'We don't have enough money to keep her in the private wing.' He took a sip of beer. 'She won't like it.'

'The NHS is fine, Dad,' I said.

It wasn't. It was grim. This time, her leg was amputated high above the knee. It was her decision. She could not, she said, face two more operations or another that did not work.

The next six months were difficult but my mother faced them with extraordinary courage and determination, getting used to her prosthetic leg and swapping the car for an automatic so she could drive again. She had scarcely found her new balance when she fell and broke her wrist.

Dad fell too, and hurt his head and knee so badly that, at one time, neither of them could walk. His cancer seemed to be in check, although the medication affected him in other ways.

I drove up and down motorways with food during that cold, bleak drawn out winter. Dad's breathing became difficult as the result of the drugs he was taking and he was admitted to hospital. In a grim echo of the previous months, he was in the ward next to the one where Mum had her leg amputated. My younger brother, Tony, became badly depressed, about that and other things.

I thought the spring would never come. The twiggy silhouettes of the shrubs I had planted in my new garden looked like barbed wire sticking out of the iron earth. I walked the length of it every day, peering at each stiff, brown branch and wondering when, or if, life would return.

As the months passed, I discovered that reading was still difficult but I managed and I started to write again, at first tentatively and then with greater fluency. For two years, Corinna Honan, my commissioning editor at the *Daily Telegraph*, had been taking me out to lunch, buying me impossibly expensive food I could not eat and encouraging me to write again. Her kindness and constancy were touching. She particularly encouraged me to write about depression.

'I can't,' I said. 'It's too much.'

'It will help. You're not the only one. You'll see.'

So I wrote, trying to inject as much hope (as much for myself as anyone else) as I could. It was incredibly painful but, curiously, the actual writing of it came easily perhaps because I didn't see it as a piece of journalism but as a way of connecting. I didn't much worry about form or style. I just wrote what I felt and what I felt was that I had never read a brutally honest personal account of how it really feels to be severely depressed. When I was very ill, that sense of understanding and connection was what I most longed for so I tried to write and do for others what I wanted done for myself. I cried as I wrote, but it did not stop me writing.

Nor did dark warnings from friends in the media who implied that such a vulnerable and exposed personal statement was a piece of professional suicide, marking me out as unreliable and unemployable. In short, labelling me as a depressive. I refused to be stigmatised or frightened because I felt it was fear (and the silence it imposes) that kept the stigma in place. Or perhaps I thought that I had nothing left to lose. I don't know. I do know that sitting down to write that newspaper article broke the deadlock I had about writing. Not immediately (it took another two years to re-establish my career as a freelance journalist but only because it took me that long to become well enough to cope with the pressures of constant deadlines), but it gave me the confidence to at least try. As for the dark warnings, none of them came true. All I was met with was support and kindness. Everyone, it seems, has been touched by depression, either personally or through family and friends.

The letters came pouring in.

> Every day is a struggle. I function, I don't live. I identified with so many of your symptoms – not wanting to be in this world, wanting the pain to end, not eating, crying myself to sleep, waking up sobbing and constantly fed up of people asking me if I am OK. I feel a failure and ashamed of what I have become. I just wanted to say THANK YOU for allowing me to see that other people have been through the same, that I am not a freak and that I AM NOT ALONE.

I read the letters with tears pouring down my face and attempted to answer each one but the effort of sitting with so much unhappiness was often more than I could bear.

> I don't know if not killing myself and rejoicing in not feeling suicidal is much of a way to live. But I do know that after reading your story, I felt a little less of a freak and think it is good to be happy for even the smallest of empathies. I can't talk to friends and family. I alluded to it once and got a blast about self-pity.

Those letters did make me understand that I was not the only one. Some of them even made me laugh. And then cry.

> A few years ago I would have dismissed your article as being typical of a neurotic woman. Since then, I have experienced what you so vividly describe. Some days I didn't get out of bed until midday. I had to force myself to eat. I was very tearful, which I felt was wrong for a man.

Reading your article has helped, because it is reassuring to know that other people can feel this way. Having cancer in 1989 didn't bother me but being depressed in 2002 was truly frightening.

Slowly, the spring began to unfold, one day bleak and frozen but the next, a morning of such brilliant, intense blue it hurt to look. Green shoots began to appear on the hard brown sticks and the garden softened and swelled as if taking a deep breath of pleasure. Then, just as suddenly, it was gone and we were back in the grip of an iron cold snap.

My moods, too, were changeable. One morning I would wake into an intense, almost electric energy, filled with good humour and possibility. It would last for a few days, during which I became euphoric and voluble – sometimes, alarmingly so – and then, just as suddenly, it would be gone.

Somehow, that was worse. The contrast between the light and the dark felt almost unbearably sharp, and the dark a colder, bleaker place than I remembered when I spent all my time encased in it.

My psychiatrist changed my medication. I had begun to hate the side-effects of the tricylic drugs I was taking, which are known to affect memory, concentration and intellectual performance. I felt drugged and slow, even when my brain was pushing for action and the bloated constipation they induce made me feel generally lousy. No wonder they're known as 'dirty drugs'.

I went on Prozac. Pretty soon, I was intensely suicidal again.

I came off Prozac.

He felt we should try one of the new breed of SSRIs, Escitalopram, which had just been launched, and was said to be a more potent and selective inhibitor of serotonin reuptake than the older SSRIs as well as having a higher tolerability profile, which he felt might suit me.

He was right. I tolerated the drug pretty well, but my moods continued to shift alarmingly. Bright days were intense but the dark days were a deep and dirty black.

I began to drink again.

I had been stopping and starting for months, attending AA meetings on and off, but I could not convince myself that I was a drunk. I was simply depressed. The past year had been difficult. Of course I drank.

At about the same time, I met Elizabeth and went back into therapy. It was tough and difficult work as I sought to unravel the knots of pain that had somehow gathered within me.

Elizabeth, among her many trainings, is a specialist in alcoholism and addiction. With her, I knew I could not avoid or evade. I knew she could smell the drink on me when I turned up, hungover and withdrawn, for our sessions.

'Your liver's packing up,' she said. 'It can't process the amount you're drinking. Once that happens, it starts coming out of the pores of the skin which, as you know, is the body's biggest organ.'

I knew that. I could smell stale alcohol on my skin, even after I had taken a bath. I was a mess, and I looked it. My face was bloated, my eyes narrow and reddened, my skin blotchy. I had constant heartburn and diarrhoea; I felt like I had been submerged in acid. Drinking made me gag. Every swallow tasted acrid and burning, like lighter fuel, but still I could not stop.

By then, I had switched from wine to vodka. I wanted oblivion, and fast. In the depth of my dirty black moods, wine took too long to have an effect. So did pouring a measure of drink into a glass. I drank straight from the bottle, usually in bed, in the afternoon. Then, I would finally fall asleep for a few hours and wake up, wretched and ill. There is only one cure for a hangover, other than time. Another drink. And so I would spend my evenings alone, cradling the bottle, slumped on the sofa in front of the television.

'I know it's a slow form of suicide,' I said to Elizabeth.

'You might die,' she said calmly, 'but you'll go mad first.'

'I thought I was already mad,' I said, trying to smile, although my heart wasn't really in it.

'Alcohol rots the brain,' Elizabeth said. 'One of the final stages of chronic alcoholism is called wet-brain. It is truly horrible.'

I carried on drinking although I did not drink every day. I would stop for a week, ten days or three weeks. And then something, anything, would give me an excuse for another drink and I'd be off again.

Spring finally came. The earth grew warm and yielding. I began to plant up the garden, but in a mood of strange indifference. I kept telling myself that I was planting for the future, for the summer, the autumn, the next spring but I could find no pleasure in it. I still could not see a future. 'The time I was really worried,' Nigel told me recently, 'was when you stopped caring about your garden.'

I called Tom, just to hear his voice. We had not seen or spoken to each other for a year.

'I wanted to say I was sorry,' I said. 'I hope we are still friends.'

'There is nothing to be sorry for,' he said. 'And of course we're still friends. My affection for you has never changed.'

He did not suggest we meet, and neither did I. Since we parted, I had felt his absence so sharply it had become a presence, huge and constant. I missed him, every minute and every hour of every day. I did not say so.

There was no going back but it seemed that I could not go forward either. My heart had broken and I knew no way to mend it, except with vodka. A few men appeared on my horizon, but either I did not take them seriously, or I was cruel in my indifference. All my affections and my certainties lay elsewhere.

I had always thought that Tom and I would be together. It had seemed so clear to me, right from the start. I was wrong. Even in my absolute certainty, I had been wrong. Yet I could not believe it. Sometimes, I felt that it was just some cruel joke or even a slip of memory. We had not parted after all. It was a nightmare, a trick of my mad, deluded mind.

I knew, though, that it was not and neither was I deluded enough to think that he would come back. I knew him too well, knew how he could pull down the steel trap of his mind and shutter away his heart.

I dealt with the pain by drinking. I dealt with all pain by drinking. Severe depression does not suddenly lift or disappear. It recedes slowly and, even as it recedes, can suddenly reappear in brief but violent onslaughts. I knew I was not helping it by drinking, but during those assaults I was in such agony, I did not know what else to do. I took to wandering the London streets late at night, buying vodka from late-night stores, sitting on walls and drinking straight from the bottle. I was not frightened of being mugged or murdered. I thought that as I had failed to kill myself, somebody else might do the job for me.

This was my private behaviour. In front of Molly and my friends, I tried to put on a good front and act as normally as I could. My worst drinking was when Molly was with Jonathan, which she was for five days at a time. Often, I would spend that time alone, avoiding the phone, never speaking to another person. On the day before Moll came home, I would stop drinking and sober up for her arrival. I would stay sober for the five days that she was with me and when she left, and I was alone again, I would drink again.

Then, one morning, when Molly was due to stay with me for the weekend, I walked up the road to buy some food. When I drank, I rarely ate so I rarely bought food for myself. The only time I ate was when Molly was with me.

So I went to the supermarket, still badly hungover and detoxing from the levels of alcohol I had been absorbing for the previous few days. The experts say that it takes a year for alcohol to leave your system entirely. I had been off drink for a day. My mood was fiercely low although the sun was shining. It was a beautiful day.

I stocked up on organic vegetables, fruit juice and good red meat. As I filled my supermarket trolley, I said to myself that I was a good mother. I knew how to take care of my child. I just did not know how to take care of myself.

I had no intention of drinking until I found myself next to a shelf full of vodka and decided that a quarter bottle would straighten me out, stop the terrible sweating, shaking and the intense pain that was always gathered at my throat.

There were no quarter bottles, they had run out. So I grabbed a full bottle, reasoning to myself that I would drink only one glass, so I could be steady and calm and happy for her when she arrived.

By the time Jonathan dropped Molly off at my flat at lunchtime, I had drunk over half the bottle of vodka. I had been crying for three hours. My mood was as black as I had ever known it, but I tried to be cheerful around her.

I managed to make her some lunch and then she disappeared downstairs, to play on the computer. I went and lay on my bed, the bottle of vodka next to me. I was very drunk and very low. I was also terrified. I was in sole charge of my child, and I was completely out of control. It had never been that bad, even in the depths of depression. I knew, then, that I would die, either by intention and taking my own life or by some stupidly avoidable accident. Either way, I would die.

I could hear Molly, downstairs, singing. As a small child, she woke up singing and went to sleep singing. It always made me smile. I took such pleasure in her happiness. Let joy be unconfined.

As I lay there, I knew that I could kill that joy stone dead if I went on as I was. Worse, I knew that I would.

I called Jonathan and told him that I had stepped over the line, that I was drunk and suicidal, in sole charge of our beloved child.

He came and sat with me, and we talked. I was incoherent and talked of nothing but depression, despair and death. Jonathan listened.

Then he said; 'I think you need to go away, into rehab. You're an alcoholic.'

I was shocked. 'Is it that bad?'

He said, simply, 'Yes.'

When he left, he took Molly with him.

She gave me a big hug. 'Get better soon, Mum.'

That night, I stopped drinking. The next morning, I got on the phone to my psychiatrist.

He said, 'You have become dependent on alcohol. It often happens in severe depression. You medicate to stop the pain, and end up with not one, but two, mental illnesses.'

I was booked into a treatment centre, an addiction unit based inside a large psychiatric hospital. My diagnosis was straightforward. Severe clinical depression with severe alcohol dependency.

I called my parents, to tell them I was going back into hospital. 'But you're better,' Dad said.

'No, I'm not.'

'Yes, you are. You're better. You seem so much better.'

'I'm not, Dad.' I didn't tell him about the alcohol. I couldn't bear to. 'Maybe this time. Third time lucky. I'll be away for a month, twenty-eight days.'

'Twenty-eight days? That seems like a long time.'

Not a long time, I thought. Not where I'm going.

'Yes, I know. I'll call you when I get out.'

'Can't we call you?' He sounded fretful. I knew then that he was really worried.

'They don't like us to take calls. I'll be fine, Dad. I promise.'

'I'll try anyway,' he said.

'Thanks Dad.'

'I love you.'

'I love you too.'

I called Jonathan. 'I'm going into rehab. I'm going to get better, I promise.'

'I know you will. Somebody asked me yesterday if I thought you had the strength to get through this. I said, if you tell Sal to turn left, she'll turn right. But if she decides to turn left, she'll turn left.'

I laughed. Then I cried. More than anything, I hoped that he was right.

23

Turning Left

We don't receive wisdom; we must discover it for ourselves after a journey that no one can take for us or spare us.

Marcel Proust

Step One
We admitted we were powerless over alcohol and that our lives had become unmanageable.

Annie works for a large, corporate law firm. She is forty-five years old and has fine blonde hair and skin so pale, it's almost translucent. She has been a heroin addict since she was sixteen. Now, she takes methadone, the legal substitute. She started taking it to get off heroin. That was ten years ago. She used to get methadone on prescription from the NHS, but these days she pays. It was too humiliating waiting in line with the other smack heads at the chemist to be given her state-approved daily allowance.

Annie's eyes are blue, I think. It's hard to tell, because most of the time they're half closed. Her head lolls forward then jerks sharply back as a counsellor asks her a question.

'Annie? Annie! Are you with us today?'

'Yes,' Annie slurs.

'How are you feeling?'

'Tired.'

'Tired is not a feeling. It is a physical state. How are you feeling?'

Annie's eyes snap open and her voice is strong and clear. 'Fucking pissed off.' I am amazed to discover she is Irish. I have never heard her speak before.

'You're obviously feeling better.'

Annie's head rolls forward again. 'Wanna sleep,' she slurs.

Until last week, Annie was drinking one and a half large (that is, duty-free size) bottles of vodka a day; a chaser for the methadone. She decanted the vodka into an Evian bottle and kept it on her desk, at the law firm. When they got her to the unit, she was half dead. Most of her major organs were on the verge of packing up. They kept her in bed for five days while they detoxed her. Three times a day she has to visit the nurse to get massive vitamin shots; mainly B12, because alcohol leaches it out of the system. A lack of B12 is implicated in depression.

Annie is not depressed, she says, except about the injections in her arse. Oh, and about being in rehab where she does not want to be. She says she likes being half dead. It suits her. She cannot imagine having, or wanting, a life without alcohol or drugs. Something to take the edge off because, 'life sucks, doesn't it?' She is only here because of the law firm. Shape up or ship out, is what they said. She can't afford to lose her job, even though she hates it. She needs the money to pay for the drugs and alcohol. It does not seem to occur to her that if she got off the drugs, she would not need the money, or even the job. She could take work that she likes. She's lucky, although she does not see it that way. Her company is paying for her four weeks in rehab – to the tune of £4,000 a week – or, at least, their health insurance is paying.

The brewery Pete works for is paying too. He is part of a team, delivering beer to pubs around London. He can't drive. He has been drinking since he was eleven, so he has never been sober enough to learn. He heaves the barrels and crates off the lorry and carries them into the pub, where he is given a pint of beer for his pains. He has his first pint at six in the morning, when he clocks on for his shift. He reckons he drinks around eighteen pints of beer a day plus a few whisky chasers in the evening, when he goes down the pub with his mates. Some nights he doesn't make it home; he passes it out on the grass verge outside the pub.

Pete reckons that eighty per cent of the blokes who work at the brewery are alcoholics. He was unlucky. He got caught, drunk on the job. Or rather, he was unlucky that somebody finally noticed. He was drunk for thirteen years on the job. Pete doesn't want to be in rehab either. What's the point? All his mates are drunks. If he doesn't drink, he won't have any mates. And what's the point of a life without mates?

'How are you feeling Pete?'

Pete scowls at the floor. 'Stupid.'

He scuffs at the brown carpet with a grubby trainer and blushes as he feels twelve sets of eyes trained on him. We are sitting in a circle, in morning therapy. The counsellor goes round the group, asking each of us in turn how we are feeling. All we talk about are feelings. They say that addicts are bad at locating feelings, or even knowing what they are. They've kept them at bay for so long. Addicts say that they are good at feelings. It's just that they don't like them much. Having too many feelings is why they drink.

Pete hates feelings. He says they're rubbish. Nobody in his family has feelings. Or, if they do, they never talk about them.

Therapy starts at 9.30 a.m. and goes on until 12.30, when we stop for lunch. At two o'clock, we start again, until 5 p.m. Then it's free time until supper at 6.30. At 7.30, we pile into a mini-bus and go to an AA meeting, or a CA meeting (Cocaine Anonymous) or an NA meeting (Narcotics Anonymous). It doesn't matter if you don't do coke or smack; you still go to the meeting. An addict is an addict is an addict.

I like the CA meetings best, even though the amounts of coke I've done in my life scarcely qualify me for the kindergarten user league. It was an eighties thing; everybody did it, hoping it would turn them into smart, funny contenders. It made me paranoid and aggressive, so I stopped. Lucky, I guess.

CA is filled with young men in their late teens or early twenties dressed in hoodies and baseball caps, crackling with testosterone and energy. Their voices are fast and loud and impatient; they rarely finish one sentence before they're tumbling over the second. Hard to imagine what they were like when they were wired on coke; a blur of sound and muscle.

One of them, Jamie, is in the unit with us.

'You all right princess?' he says, whipping off a baseball cap and bowing a shaved head low over my hand. He looks up with liquid brown eyes. 'You're new. They treating you right?'

I smile at him and shrug.

'They've got to be tough, see.' He jabs a brown finger at his skull. 'They've got to get in here and get the addict out.'

Jamie is seventeen and has been doing drugs since he was thirteen. 'Only skunk, in the beginning.' Skunk is the super-strong version of dope, also known as weed, pot, or marijuana, depending on your age. It is thought to cause psychosis or, in some cases, schizophrenia in young men; or at least in young men who may have a predisposition to mental illness. And who's to know?

From skunk, Jamie graduated to coke and alcohol, sometimes doing twelve grams of coke a day. My head reels at the thought, not to mention the expense. Jamie's parents are rich; he gets what he wants, when he wants it. As a lark, he liked to drink cocaine in slammers, a gram of coke dumped in a glass of champagne and straight down the hatch. 'I was stupid,' he says, although whether he is referring to the drugs poisoning his young system or a waste of good coke is hard to say.

Jamie bottled a bloke because he didn't like the way he was looking at him. He regrets that. He picked up the nearest bottle off a bar, smashed it and rammed the jagged glass edges straight into the man's face. It wasn't the first, or the only time. He smashed up a car, a Merc, because it was parked in the wrong place outside his parents' house and he has been banned from so many clubs for violence, he can't remember all their names.

Now he is staring into my eyes in drama therapy. We have been paired up in role play. His face is two inches from mine.

The therapist says, 'Everyone, I want you to say out loud the emotion you are feeling right now.'

Jamie doesn't blink. 'Love,' he says.

Two days later, Jamie leaves. He has done his twenty-eight days.

Timothy stares after him. 'I hope he makes it.'

Timothy is gay and smiling. He is in his forties, with glasses and sandy brown, clean-cut hair. His shirts are laundered and his jeans pressed to sharp creases. He is meticulously well mannered, except when he's drunk. When he arrived at the unit, they had to carry him up the stairs, fighting and swearing like a trooper.

'Get angry,' the counsellor says. 'You won't get sober until you acknowledge the way you really feel. Get in touch with your emotions. Stop being so pissing polite.'

Timothy sighs. 'Fuck off and leave me alone.'

'You're faking it,' the counsellor says.

'I'm not,' Timothy says mildly. 'Really, I'm not.'

Timothy worked around the world, moving from one foreign posting to another. He loves to live abroad but he has been transferred back to head office in the UK, where they can keep an eye on him. Timothy is clever and learned but often passed over for promotion because of, 'a few little incidents'. Only his desperation to get sober reveals how much those lost promotions hurt. 'I'm fine,' he says. 'Really.'

'No, you're not,' Rosie says. 'You're well pissed off.'

Timothy smiles. 'Probably. But I only know that when I'm drunk.'

Just before she was admitted to the unit, Rosie smashed up her flat in a drunken rage. She doesn't drink every day, only every few weeks or so, but when she starts, she disappears into a drunken binge that lasts for five days. 'I lose myself,' she says. 'I turn into somebody else.'

Rosie is funny and clever and lives with Sam, who she loves very much. She has a good job and two cats, who she also loves very much. She is in her early thirties and very pretty: blue eyes, peachy skin, glossy auburn hair. When she's drunk she smashes her fists through doors, screams abuse at strangers and wakes up in unfamiliar beds with naked men, one or sometimes two, who she does not recognise. Her peachy skin is often covered in bruises.

She thinks she is worthless and rotten; somewhere deep in her soul there is a writhing mass of maggots that eat away at her. Sometimes, she gets drunk, to try to kill them. And when she gets drunk, she gets very angry.

Rosie is in the middle of a police case, trying to get a family friend convicted for the sexual abuse he inflicted on her between the ages of eight and thirteen. When she told her mother, her mum didn't believe her. Or, she said she did, but then she went on being friends with the man who had raped her daughter.

It wasn't her mum but Rosie who went to the police, when she was in her late twenties. It has taken four years to gather sufficient evidence to build a case. The police are hopeful, even though it happened many years ago.

Rosie wants to be sober when they take the man to court and sentence him. 'I want to see his face clearly, when they send him down,' she says. 'I want to know that I am believed, that somebody is listening to me.'

'What if they don't send him down?' the counsellor says.

Rosie looks away.

In rehab, we spend twenty-eight days getting acquainted with the first three steps of the Twelve Step programme. This is the system of recovery devised by the founders of AA, themselves all former, chronic alcoholics, back in the 1930s. It is based on both practical and spiritual principles and involves acceptance, accountability, faith, trust, self-examination, responsibility and, crucially, helping others. It is believed by its adherents (and by most experts in the field of addiction) to be the best treatment for alcoholism and drug addiction, which is why it is practised in so many drug and alcohol rehabilitation and treatment centres across the world.

There are, obviously, twelve steps in the programme and successful recovery from alcoholism involves learning as well as putting into practice each of the steps and using them as a blueprint for living. As in any other practical (or spiritual) programme, it can take months or even years to fully grasp the principles that lie behind what seems, at first, an intensely simple collection of ideas.

Our first task in rehab is to complete Step One, which we are asked to repeat daily, if not hourly: *We admitted we were powerless over alcohol and that our lives had become unmanageable.*

We do that by telling our life stories, unvarnished, unblemished, no grubby little detail spared. We tell them out loud in front of the group, and then we write them down; five examples of how powerless alcohol has made us and five examples of how unmanageable our lives have become because of alcohol.

And then we read out loud what we have written and we tell it over and over again until, finally, we might be able to see (though not everyone can; denial is a powerful component of addiction) how powerless we are over alcohol, and how unmanageable our lives have become.

We write down the time, say, that we had an important early morning meeting at work and how we said we'd have just one drink the evening before. And how that drink turned into five, or ten, and we were so trashed in the morning that we forgot the meeting. Or pretended to forget. And how we had another drink to make us forget that it mattered or to stop the shakes enough to allow us to crawl, late, into the office. The unmanageability is how we lost our job because we forgot the meeting and appeared in the office, reeking of drink but claiming flu.

We needed another drink to forget how we shouted at the MD for being an uptight arse for sacking us over a little bit of harmless fun. And then we seethed with resentment against that MD and blamed everyone else, except ourselves, and most particularly not the drink.

We didn't blame the drink because we needed another drink to stop the guilt and the shame which came from shouting at the boss about stuff that was our fault and about letting everybody, but most particularly ourselves, down. We needed the drink so we could hide the truth from ourselves and say it didn't matter.

And then, of course, we needed money to buy the drink. So we took some grubby little job that was way beneath us. Then we needed another drink to forget the time and the energy that had been spent on our education to turn us into the smart, functioning human beings who we're fast pissing away on drink, and to forget the love that our mum and dad lavished on us and the sacrifices they made on our behalf. We needed another drink to stop that shame too, and then we needed another because our lives were so piss-awful, who wouldn't drink?

And then we write down in our notebooks, and across our hearts and our minds,

'It's the first drink that does the damage. If you don't take a drink, you can't get drunk.'

And then, because it's so hard to think that we cannot take another drink, ever, we write down,

'Just for today.'

Just for today, I will not drink. I might drink tomorrow, or next week, but just for today, I will not drink.

And then the days and the weeks and the months and the

years add up, because there is only today. Yesterday has gone and tomorrow has not yet arrived.

Or, at least, that's the theory.

It's tough, though. Some people, particularly in the early days, adopt a more immediate timetable.

'Just for this moment.'

'Just for this hour.'

Nobody likes to admit that they are powerless. We live in a culture of control and success. The most money, the best job, the biggest car, the fanciest handbag. Powerlessness is weakness, failure is pathetic and surrender is giving up. I found Step One almost impossible at first but then, like most people, I like to be in control. I hate to feel needy or powerless.

'Turn your head around, Sally.' That's what, Elizabeth, my therapist used to say to me. 'Try a new way.'

'Why?'

'Has your way worked?'

I think about this, long and hard. 'No.'

'Then let's try another.'

Trying another way means understanding that there are times when a fight is not worth fighting. It cannot be won. Admitting to being powerless is not an admission of defeat, but one of liberation. You begin to understand that we are powerless over so much, even though we like to believe otherwise.

We cannot, for example, change other people; we can only change our responses to them. People rarely behave in the way that we wish. We cannot make them love us. We cannot stop them leaving us. We cannot live our children's lives for them. We cannot change life either; cannot undo the past or predict the future. Life rarely turns out in the way that we would wish it to, or that we have dreamed it would. We are powerless to do anything about that except to make the best, or the worst of it. Once we accept that we are powerless, not just over alcohol but over people, places and things, we accept life and all that goes with it.

Powerlessness is acceptance. It is not just a part of the Twelve Step programme, but every belief from Buddhism to Christianity.

Acceptance is not giving up on action or a resignation to events. Acceptance is facing reality without illusion.

Acceptance is watching the plants in my garden grow. Acceptance is not digging them up to see how their roots are growing. They will develop in their own sweet time and there is absolutely nothing I can do about that. I can encourage them, with water and fertiliser, but I cannot make the sun shine or the days grow warmer.

I accept that I am powerless.

It is a rare sort of freedom.

Step Two
We came to believe that a power greater than
ourselves could restore us to sanity.

'I'm not insane,' Pete says belligerently. 'How can I be restored to sanity?'

The counsellor looks at him. 'Is it sane to drink eighteen pints of beer a day?'

Pete swaggers in his chair. 'Yeah, where I come from.'

'And is it sane to pass out in the hedge in your front garden and wake up covered in vomit?'

Pete shuffles uneasily.

'Is it sane to still be living with your mum and dad, aged thirty-five, because you spend every last penny you have on alcohol?'

Pete blushes and ducks his head. 'They don't mind,' he mumbles, but the fight has gone out of him.

'And what about you?' the counsellor presses. 'Do you mind? How does it make you feel?'

Pete sways in his chair, like a boxer ducking a punch.

The counsellor persists. 'What are you feeling now?'

'I'm feeling that I'm fucking sick of talking about fucking feelings,' Pete mutters. 'And there ain't no power greater than myself.'

The counsellor gestures at the open window, at the trees and landscape beyond. 'So you created all this, did you? You have the power to do that?'

'Fucking god squadders,' Pete says.

'It doesn't have to be God,' Timothy says gently. He has taken a shine to Pete. 'It can be anything you want. I particularly like the acronym, Group Of Drunks.'

Pete perks up appreciably. 'I don't mind that,' he says, 'believing in a bunch of pissheads.'

'Every time you want a drink, call another pisshead,' Rosie says. 'When you think you can't do it on your own, go to a meeting with the other pissheads, who also think they can't do it on their own. Tell them how you feel.'

'Fucking feelings,' Pete says, but he looks at her with a shy grin.

Timothy says, 'Or you could use, Good Orderly Direction.'

Pete snorts.

'Or perhaps not,' Timothy says.

'No,' Pete says. 'You're all right. Thanks.'

Molly came to visit me at the clinic. We were allowed visitors only one day a week, on a Sunday afternoon. This made her quite cross.

'Why can't I see you whenever I want?' she said. 'I could in the other hospitals.'

'This one's a bit different.'

'Why?'

I did not particularly want to tell Moll about my drinking. I felt she should have something left to admire in her mother. But better the truth than a lie.

'My mum? Well, she's a depressive and a drunk. Oh, and a liar too.'

So I said, 'As well as suffering from depression, I've been drinking too much. I've come here to get help to stop.'

Molly was outraged. 'You don't drink much.'

'Darling, I've always got a glass of wine in my hand.'

'I thought you were just partying.'

I laughed. 'Well, I was, but I was partying alone which is not good. I got addicted to alcohol, which is not good either. It makes depression much, much worse.'

'Well, you'd better stop.'

'Yes, darling. I will.'

There was a long silence.

'Actually, I'm much more worried about your coke habit.'

My voice went up an octave. 'My coke habit?' Had I got so drunk that I had taken coke in front of Molly? I couldn't remember the last time I'd taken coke. Before she was born, surely? Perhaps I'd blacked out. I had never blacked out, had I? Or, perhaps I drank far more than I thought I did.

'You drink at least six cans a day and Diet Coke is really bad for you.'

I hugged her. 'You're right. I should stop.'

She held out her hand.

'OK, if you stop drinking Coke, I'll stop eating sweets.'

'You don't have to do that.'

She smiled, a smile sweet enough to break your heart. 'I know I don't have to. I want to.' She slapped her hand in the air. 'Give me a high five.'

Step Three
*We made a decision to turn our will and our lives over to the care of God **as we understood him**.*

One definition of addiction is, 'doing the same thing over and over again, and expecting a different result.'

It's a borrowing from Albert Einstein (attributed, the jury's out on whether he actually said this), 'The definition of insanity; doing the same thing over and over again, expecting different results.'

Either will do for me. Addiction? Insanity? It's a close run thing.

The God question, though, was tricky. I have been a fully paid-up and passionate atheist all my life. God is for other people. I still believe that, in the sense of any organised religion, but I have come to believe in the possibility of a spiritual community. Perhaps that's why, like so many depressives before me, I was drawn to Buddhism, which follows an atheistic principle in that Buddha was not a god, he was a man, and a flawed one at that. I am not a Buddhist. I simply admire some of the beliefs and practices it follows, although not all of them.

I follow a similar adherence to the Twelve Step programme. I admire some of the principles, but not all. I take what I need, and the rest I leave behind. But, as somebody who has suffered from severe depression and alcohol dependence, I also know the terrible nihilism of hopelessness. I lost belief in everything, in myself, in other people, in the future and in life itself. The only antidote to hopelessness is faith, trust, belief – call it what you like – and, through attending AA and seeing the love, kindness, compassion and respect that people regularly show each other in the meetings, I began to believe again in the kindness of strangers and in community. You might say that AA restored my faith. It taught me not to interrupt, to listen to other people and look at them without judgement. It taught me compassion, forgiveness, tolerance and understanding and not just for other people, but for myself. Most of all, it taught me about the redemptive power of love and friendship.

'I hate that name, AA,' Molly said. 'Alcoholics Anonymous. It makes you sound like a loser.' She made an L shape with her fingers and held it to her forehead. 'And you're not. You're cool.'

I laughed. 'Its other name is "The Fellowship". It's the

name I prefer because that's what it is, a fellowship of men and women who look out for each other.'

Moll considered this for a moment. 'I like that. I'd like to belong to a fellowship. It's wicked. I might start one of those at school.'

'Perhaps not,' I said, thinking of the other parents and the amount of money they were spending on setting their little darlings on the right road. On the other hand, a London girls' day school: top of the league, filled with bright, competitive, relentlessly driven type-A personalities susceptible to drugs, drink, eating disorders . . .

If I am forced to name a Higher Power (and I resist that directive, even in AA) it is other people. More importantly, it is life. I knew, when I was drinking heavily, that it was no life. It was a dark, despairing living death. So was depression, and alcohol was keeping me there. So, when I finally decided to stop drinking I decided that I had two choices. I could choose to go on drinking myself to death, or I could choose to live.

Or, to put it another way, life or death?

I choose life.

Critics of AA will say that it is a cult; that it peddles a dangerous, addictive form of religion. That is not my experience. Alcoholics tend not to be meek, agreeable sorts; most dislike intensely being told what to do or what to believe in. That's why there are no rules in AA, only suggestions. That's why there is no one god, only the god of somebody's individual understanding.

It is not, anyway, a religious programme but a spiritual one that has its roots in a conversation between the psychiatrist Carl Jung and one of the founders of AA, who went to Jung for help. The conversation is printed in the Big Book (the nickname for the AA book containing the principles of the Twelve Step programme). The Big Book was first printed in the 1930s, so some of its wording may sound quaint. The meaning, though, is entirely modern.

The doctor described in the following extract is Carl Jung.

Some of our alcoholic readers may think they can do without spiritual help. Let us tell you the rest of the conversation our friend had with his doctor.

The doctor said: 'You have the mind of a chronic alcoholic. I have never seen one single case recover, where that state of mind existed to the extent that it does in you.'

Our friend felt as though the gates of hell had closed on him with a clang.

He said to the doctor: 'Is there no exception?'

'Yes,' replied the doctor, 'there is. Exceptions to cases such as yours have been occurring since early times. Here and there, once in a while, alcoholics have had what are called vital spiritual experiences. To me those occurrences are phenomena. They appear to be in the nature of huge emotional displacements and rearrangements. Ideas, emotions and attitudes, which were once the guiding forces of the lives of these men are suddenly cast to one side, and a completely new set of conceptions and motives begin to dominate them. In fact, I have been trying to produce such emotional rearrangements within you. With many individuals the methods which I employed are successful, but I have never been successful with an alcoholic of your description.'

Upon hearing this, our friend was somewhat relieved, for he reflected that, after all, he was a good church member. This hope, however, was destroyed by the doctor's telling him that while his religious convictions were very good, in his case they did not spell the necessary vital spiritual experience.

Here was the terrible dilemma in which our friend found himself when we had the extraordinary spiritual experience, which as we have already told you, made him a free man.

We, in turn, sought the same escape with all the desperation of drowning men. What seemed at first a flimsy reed,
has proved to be the loving and powerful hand of God. A
new life has been given us or, if you prefer, 'a design for
living' that really works.

The 'extraordinary spiritual experience' which made the
writer a free man was a blinding and sudden belief in a
power greater than himself, and which convinced him that
there was a better way than killing himself with alcohol.

I had no such experience and nor do I expect one, although
I did (slowly) become convinced that there was a better way
than alcohol. My belief in AA does not involve God but,
rather, that 'design for living' mentioned above. I remain an
atheist. I put my faith firmly in people and the power of the
group. In that spirit, nobody in the fellowship has ever taken
issue with my beliefs, and I have never taken issue with theirs.
One of its guiding principles is non-judgement, or taking
one's own inventory (paying attention to your own faults)
and nobody else's.

I also like Jung's 'emotional rearrangements' which is
pretty well what I was after, not just for alcoholism, but
for depression too. As research indicates that large numbers
of depressives abuse alcohol or drugs in order to medicate
pain, the AA Twelve Step programme of emotional rearran-
gement seems to me a blessed thing. It is group support and
therapy (for lack of a better word), based around sound
psychotherapeutic and spiritual principles, offered on a massive, global scale. It embraces every creed, gender, colour,
nationality, religion and social and economic background.
And it's free: going to AA costs nothing.

I'm sure that if most modern therapists, particularly CBT
practitioners, took the Twelve Step programme apart, they
would recognise many of the principles embedded in their
own disciplines.

This is particularly true of two of the newest and most

exciting forms of therapy emerging at present; Positive Psychology (emerging out of the US and based on practical solutions that encourage mental health rather than dwelling upon the symptoms of mental illness) and Cognitive Mindfulness Behavioural Therapy (a step on, and up, from the drier scientific model of challenging negative thinking used in CBT to include Buddhist principles of acceptance, faith and self-governance).

These therapeutic models prefer to play to people's strengths, rather than their weaknesses. They maintain that we need to look to a better future in preference to living in a difficult past. We might consider the past and our part in it, but once we have done so, we need to move on.

And so it is with the Twelve Step programme. It encourages people to look at their own behaviour, and how they might be sabotaging their own happiness. It asks them to look at how they might be at fault, rather than casting blame on others. It asks them to examine and to know themselves, and to work persistently at changing their more destructive behavioural patterns. It does, in essence, what psychotherapists of all sorts encourage.

Here are the principles of the Twelve Step programme, presented as a list. There are more principles included here than there are steps, because each step embraces many principles. I use them on a daily basis to help me with depression, or with any emotional pain that might make me want to self-medicate or drink. Nor are they just for depressives (we have no favourites here) but for anyone who might want a better design for living.

Open up.
Ask for help.
Accept help.
Accept yourself.
Be completely honest.
Take a daily inventory.

Whenever you are in the wrong, make amends.

Face reality.

Reach out.

Communicate.

Show kindness.

Share your concerns and your worries with another human being.

Help another human being, on a daily basis.

Count your blessings, not your failures.

Don't live in regret or in yesterday.

Don't project your fears into tomorrow.

Take action, when action is needed.

Deal with your feelings if and when they arise. Don't sit on them.

People talk about alcoholism as if it were a disease. It is not. You cannot catch it. It is a condition, an emotional illness or a behavioural disorder. It is, if you like, an inappropriate response to difficulty or pain. It is the messenger, not the message. At AA meetings, people rarely talk about alcohol. If they mention sobriety, generally what they mean is emotional sobriety. Meetings, or the support group, exist to help people to express and deal with the pain that might otherwise become so unmanageable that they try to dull it with drink.

For some people, depression is a result of alcohol abuse. Once they put down the alcohol, the depression lifts. For others, depression is a co-existing disorder, known as a co-morbid condition, and is often undiagnosed. When they stop drinking, their depression may worsen. They no longer have an anaesthetic to mask their pain and so they are more aware of it than ever. People have been hospitalised with severe depression two years after becoming sober.

Depressive illness and alcoholism are enduringly inter-twined. Studies indicate that where both conditions are present, depression or a mental illness is usually the primary disorder. A report published in the *American Journal of Drug and Alcohol Abuse* states:

> Among psychiatric disorders, alcoholism has been linked particularly to depressive conditions. In a study of psychiatric patients, those with major depressive disorder were among the highest substance abusers. Patients with severe depressive symptoms presumably are strongly motivated to find relief from their symptoms, and some may seek it through intoxication. Conversely, among alcoholic populations, those with depressive or other affective symptoms are likely to abuse alcohol more than those without such symptoms.
>
> Thus, within both psychiatric and alcohol-abuse populations the presence of depressive symptoms is associated with increased alcohol use. Also, when depression and alcohol abuse occur together – apparently regardless of which condition is clinically primary – the prognosis is worse than when either problem occurs alone. In a study comparing subgroups of depressed patients only, alcoholic patients only, and depressive patients with alcoholic disorders, the co-morbid group had the most severe psychopathology. One interpretation of this finding is that the co-morbid condition (depression with secondary alcoholism) produced more severe psychopathology. Another possibility is that those patients with more extreme psychopathology became alcoholic in attempting to cope with the noxious and stressful effects of their symptoms.

Alcoholism is also a physiological illness, inasmuch as the body becomes habituated to alcohol and craves more. I am sure, too, having watched closely for the past five years or so, that there are intuitive alcoholics: people whose systems are so sensitive to alcohol that it will cause them to malfunction, almost from the first drink. The route into alcoholism takes many paths but one of them seems to follow an inherited tendency. I have heard numbers of people in AA (usually with an alcoholic parent or sibling) describe how, at the age of thirteen or even younger, they took their first drink and immediately wanted another, drinking until they passed out. Vomiting, blackouts, toxic poisoning; nothing dissuaded them from pursuing another drink, and then another.

As is the case for most addictions, once the physical addiction is broken, the psychological one may continue. Or it may not. Not everyone who becomes dependent on alcohol stays dependent. I may not, as so many of my friends have pointed out, be an alcoholic, at least in the sense that they understand it. I have never passed out from drink. I do not vomit, smash up furniture, hit people, become abusive, shag strangers or exhibit any of the malfunctioning behaviour popularly associated with alcoholism.

That does not mean that I am not an alcoholic. If I am in emotional pain, my instinct is to take it away. My way of doing that is to drink, as I know that it relieves (if only temporarily) my pain. I have learned a disordered habit of behaviour that, once learned, is difficult to dismantle.

Now that I am well again, perhaps I could drink again. It is simply a risk that I am not prepared to take. After a long and severe episode of depressive illness, the possibility of relapse is high. Alcohol may precipitate depression by disrupting the already fragile chemical pathways in my head. On top of that, in order to guard myself against intuitive patterns of thinking and behaviour that may lead me back into depression, I need to be alert to my behaviour and thinking at all times. Alcohol is unlikely to help me in that clarity. It is, for me, no solution.

Once I had accepted that, it ceased to be a problem. I never drink alcohol and nor do I crave it. I love somebody who drinks. I always have drink in the house for him. As far as I'm concerned, it's just another grocery, like milk.

Very occasionally, on a hot summer's day when friends are drinking cold glasses of champagne I think, oh, wouldn't that be nice. Or perhaps, at a party where I am feeling nervous, I'd like to be able to have a drink to dull my anxiety or at a dinner where everyone around me is garrulous and repetitive (and, eventually, fantastically dull), I'd like to inhabit the same dimension in order to make the time pass more quickly.

But otherwise, no. Even when my mood is very low and I'd like a sedative or an anaesthetic to blunt the pain, I never consider having a drink. Alcohol reminds me of only one thing. It smells to me of despair.

24

The Useful Stuff

Whatever you think you can do or believe you can do, begin it. Action has magic, grace and power in it.

Johann Wolfgang von Goethe

Once I had got myself off alcohol, I began to address what my psychiatrist called low mood. This is what passes as ordinary, everyday depression. It is no longer clinical, or severe or major. It is what healthy people mean when they say that they are depressed; that low, weary feeling of things being disjointed and difficult, but not impossible.

For me, it felt like an interminable, grey summer. You know the sun is there and you long for it to appear but every morning you wake to a flat, low cloud. After I left rehab, this dragged on for eighteen months, the grey sometimes relieved by a tantalising glimpse of sunlight or a sudden, shockingly blue sky. Those brief passages of normality (or what I call normality) seemed both intolerable (would I be that way for ever?) and a reason to hope. I was further up than I had been for four years, and there seemed no reason why I could not go higher.

I was scared, though, nervous of one of those dizzying relapses with which depression literature is filled. According to research, most depressions go into spontaneous remission.

There are those, too, that spontaneously recombust. A longitudinal study of patients who had recovered from an episode of major depression showed that eighty-five per cent had a recurrence over the fifteen years of the study, and even in those who remained well for five years, there was a fifty-eight per cent chance of relapse. The longer the episode of depression, the higher the chance of a relapse.

Then again, every case of depression is unique, just as every individual is unique. And a scientific study, by its nature, relies on a large group of people doing exactly the same (proscriptively limited), thing over a determined period of time. What might be true for that control group may, or may not, be true for me. Or you.

Believe nothing.

Try everything.

That was my psychiatrist's view.

'We simply don't know,' he said.

And so I became determined to pull myself out of that low, grey mood in whatever way that I could. Now that I know so much more about depression, I look at it like this. It doesn't much matter how you manage the illness. It just matters that you do.

I manage it in a number of ways, which I include here. Some may work for you and some may not. We are all different.

They are all, though, worth trying.

The first is therapy, which, after my early furious attempts to engage with, I have come to value highly. Yes, even CBT. Anything that challenges the negative thought processes and hopelessness that define depressive illness is valuable. I think of therapy as reprogramming, overwriting the faulty script and replacing it with a fresh, more balanced take.

Scientific studies are beginning to back this up. Recent research demonstrates that psychotherapy significantly changes functions and structures of the brain, in a manner that seems to be different from the effects of medication.

Neuroscientists are discovering that major depression and bipolar illness (manic depression) are more than mere mood disorders. The impairments to function and cognition may last far beyond the course of an actual episode. Although they are not 'classic' neurodegenerative diseases such as Parkinson's and Alzheimer's, they are illnesses clearly associated with brain cell loss.

In the brain, a horseshoe-shaped structure known as the hippocampus is a centre for both mood and memory. Loss of neurons in the hippocampus is found in depression and correlates with impaired memory and low mood. According to research, when the brain is stressed (the 'stressors' known to be so implicated in depression), neurons shrink in the hippocampus, and that seems to impair memory. More recent research suggests that the same thing happens in the prefrontal cortex, which is crucial for decision-making and attention. The other profound loss is mental flexibility. Long-term stress can also enlarge the amygdala, the part of the brain that governs emotional and traumatic memory. If it becomes overactive, it is possible to develop what research scientist Bruce McEwen calls, 'an emotional memory that is not strongly attached to the world around you.'

In other words, the depressive's perspective may become shrouded with an excess of intensity and negativity or what we depressives know as 'stinking thinking'. That's the sort of thought process that keeps us dwelling on old emotions or hurts and, literally, playing the same track over and over again. It has little to do with reality but is simply a malfunction of thinking. It is that sort of thinking that therapy seeks to correct.

The good news is that it is no longer correct to talk about our brains as if they are the hard disk of a computer (although it is tempting) or that we are hardwired to behave in certain ways because our brains are not, as was once thought, immutable. They change. They are plastic, or flexible (neuroplasticity as it is known). The cells can grow again (neurogenesis). The self is constantly reinventing itself. The brain can heal itself and one of the ways it can do that is through the talking therapies. Here's Bruce McEwen, speaking at the 2006 Annual Convention of the American Psychological Association:

> The brain is very resilient. Give it a chance and it will make every effort to repair itself. A combination of psychotherapy, cognitive behaviour therapy and pharmaceuticals could actually change the brain and restore it more or less to normal.

When even neuroscientists are telling us that therapy can restore the brain to normal function, we should sit up and take notice.

Or start talking.

The point is, though, that we have to engage. We tend to think that we go to see a therapist in order to get fixed. In other words, we believe that someone else will make us better. This is not so. A therapist can only show us the faults in our thinking. He or she cannot actually change them. It is down to us to do that.

For that reason, therapy is hard, slow work and it is the sort of work that many people avoid or abandon when they are only partway through on the grounds that it is too difficult and frustrating. Well, so is depression.

We learn through repetition. Every skill or talent is the result of a repetitive action, done over and over again until it feels like second nature. Research shows that it takes 10,000 hours to truly master a skill, but far less than that to become somewhat proficient. If the same is true of therapy or learning to think in a new way (and why would it not be?) then both time and repetition are essential.

For two years, I did intensive therapy for four hours a week. On top of that, I attended AA meetings (which last for between an hour and an hour and a half) three times a week.

More than seven hours of therapy a week might sound excessive. Well, so was the severity of my depression and if medication couldn't make my neurons grow, I had to find another way.

I have stopped therapy, but I still go to AA meetings, at least two or three times a week. I go because I need to keep a constant check on my head, which is liable, at any time, to start misfiring, perhaps as a result of those pesky neurons shrivelling up. The meetings help me to correct my faulty thinking. They offer antidotes to my black thoughts, suggestions of ways in which I might think myself around or out of my most difficult responses. They suggest answers and remind me to live, as they say in AA, 'in the solution, not the problem'.

Group therapy (of whatever sort whether it is AA, CBT or any other form of structured, therapeutic talk) is, I believe, crucially important to the depressive. We get stuck in faulty thought patterns. We start running, faster and faster, on that hamster wheel in our own heads. The nature of depression is that it narrows our focus until we believe that our problems are insuperable and we are the only people who feel the way we do. Understanding that we are not alone and hearing other people express similar thoughts and feelings is quite possibly the best pain relief there is. In depressive or low moods, we are inclined to shut down, believing either that we have nothing to offer or that our moods are contagious to other people. In one way that is true, as anyone who has ever loved or lived with a depressive knows only too well. But the converse is true too; other people are contagious to our moods. Being with other people makes us feel better. It also makes us think better, or more realistically, about our own situation.

Here's a neat piece of research. It's about running, rumination and rats but think no less of it for that. Exercise can restore a depressed mind, rumination is proven to be both bad for (and intuitive to) the depressed mind and rats are social creatures, like us. In the study, published in the scientific journal, *Nature Neuroscience*, rats were divided into two groups: one lot was housed and exercised together and another housed and exercised in isolation.

Both groups of rats exercised for twelve days but the impact on brain health was dramatically different. The group of rats that exercised together showed increased neuron growth, i.e., new brain cells. The rats in isolation had suppressed brain cell growth.

Additionally, the study measured blood levels of the stress hormone, corticosterone. Both groups showed similar elevations, but only the isolated rats were vulnerable to a negative influence on new brain cell growth. They also showed higher levels of stress hormones in response to stressful stimuli when compared with the group-housed rats. People with chronic depression have high cortisol levels, which negatively affect brain cell growth. It could be that isolation in the rats led to greater depression, which negatively affected brain growth, whereas the group, or social, rats showed no increase in stress hormones.

Even if you ignore the science, the meaning is clear. We depressives need to get out more.

This, for most of us, is horribly difficult, particularly when we are enduring our blackest Garbo moments. In that state it doesn't do to be in a group of people who are unlikely to understand our more exotic thoughts such as suicide. But being with a group of people who do understand, and are willing to share that understanding, is undoubtedly helpful.

I no longer take medication, in part because my relationship with it was always so fraught but also because, most of the time, my brain seems to run along quite happily without it.

I took myself off it a year after I came out of rehab. While I was conscious that my mood was sometimes low, I knew instinctively that the depression had lifted. The first time I understood that was when I cried. The tears lasted for five minutes, and afterwards, I felt better.

I rang Nigel.

'I cried for five minutes.'

'Well done, Sal. That's fantastic.'

Now, it might sound mad to call one of your closest friends and boast that you have been crying but in the language of depression, five minutes of tears is healthy crying. Depressive crying has no limits. It can last for hours. It does not make you feel better. It comes for no reason. It does not stop. Any reprieve is merely temporary. Those five minutes of tears taught me one thing; I was getting better.

Shortly after I came off antidepressants, I took myself off sleeping pills too. I was terrified. When I was ill and taking the highest dose, I could not sleep for more than four hours a night. I did not get a full night's sleep for three years. I was so frightened of not sleeping and the black, blank terror that went with it, that I never forgot my prescription.

One day, I did. It was late at night and I had run out of sleeping pills. It occurred to me then that I no longer needed them. My brain was no longer on full alert.

And so it proved. It was difficult, at first. Insomnia had returned. But it was the insomnia of old, the insomnia that stopped me getting off to sleep, rather than woke me up at three twenty in the morning. I loved it, loved the hours of not being able to go to sleep. My brain was back to normal.

As for antidepressants, I would not rule them out, should I ever need them. I remain optimistic that a new form will be developed for people like me who are resistant to the present variety. Nor would I encourage anyone else to come off their drugs, simply because they feel they ought to. I have never quite understood the 'ought' in that sentence. Or the logic in this one: 'I don't like feeling dependent on drugs.'

Well, why ever not? If they keep you stable and you tolerate them happily, if coming off them might mean weeks and months of misery, then why even consider it? SSRI medication is not a magic drug – although it may feel like it to somebody who responds well to it when he or she is drowning in the black depths of depression. I feel a sort of yearning as I write that sentence. If only I was one of those people. I am not. But I know people who are. I have known them before taking medication, and after, and the effects are, frankly, miraculous. They can restore somebody to normal functioning. What they cannot do is turn somebody into a person that they are not. They are not character altering. They are character restoring.

Nor are they mind altering. In the same way that depression is an illness and not a character flaw, drugs treat an illness; they do not remedy a personality. The personality was always there. It may have been disguised or distorted by depressive illness but it is, in essence, changeless.

I am, anyway, dependent on drugs. Every morning I take thyroxin and will do so for as long as I live. If I don't, everything about me including my mood will get slower and slower until, eventually, I shall cease to work.

An underactive thyroid (hypothyroidism) is apt to be dismissed as a minor complaint. It should not be. The symptoms can mimic depression in that they show up as extreme fatigue, lack of focus or concentration, abnormal sleep patterns (often much longer and heavier sleep) and a general greyness of mood. The sharp psychic pain of severe depression is absent, though, and so are the long wearying bouts of crying. But as hypothyroidism may precipitate an episode of depression, it is always worth asking your GP for a thyroid test if you are feeling very low. Some cases of what appears to be depression have turned out to be untreated hypothyroidism.

I also take omega-3 oil, on the advice of my psychiatrist. When I was in hospital, he ordered some tests on my fatty acid levels and discovered that they were alarmingly low. This finding was in line with numerous studies showing decreased omega-3 content in the blood of depressed patients. In one study, medication-free depressed patients, tracked over a two-year period, showed that low blood levels of omega-3 predicted the risk of suicidal behaviour.

Over sixty per cent of the human brain consists of fat, which insulates nerve cells to support proper electrical signalling. More than one third of the brain's fat is composed of omega-3 fatty acids such as those found in fish oil. Neuroscientists believe that deficiencies of essential fatty acids may upset the fatty make-up of the brain and contribute to mood disorders.

The crucial ingredient seems to be EPA (eicosapentaenoic acid; an omega-3 fatty acid), and research seems to indicate that to have an effect on depression you need to take 1,000 mg (1 gram) of EPA a day. You could, of course, get that amount from eating fish if you were prepared to stomach more than half a kilo of wild salmon daily. Farmed salmon is thought to contain less beneficial fats and is also implicated in high levels of toxins.

EPA supplementation is also particularly good for people with depression that is resistant to treatment with SSRI medication. It appears to improve the accessibility of the brain to the antidepressant and allow it to do its work. It is important, though, to take pharmaceutical-grade oil with a high content of EPA, so it's worth searching around. The Internet is a good source. As EPA is only one constituent of omega-3, you need to work out the number of capsules or the amount of pure oil you need to take in order to get the therapeutic dose of one gram of pure EPA. You should allow three months for it to have any effect and it does not work for everyone.

I also take complex B vitamins daily. I had not considered taking vitamins until I had a blood test for a quite unrelated condition, last year. The doctor asked me if I was eating well because my vitamin B12 levels were abnormally low. I have always eaten well but, since my illness, I am particularly careful about my diet since poor nutrition seems to me an obvious link to poor mood.

So I was somewhat surprised until I discovered that low levels of vitamin B12 are often linked to higher incidences of depression. A report, published in *BMC Psychiatry* and the result of a study undertaken by researchers at Kuopio University Hospital, Finland, suggests that there is a link between vitamin B12 levels and the probability of recovery from major depression. A further report maintained that B12 makes antidepressants work more effectively although researchers are still puzzling over why some depressed people have lower B12 levels and recommend further investigation.

All I know is that taking B12 works for me. On a couple of occasions I have run out of vitamins and omega-3 or grown bored of taking my daily dose of pills and oils. On both occasions, within a couple of weeks, my mood plummeted. Sometimes, we are our own best evidence.

I have learned to calm my mind in other ways too. One of those is meditation.

There are many different forms but I practise Transcendental Meditation (or TM), which I took up in order to counteract the early morning waking, which I did not at the time realise was the first symptom of my illness. I thought it would calm my frantic mind but I think now that it had other, less enjoyable effects.

My teacher warned me that meditation is not entirely benign and that it has the power to disturb long-repressed feelings so I was not to be too concerned if I experienced sudden flashes of anger or grief. In me, it seemed to uncover much more than that but whether it simply foreshadowed the depressive storms that were already gathering on the horizon, I do not know.

I do know that when I was very ill, I was unable to meditate. Simply closing my eyes set off such storms of grief and terrible imaginings that I became frightened of doing it at all. This, apparently, is quite common in severe depression and many meditation and yoga teachers advise students not to close their eyes if they experience it.

I simply abandoned meditation altogether and I would say to anyone in the middle of a depressive episode that it would be best not even to attempt it. If you do want to practise some form of self-soothing then gentle breathing exercises performed with your eyes open are far kinder.

As a part of recovery, however, meditation has proved invaluable. Once the worst of my illness had passed, I began to meditate again, at first tentatively and now, regularly for twenty minutes every morning. If I find the time, I meditate in the evening too, as twenty minutes, morning and evening, are described as having the most powerful benefit. The effect appears to be cumulative but for me the most obvious benefit has been a deep-seated feeling of calm. It is, fanciful as it sounds, as if somebody has turned the volume down a little. There are acres of research on this but I simply feel that as depression is precipitated by stress, it makes sense to do anything that one can to reduce that.

As to which form of meditation, it is best to go to a class or a teacher and learn the discipline properly. As a group practice, it is formidably powerful and, once again, a connection to other people is profoundly helpful to the depressive.

The last, persistent symptom of my depression was the throat monster, good old *Globus hystericus*.

One morning, when I was meditating, it was particularly bad. It had been, for weeks. I thought, I can't go on like this.

A little while later Maggie, a friend, telephoned.

'How are you?' she said.

'Really low. It's this thing at my throat. It's dragging me down. Every time I feel it, which is every day, it reminds me of the way that I used to feel when I was really sick with depression. It makes me believe that I'll never be right again.'

'Go and see my pin man,' she said. 'He's brilliant at stuff like that.'

'What? Mad people?'

She laughed. 'And the rest.'

I went to see the pin man. His name is Robert.

'I can get rid of that for you,' he said. 'The Chinese call it plum stone.'

'You can?' I said, wondering if a few acupuncture needles would succeed where one psychiatrist, five therapists, three psychiatric units, two tons of antidepressants, Xanax, Valium, and five vats of pure alcohol had failed.

'Sure, although it may take two or three sessions.'

It took two.

I go and see Robert every two weeks, without fail. I have no idea what he does or how acupuncture works, although he did try to explain it to me.

Actually, I don't care. I just know that his needles work, that they keep me, in some mysterious way, in balance. But, like any other treatment, consistency is crucial. One session is not enough. It is a commitment to health and, like any other commitment, requires steadiness of purpose.

Acupuncture is one of the few alternative therapies to have found some sanction from science. In the first study of its kind in the West, reported in the *Psychiatric Times* in 2000, Dr John Allen, associate professor of psychology, cognitive science and neuroscience at the University of Arizona, got together with acupuncturist Rosa Schyner to compare the reduction of major depression in three groups of women. For eight weeks the first group of women received specific acupuncture therapy for depression. The second group received acupuncture treatment for symptoms not associated with depression. The final group was put on a wait-list. The women in the first two groups were not told which treatment they were getting.

At the end of eight weeks, the women who received specific acupuncture treatment for depression were significantly less depressed (sixty-four per cent experienced full remission according to *DSM-IV* criteria) than the women who received acupuncture treatment for symptoms not related to depression.

There are now many more trials under way. They look promising. It seems that acupuncture may well be able to deliver a release from severe depression at least as good as antidepressants. There are, though, two other variables; the acupuncture practitioner and the patient. It is worth searching out a good acupuncturist and it is sensible to understand that it may not work at first. Try, try and try again. It is the mantra of recovery, in all things.

25

Coming Through

We shall find peace. We shall hear the angels, we shall see the sky sparkling with diamonds.

Anton Chekhov

If there is any lesson I have learned from depression, it is this.

We have to let go – of self-pity, anger and blame. We are what we are. Life is what it is. It will be what it is, however we are, and the best way to deal with it is gently. It took me a long time to learn that. In every psychiatric hospital all the psychiatrists, therapists and nurses kept saying the same thing.

'You must let go, Sally.'

The trouble was, I did not understand what they meant and nor could they tell me how to do it. Whenever my mind wrapped in coils so black and tight and knotted that I thought they could never be undone, I tried to do as they suggested.

The harder I tried, the more my mind seemed to hold on.

And then I came across the writings of a Buddhist teacher, Jack Kornfield, an American who went to Tibet as an adolescent and became a monk, in part to calm the agonised tangle of his mind. He went on silent retreats, spent long hours in meditation, learned humility, acceptance and non-judgement. He was happy. And then he returned to New York, and discovered all that he had learned sitting peaceably halfway up a mountainside in Tibet was no match for the tense speed and aggression of Manhattan. He retrained, as a psychologist, and began to match the teachings of the East to the knowledge of the West.

Here is something he wrote:

Letting go is not getting rid of.
Letting go is letting be.

When I read that I felt one of those rare moments of clear, lucid understanding. It was a moment of light.

Years of clenched meaninglessness slipped into place. The coils loosened and fell away. It did not last, of course. Nothing does. But it gave me a sufficient understanding to know that when I get into difficulty, the best way for me is not to try to let go, but to let it be.

And so it is with my illness. I know that I am fragile in some way. People often say, 'Are you frightened it will come back?'

Of course.

Do I worry about it?

No. Worrying is a holding on to, a tightening of the coils. I take action to avoid a relapse. That's different from worrying about it. Worrying is inaction, a paralysis of fear. It is an agitation about a future that has not happened, and a past that cannot be changed. It can be understood, explained, even apologised for. But it cannot be changed.

Here is another story I find useful.

It is about a young Buddhist novice who was learning meditation with his master. It was a hot day so the windows were wide open. Across the way, a car engine was being persistently revved. The young novice squirmed and shifted on his cushion. He peeked at his master who was motionless, his eyes closed in beatific peace. Finally, the novice could stand it no longer. He approached his master.

'How can you meditate with such a noise?'

The master did not open his eyes. 'What noise?' he said.

'That car!' exclaimed the novice. 'Isn't it bothering you?'

'Is it the car that's bothering you?' said his master. 'Or is it you that's bothering the car?'

The novice thought about this for a while, then walked silently back to his cushion and sat down and closed his eyes.

I often think of that story when some detail of life (sometimes an event but more usually a person, as in the spirit of Sartre; 'hell is other people') irritates me. Are they bothering me? Or have I fixed on something about them in some part of my mind and it is, in fact, me who is bothering them?

Even the thought is usually sufficient to stop the bother.

The last method I practise regularly is gratitude.

I know, it sounds too cute for words.

It works.

Other than this book, I write regular columns for newspapers and magazines.

Sometimes, the deadlines get crazy. Sometimes, I want to pay attention to the rest of my life. Sometimes, I do not want to write at all.

When that feeling of stress – trapped by work; cut off from pleasure – becomes too overwhelming, I let loose the gratitude theory.

It goes something like this.

I am grateful for the talent to write.

I am grateful that people pay me to write.

I am grateful that I have the ability to write, after losing it in depression.

I am grateful that something that gives me so much pleasure also gives me the ability to earn a living.

I am grateful that people are sufficiently interested in what I have to say to publish it.

I am grateful that I can take my work anywhere and do it everywhere; up a mountain, in the middle of the night.

By the time I have finished, I am generally able to settle down happily to work. I use it in other ways too. Every night, before I sleep, I run through a gratitude list in my head. The trick is to stay with the details; otherwise the great temptation is to scurry past the more obvious objects of gratitude. For example, I am always, eternally, grateful for my daughter so it's curious how easily she can get passed by in my head. But if I concentrate on some detail of Molly and focus on the fact that she had a happy day at school that day or remember that she and a friend had made up a quarrel, I see and appreciate her presence in my life with greater clarity.

Nor do we need to be solely grateful to the people we are most intimate with. I often find myself grateful for the comfort of strangers; a man who gave up his seat for me on the bus, a woman who helped me out with a heavy shopping bag. Remembering small acts of kindness puts the world in a finer, sweeter order.

Some people write a daily gratitude list, but however you do it the consistency of habit has undeniably positive results. It teaches you to see life as a blessing rather than a trial, or a punishment, which is where the depressed mind is inclined to go. Obviously, gratitude as a daily practice is not new. It has been used by every spiritual discipline from Buddhism through Islam to Christianity. However, the scientific study of it is new, most prominently spearheaded by Martin Seligman, a professor of psychology (with a string of other degrees to his name) at the University of Pennsylvania and author of *Authentic Happiness*. According to Seligman, 'Empirically the amount of gratitude is related to baseline levels of happiness. The less gratitude you have in life the more unhappy you are, interestingly.'

It was Seligman who first defined the term 'learned helplessness' when he was working in animal-behaviour labs. Dogs were given electric shocks. When they learned that no matter what they did, they couldn't avoid the shocks, they simply gave up trying. Later, even when they could easily escape, they passively endured the electric shocks. Seligman went on to apply this finding to humans and developed the theory of learned helplessness as a model for depression.

In an interview published on *Edge*, a website devoted to an interplay of science, society and culture, he explained that:

> I spent the first thirty years of my career working on misery. I found helpless dogs, helpless rats, and helpless people, and I began to ask, almost forty years ago now, how do you break it up? What's the neuroscience of it? What drugs work? While working on helplessness there was a finding I was always brushing under the rug, which was that with people and with animals, when we gave them uncontrollable events, only five out of eight became helpless. About a third of them we couldn't make helpless. And about a tenth of them were helpless to begin with and we didn't have to do anything. I began to wonder why.

The wondering why became the Positive Psychology movement, which teaches people what Seligman calls, 'learned optimism'.

> I started working on optimism versus pessimism, and I found that optimistic people got depressed at half the rate of pessimistic people, that optimistic people succeeded better in all professions that we measured except one, that optimistic people had better, feistier, immune systems, and probably lived longer than pessimistic people. We also created interventions that reliably changed pessimists into optimists.

Those interventions consist, in brief, of expressing gratitude, knowing your strengths and crafting everything you do to use them as much as possible and discovering an activity that consistently challenges and entertains you. For some people that might be studying nuclear fission, for others it could be doing a jigsaw puzzle. It doesn't much matter. What matters is that it is sufficiently absorbing to lose yourself in and sufficiently challenging to keep you eagerly anticipating the next moment. Mine is gardening. When I am in the garden, I forget everything but the task in hand. Seligman also discovered that a single act of kindness makes people feel far better about themselves (for a full day) than any transient act of pleasure, such as buying a new pair of shoes or going to the movies. He calls the feeling it inspires, elevation. An act of kindness might be helping an elderly neighbour to do their shopping or standing aside to let somebody pass instead of barging past them and making them feel they don't matter or exist.

When we think about how other people are feeling, we stop concentrating so hard on ourselves. We expand rather than contract, and so the world expands along with us. We can change our whole day (and other people's) with a single kind word, or ruin it by an angry exchange. By thinking outside ourselves, we also stop thinking about how life isn't giving us happiness and how we might give a little happiness to life.

There is, though, a final route to optimism. Here's Seligman again:

> There's a third form of happiness that is ineluctably pursued by humans, and that's the pursuit of meaning . . . There is one thing we know about meaning: that meaning consists in attachment to something bigger than you are. The self is not a very good site for meaning, and the larger the thing that you can credibly attach yourself to, the more meaning you get out of life. There's no shortcut to that. That's what life is about.

Whether we feel that way through a spiritual practice, a walk in the park or (as in my case) sitting around with a bunch of depressives or alcoholics doesn't much matter. What matters is to feel that we are not alone.

Every story deserves a happy ending. Here is mine.

Tom and I met again, three years after we parted. We had not seen each other at all during those years but he was never far from my mind – or from my heart. We met in a pub. He bought me a drink, lime and soda. Then he bought me a cup of tea.

'You're a cheap date these days,' he laughed, but I noticed his hands were shaking. So were mine.

He said, 'How's your love life?'

I felt as if I was about thirteen. Was he asking me as an old friend, or because he wanted to know if I was available? I searched for a right answer and then, because I could find no right answer except the truth, I said, 'Non-existent. We were too much of a hard act to follow. How's yours?'

He was silent for a while, and then he smiled at me. 'The same.'

Two years later, we were married. It is, in its own particular way, bliss.

Notes

4 **To wage war** Andrew Solomon, *The Noonday Demon*, Chatto & Windus, London, 2001

7 **personal account** Sally Brampton, *Daily Telegraph*, 5 March 2003

19 **The dirty little secret** Interview with Martin Seligman, 'Eudaemonia, The Good Life', 23 March 2004. *Edge* magazine. Edge is also a website devoted to an interplay of science, society and culture. www.edge.org

21 **Around 5 million** Study of treatment-resistant depression at the Clinical Neuroscience Research Centre, published in *Biological Psychiatry*, 15 October 2003. The Clinical Neuroscience Centre, Dartford, UK, is headed up by Professor Tonmoy Sharma and dedicated to innovative research into more accurate diagnoses of, and more effective treatments for, a range of conditions including depression, schizophrenia, mild cognitive impairment, and Alzheimer's disease.

24 **If by 'cure'** Interview with Professor John F. Greden, director of the University of Michigan Depression Center, published in *Medicine at Michigan*, Volume 4, Summer 2002. John F. Greden is Rachel Upjohn Professor of Psychiatry and Clinical Neuroscience, Chair of the Department of Psychiatry and Senior Research Scientist at Michigan's Mental Health Research Institute.

33 **My creative powers** Johann Wolfgang Goethe, *The Sorrows of Young Werther*, 1774. Goethe was famously a depressive.

41 **Mild to moderate depression** *The Diagnostic and Statistical Manual of Mental Disorders, Fourth Edition (DSM-IV)* is published by the American Psychiatric Association and covers all mental health disorders for both children and adults. It lists known causes of these disorders, statistics in terms of gender, age at onset, and prognosis as well as research concerning optimal treatment approaches.

72 **Most depressives** Smoking and depression. Dr Gregory A. Ordway, a professor of psychiatry at the University of Mis-

sissippi Medical Center, and collaborator Dr Violetta Klimek, compared brain-tissue samples from long-term smokers with samples from non-smokers and concluded that chronic smoking produces 'antidepressant-like' effects on the human brain. This may contribute to the high incidence of smoking and difficulty to quit in those who are depressed. *Archives of General Psychiatry*, September 2001. In September 2006 researchers at Duke University Medical Centre gave nicotine or placebo patches to a group of non-smokers diagnosed with depression, then measured their symptoms using a standardised questionnaire. They found that who wore the nicotine patch for at least eight days experienced significant declines in depressive symptoms.

78   **Beck Depression Inventory** The Beck Depression Inventory (BDI, BDI-II), created by Dr Aaron T. Beck, is one of the most widely used instruments for measuring the severity of depression. There are three versions of the BDI – the original, first published in 1961 and later revised in 1971 as the BDI-1A, and the BDI-II, published in 1996.

84   **The severity of depression** Kay Redfield Jamison, *Night Falls Fast: Understanding Suicide*, Alfred A. Knopf, New York, 1999. Kay Redfield Jamison is Professor of Psychiatry at the Johns Hopkins University School of Medicine and Honorary Professor of English at the University of St Andrews in Scotland. She has bipolar disorder and wrote a first hand account of her illness in her first book, *An Unquiet Mind*, Picador, London, 1995.

97   **By 2020** Facts on depression taken from the the World Health Organisation (WHO). Depression was the leading cause of disability as measured by YLDs (years lived with disability) and the fourth leading contributor to the global burden of disease, measured by disability-adjusted life years (DALYs), in 2000. By the year 2020, depression is projected to reach second place in the ranking of DALYs calculated for all ages and sexes. Depression is already the second cause of DALYs in the age category 15–44 years for both sexes combined. It is common, affecting about 121 million people worldwide but can be reliably diagnosed and treated in primary care. However, fewer than twenty-five per cent of those affected have access to effective treatments.

100   **Bruce Charlton** Bruce Charlton, research psychiatrist at the Department of Psychology, University of Newcastle upon Tyne. 'The Malaise Theory of Depression: Major Depressive

Disorder is Sickness Behaviour and Antidepressants are Analgesic', *Medical Hypotheses*, 2000.

113 **According to a study** 'A Swedish National Twin Study of Lifetime Major Depression', Kenneth S. Kendler, MD, Margaret Gatz, PhD, Charles O. Gardner, PhD, and Nancy L. Pedersen, PhD. Objective: substantial evidence supports the heritability of lifetime major depression. Less clear is whether genetic influences in major depression are more important in women than in men and whether genetic risk factors are the same in the two sexes. *American Journal of Psychiatry*, January 2006.

114 **Because parents may** A three-generation study showing new evidence that major depression can afflict families from one generation to the next. The twenty-year longitudinal family study found twice the rate of depression or anxiety in children whose parents and grandparents also had depression than in children without such a history. Myrna M. Weissman et al., *Archives of General Psychiatry*, 2005.

115 **conducted a study** News Archive, 2003, King's College London. 'Variations in a region of DNA next to the serotonin transporter gene help to determine whether stressful events will make you depressed', lead author Professor Terri Moffitt at the Institute of Psychiatry. Published in *Science*, published by the American Association for the Advancement of Science, July 2003.

119 **'adapted child'** Eric Berne (1910–70) was a prominent psychiatrist and author who felt increasingly frustrated with the psychoanalytic approaches of the time. As a result, he began developing a new and revolutionary theory, which he called Transactional Analysis. In 1958 he published the paper 'Transactional Analysis: A New and Effective Method of Group Therapy', where he outlined this new approach. After creating Transactional Analysis, Berne continued to develop and apply this new methodology, most prominently in his book *Games People Play*, Penguin, London, 1964.

120 **Depression is the price** Alice Miller, *The Drama of Being a Child*, Virago, London, 1987. Miller, a psychoanalyst, became strongly disenchanted with her chosen field after many years in practice. Her first three books stemmed from a reaction to what she felt were major blind spots in her field. By the time her fourth book was published she no longer believed that psychoanalysis was viable.

143 **an emotional cue** The paper on emotional memory and a self-reinforcing 'memory loop', by Florin Dolcos, Kevin LaBar

and Roberto Cabeza, was published online 9 February 2005, in *Proceedings of the National Academy of Sciences*. The researchers are in Duke University's Center for Cognitive Neuroscience, Department of Psychological and Brain Sciences, and Brain Imaging and Analysis Center.

159 **A study by** E. Mark Cummings, the Notre Dame Professor of Psychology, and researchers from Rochester University and the Catholic University of America examined the effect of marital conflict on the 9- to-18-year-old children of 226 parents for three years. A second study also examined the connection between marital conflict and emotional problems over a three-year period, with a different group of 232 parents and kindergarten-aged children. The researchers again found that destructive marital conflict led to similar problems. Published in the Jan/Feb 2006 issue of the journal *Child Development*.

159 **According to research** Dr Alan Booth, Distinguished Professor of Sociology and Human Development, and co-researcher Dr Paul R. Amato, Professor of Sociology, Penn State University, in 'The Legacy of Parents' Marital Discord: Consequences for Children's Marital Quality', published in the October 2001 issue of the *Journal of Personality and Social Psychology*. Their data were based on a longitudinal study of marital quality spanning twenty-one years, analysing a sample of 297 parents and comparing the quality of their marriages in 1980 with those of their children in 1997.

161 **Difficulty understanding** 'Asperger's Syndrome', Stephen M. Edelson, PhD, Center for the Study of Autism, Salem, Oregon, 1995. www.autism.org/asperger

162 **Whether a child** *John Bowlby and Attachment Theory*, Jeremy Holmes, Taylor & Francis, Oxford, 1993.

171 **Madness need not** R. D. Laing, *The Politics of Experience*, Penguin, London, 1967. One of the most famous and controversial psychiatrists of his generation, Ronald Laing admitted to suffering from periodic bouts of alcoholism and clinical depression during a BBC interview for *In the Psychiatrist's Chair* with Dr Anthony Clare in 1983.

243 **Suicidal thoughts** Interview with Professor John F. Greden, director of the University of Michigan Depression Center, published in *Medicine at Michigan*, Volume 4, Summer 2002.

245 **pilot clinical trial** University of Texas Southwestern Medical Center, Dallas, pilot clinical trial; adding exercise to antidepressant medications significantly reduces depressive symptoms in patients with major depressive disorders. Study led by

Dr Madhukar Trivedi, professor of psychiatry and director of UT Southwestern's mood disorders research programme. News release, Society for Neuroscience, 2003.

246 **Another study** Thirty-minute aerobic workouts done three to five times a week cut depressive symptoms by fifty per cent in young adults. Study led by Dr Madhukar Trivedi, professor of psychiatry and director of UT Southwestern's mood disorders research programme. Results published in the January 2005 issue of the *American Journal of Preventive Medicine*.

246 **while research at** Exercise as effective a treatment for depression as antidepressants. Study led by psychologist James Blumenthal, Duke University, North Carolina. Results published in the journal *Psychosomatic Medicine*, October 2000.

252 **A study carried out** Study of depression as a risk factor for the onset of severe neck and lower-back pain. Study led by Dr Linda Carroll, professor in the University of Alberta Department of Public Health Sciences, published in the journal *Pain*, March 2004.

252 **In a study** Seattle study findings that fifty per cent of all depressed patients worldwide report multiple unexplained physical symptoms. 'An International Study of the Relationship between Somatic Symptoms and Depression' published in the *New England Journal of Medicine*, October 1999.

252 **As with any** 'Some of the most extensive medical research on yoga therapy is being done in India but will it ever be accepted by Western medicine?' Timothy B. McCall, MD, *Yoga Journal*, January/February 2003.

252 **pranayama** The National Institute of Mental Health and Neuroscience (Demeed University), India. The yoga research group in NIMHANS has been studying the therapeutic use of yoga in various psychiatric conditions for some years, with active collaboration from the Art of Living foundation and the Swami Vivekannada Yoga Anusandhana Samsthana (SVYA-SA).

253 **an accessible form** Stephen Cope, *Yoga and the Quest for the True Self*, Bantam Dell, New York, 2000. Cope is a psychotherapist, senior Kripalu yoga teacher, and Senior Scholar in Residence at the Kripalu Center for Yoga and Health in Lenox, Massachusetts.

253 **You don't take** Amy Weintraub, *Yoga For Depression*, Broadway Books, New York, 2004. Weintraub is a senior Kripalu yoga teacher and founder and director of the LifeForce Yoga Healing Institute. She is also a consultant to the Program in Integrative Medicine at the University of Arizona.

288 **Among psychiatric disorders** Extracts from 'Anxiety and Alcohol Abuse in Patients in Treatment for Depression', Edward H. Fischer and John W. Goethe, *American Journal of Drug and Alcohol Abuse*, August 1998.

292 **study of patients** 'Recurrence after Recovery from Major Depressive Disorder During Fifteen Years of Observational Follow-up', T. Mueller, A. Leon, M. Keller, D. Solomon, J. Endicott, W. Coryell, M. Warshaw and J. Maser, *American Journal of Psychiatry*, July 1999.

293 **an emotional memory** Bruce McEwen is the Alfred E. Mirsky Professor and head of the Harold and Milliken Hatch Laboratory of Neuroendocrinology at the Rockefeller University. McEwen is a major figure in behavioural neuroendocrinology and the roles of steroid hormones in reproductive behaviour, brain development, gene expression in the brain, brain plasticity in adulthood, and the effects of stress on the brain. He is the co-author, with science writer Harold M. Schmeck, Jr, of *The Hostage Brain*, Rockefeller University Press, New York, 1994, and co-author, with science writer Elizabeth N. Lasley, of *The End of Stress as We Know It*, National Academies Press, Washington DC, 2002.

300 **A report** 'High Vitamin B12 Level and Good Treatment Outcome May Be Associated in Major Depressive Disorder', J. Hintikka, T. Tolmunen, A. Tanskanen, and H. Viinamäki, *BMC Psychiatry*, 2004.

302 **first study** 'Depression and Acupuncture: A Controlled Clinical Trial', John J. B. Allen, PhD, *Psychiatric Times*, March 2000.

304 **a Buddhist teacher** Jack Kornfield, *The Art of Forgiveness, Lovingkindness, and Peace*, Rider, London, 2002.

307 **Empirically the amount** interview with Martin Seligman, 'Eudaemonia, The Good Life', 23 March 2004, *Edge* magazine.

Helpful Reading

Beck, Charlotte Joko, *Everyday Zen* (HarperCollins, 1997)

Bradshaw, John, *Healing the Shame That Binds You* (Health Communications, 1991)

Csikszentmihalyi, Mihaly, *Flow: Psychology of Happiness* (Rider, 1992)

Fromm, Erich, *The Art of Loving* (Thorsons, 1995)

Goleman, Daniel, *Emotional Intelligence* (Bloomsbury, 2004)

Haidt, Jonathan, *The Happiness Hypotheses: Putting Ancient Wisdom to the Test of Modern Science* (Heinemann, 2006)

Jamison, Kay Redfield, *An Unquiet Mind: A Memoir of Moods and Madness* (Picador, 1997)

Jamison, Kay Redfield, *Night Falls Fast: Understanding Suicide* (Picador, 2001)

Kornfield, Jack, *A Path with Heart* (Rider, 2002)

Kornfield, Jack, *After the Ecstasy, the Laundry* (Rider, 2002)

Manning, Martha, *Undercurrents* (HarperSanFrancisco, 1995)

Martin, Philip, *The Zen Path Through Depression* (HarperSanFrancisco, 1999)

Miller, Alice, *The Drama of Being a Child* (Virago, 1995)

Puri, Dr Basant K., and Hilary Boyd, *The Natural Way to Beat Depression* (Hodder Mobius, 2004)

Ricard, Matthieu, *Happiness: A Guide to Developing Life's Most Important Skill* (Atlantic Books, 2007)

Ridley, Matt, *The Origins of Virtue* (Penguin, 1997)

Rogers, Carl, *On Becoming a Person: A Therapist's View of Psychotherapy* (Constable, 2004)

Rowe, Dorothy, *Depression: The Way Out of Your Prison* (Routledge, 2003)

Schaef, Anne Wilson, *Escape from Intimacy* (HarperSanFrancisco, 1990)

Seligman, Martin E., *Authentic Happiness* (Nicholas Brealey, 2003)

Servan-Schreiber, David, *Healing without Freud or Prozac: Natural Approaches to Curing Stress, Anxiety and Depression without Drugs and without Psychoanalysis* (Rodale International Ltd, 2004)

Solomon, Andrew, *The Noonday Demon: An Anatomy of Depression* (Chatto & Windus, 2001)

Styron, William, *Darkness Visible* (Vintage, 2001)

Weintraub, Amy, *Yoga for Depression* (Broadway Books, 2003)

Wolpert, Lewis, *Malignant Sadness: The Anatomy of Depression* (Faber & Faber, 1999)

Wright, Robert, *The Moral Animal* (Abacus, 2004)

Thank You

This book should be dedicated to all my friends, not just two, but the list would be too long. Thank you all for your love. It is returned, in full. Thank you for being there and for believing in me when I could not do it for myself. It was that, most of all, which pulled me through.

In no particular order, I should like to thank the following for their love and kindness during those dark days. Jasper Conran, Jules and Thomas Hughes Hallett, Maggie Mullen, Emma Turner, Lesley White and Jim Gee, Betty Jackson and David Cohen, Lulu Guinness, Maureen Doherty, Caroline Broadbent, Alastair Blair, Delia and John Rothnie-Jones, Charles Elton, Lucy Heller, Claire Lloyd, Matthew Lauder, Gideon Kopell, Julie Lynn Evans, Aly Brown, Emma Duncan, Nicholas Myers, Mary Sackville-West and Rosie Boycott.

Thank you to my family, who suffered and worried a great deal. Thanks, too, to my brothers, for reading the manuscript of this book, and for suggestions.

My thanks to all at Bloomsbury, but in particular to Alexandra Pringle and Rosemary Davidson, for their faith in me and in this book. Thank you, too, to my editor, Michael Fishwick, for making this book better, for taking endless cigarette breaks with me, and for being as crazy about gardening as I am. When talk of depression became too much, we started on the roses. And to Trâm-Anh Doan, for her tireless patience in seeing the book through.

Thank you to my agent, Pat Kavanagh, for her kindness and support and those odd, whimsical postcards that appear from time to time, which always cheer me up. Most of all, thanks for twenty years of friendship. My European agents at ILA, Sam Edenborough and Nikki Kennedy, were unfailing in their patience and kindness when I could not write and wonderfully encouraging and enthusiastic when this book was finally finished. Thanks, too, to my US agent, Zoe Pagnamenta, for her support and for working so hard on my behalf.

Thank you to Corinna Honan, my editor at the *Daily Telegraph*, who encouraged me to write, even when I couldn't. And who paid me to write, when I could.

With thanks to my psychiatrist for his unfailing optimism and frankness, and for encouraging me to write this book. When I was fretting that I was no expert, he reassured me that there was no better qualification than experience. My therapist, Elizabeth Hearn, taught me about trust, love and acceptance, and her continuing friendship means a great deal to me.

My yoga teacher, Catherine James, was a constant source of strength and hope, encouraging me to believe that anything is possible, even being able to stand on my head: 'There is no such word as can't.'

Thank you to my acupuncturist, Robert Ogilvie, for his compassion and belief in me, and for finally vanquishing the throat monster.

Jonathan Hinde taught me how to keep my mind still and not to attach to my darkest fears. I might have given up were I not so wholly comforted by the sight of a meditation teacher in a suit, tie and bare feet.

My ex-husband, Jonathan Powell, showed me that friendship and affection are not limited by or to marriage. Thank you for that, and for never failing to make me laugh.

Thank you to my husband, Tom Wnek, for complete and enduring love. Until I met you, I did not know such happiness was possible.

Most of all, thank you to my daughter, Molly, whose luminous presence kept me going through the long, dark nights. You are the most constant and the loveliest light. I love you, Moll.

Index

Note: the abbreviation SB in the index refers to the author